BECOMING
THE
ICEMAN

PUSHING PAST PERCEIVED LIMITS

BECOMING
THE
ICEMAN

PUSHING PAST PERCEIVED LIMITS

WIM HOF
JUSTIN ROSALES

EDITED BY JUSTIN ROSALES AND BROOKE ROBINSON

Mill City Press, Inc.
212 3rd Avenue North, Suite 290
Minneapolis, MN 55401
612.455.2294
www.millcitypublishing.com

ISBN-13: 978-1-937600-46-4
LCCN: 2011942054

Cover Design and Typeset by Ryan Nygard

Printed in the United States of America

FOREWORD

*B*ecoming the Iceman is a project inspired by Wim and Justin to show the world that anyone can adopt the ability to become an Iceman or Icewoman. The project's goal is to show that the ability to control the body's temperature is not a genetic defect in Wim, but an ability that can be adopted by anyone.

For many generations, we have been taught to fear the cold:

"Don't forget your jacket! You don't want hypothermia, do you?"

"Put your gloves on before you get frostbite!"

Of course, these are consequences of extreme cold exposure, but with the proper understanding, anyone can learn to use the cold as a natural teacher.

You may have seen Wim running around on television, barefoot in the snow or swimming in ice-cold waters. While he is doing those incredible feats, he isn't worried about how cold it is; he is enjoying himself.

Like any new tool, you must understand how it works before you can use it efficiently. This pertains to the cold as well. Wim is the epitome of what can happen if someone uses the cold to train the body.

You might ask, "How can you prove that anyone can learn this ability?" We're glad you asked...

As of Fall 2009, Justin Rosales had no experience with the cold whatsoever. He was a college student attending Penn State University. After Justin's friend, Jarrett, showed him one of Wim's videos on YouTube, they became exceedingly interested in understanding this ability. They wanted to see if it was possible for anyone to learn. So they thought, "Why not test it on ourselves?"

In Spring 2010, after speaking to Wim for several months via email, Wim invited Justin to attend a workshop in Poland for ten days. After many days of working as a dishwasher, Justin was able to pay for his trip to Poland and learn the technique of the Iceman.

With more training and countless experiences with the cold, Justin began to slowly adapt. The length of time he could remain exposed to the cold increased dramatically. He quickly realized that the technique to withstand the cold was, indeed, an ability that could be harnessed by anyone.

This book tells the tale of Wim and Justin's journey to *Becoming the Iceman!*

CHAPTER 1:
BREAKING THE ICE

"Just do it! Right on! Go for it!" That's what I always say.

I have come to a point in my journey where I can finally say, "I did it." Now is the time to write about my experiences. I have been a pioneer all my life and I think it is best to finally share my wisdom with the rest of the world.

Fear and trust are the components of the human psyche. Though the path may be to ascend up steep mountains, I use no auxiliary tools, only my mind.

Many years ago, I lived in the Spanish Pyrenees, making money by working as a canyoning instructor. The beautiful canyons that surrounded me were made when water excavated natural doorways into the massive mountains of the Spanish Pyrenees.

To go canyoning safely, you need ropes, wetsuits, watertight buckets, backpacks, and a lust for adventure. These are the essential things needed to safely guide people through the labyrinths of rocks and steep walls.

The feeling is always good after a strenuous day in the canyons, simply because you have to comply with whatever nature dictates. The aching muscles are signs of a hard day's work.

When traveling through the canyons, it's important to stay centered and focus within. Don't worry about the fear; embrace it. Centering, instead of thinking too much, creates a physiological process that affects both the body and the mind. If you're centered, vertigo is controlled and every descent teaches you to trust the equipment and yourself.

There comes a point when the vertigo is nothing but a mathematical problem within the mind. Once you know the proof, you can reach the solution with practice. Doing this gives control over the mind and an understanding of your limits.

Using that serene point of view, anyone can begin to enjoy the grandeur of their surroundings during their descent. This is the moment that most people enjoy when they come to the Pyrenees.

I know the paths through mountains like a child knows the shortest and nicest way to his favorite spot. During our expeditions, I would point out the flora (plants), fauna (animal life) and the geological structures of the Pyrenees. In a way, it soothed the people that I led because it gave them an understanding of my experience and hopefully gave them more of a reason to trust me.

When we would finally reach the upper part of a canyon by focus, concentration and strength, my followers would begin to feel the fear inside of them. It is at this time that I would explain to them that the journey was about overcoming that fear and becoming stronger.

Overlooking the mountains, there are many beautiful monoliths standing alone, as if an enormous artist sculptured them. In my mind, one monolith stands out among the rest: El Huso (The Spindle). To me, it looks like one of the Stone Heads on Easter Island. It is the mysteriousness that catches my attention. Like a magnet, it draws me in.

One day, while I was traveling through the Pyrenees alone, I decided to examine the behemoth. As I got closer, the rock seemed bigger and bigger. Touching it from all sides, I calculated her height and the possible climbing routes. I then decided that I would soon tackle this majestic entity and climb this amazing rock with no rope or safeguards.

My fear and trust began to initiate their irrational beliefs of a near-death reality. My body tightened at the thought of falling. Now was not the time to climb.

Descending back the way I came, I contemplated how I would approach my climb. I went deeper into myself as I felt my determination growing stronger. I told no one of my plan to ascend the mysterious rock. It was my challenge and I had hoped that it would help me look deeper into my soul.

I began to train my body, doing pushups on my fingertips, pulling myself up on doorways using only my fingertips, and meditating on the single thought of climbing.

That's when the nightmares began. I dreamt that I was climbing El Huso and I was controlled by fear. It was an overwhelming sense of powerlessness that seemed too impossible to overcome.

Fear does not go away by itself. You have to confront your fear, mold it, then learn to control it in it's own irrational reality. Every human being has the power to do just that. To go deep within and confront your inner being is a powerful act. Going deep and developing the will power is the only way.

For days I continued training, visualizing the climb, concentrating on the hunger inside of me. I developed a determined focus that I knew would only grow stronger. The nightmares slowly began to fade, telling me that it was almost time to climb.

The day my nightmares stopped, I realized that the fear was gone and my trust had replaced it. Trust is the element needed to conquer fear. I went to where El Huso was located and eyed up my worthy adversary one last time. It was at that point that I realized I forgot my climbing shoes, but there was no turning back now!

I emptied my mind and just let go. It's important to be mentally prepared before beginning. Being badly prepared or not confident in something this dangerous could lead to serious injury.

As I started to climb, I realized a light feeling of being inside of me. I had a powerful grip in my hands and there were no anxious thoughts holding me back. *Just do it*, I thought.

Silence and emptiness aided my conquering of fear. These elements are also present in meditation. In a way, this was my own form of meditation.

After reaching the top I felt a wave of self-worth and excitement! I climbed down and back up several more times. I felt like a child and El Huso was my playground.

A couple of years later my photographer, Henny Boogert, traveled with me to the Pyrenees to do some solo pictures for an outdoor magazine. We went back to El Huso and Henny began to take many pictures as I climbed without the aid ropes or gear. He took a lot of beautiful shots, but I asked him if he thought anything could be done better. He mentioned that the lighting was a bit off, so the pictures were a bit dimmer than he would have liked. So I said, "Then I will climb it tomorrow!"

The next morning we returned and I prepared myself as I had before. After climbing for a bit and reaching a height that would definitely kill me if I fell, I developed a cramp in my right calf! I was rendered motionless as the pain quickly became crippling. I really could do nothing but hold on to the rock for dear life. I tried to shake my leg, but there was no space, only a few centimeters.

I had no room for error; otherwise, I would quickly meet my demise. I was on the edge of losing control and one mistake could end it all.

Out of options, I tried something new. I tried to *think* my cramp away. Visualizing the part of my leg that was throbbing, I began to loosen that area in my mind. Soon enough, the muscle in my leg

began to relax. For the first time ever, I realized that I could consciously think away a muscle cramp. I believe it was a direct result
of knowing the body with my mind.

   That experience made me realize that overcoming fear, by trusting the body and mind, can increase the potential for success as long
as you *just do it.*

CHAPTER 2:
PHILOSOPHY - THE LOVE FOR KNOWLEDGE

When I was thirteen, I spent my autumn holiday reading a book about Psychology. It was a book with mysterious concepts that I hoped I would soon understand. I knew the text held value, so I committed my time and separated myself from the world to gain a better understanding.

The psychological terminology gave birth to my inquisitive mind and the urge to philosophy everything around me. It was then that I began to see the world in a different light. All at once, I wanted to learn about different cultures, traditions and new languages.

I applied for a passport as soon as I was of age, excited when I finally received it. I packed my bright orange backpack and with my thumbs up, I hitchhiked to Morocco.

When I was traveling through Belgium, I thought it would be helpful to learn a few catch phrases that would help me survive. I was taught French in school, but it wasn't enough to get by. Luckily, the people I met while traveling were willing to teach me a few important phrases, like:

"Are you going to Paris?"

"Thank you."

"Where is the bathroom?"

"Where am I?"

Using this method, I progressively learned French. Later on in my life, I came to learn many other languages through similar methods, such as Spanish; Portuguese; Italian; Japanese; Sanskrit (from a teacher), and Polish. I had also learned German from living one kilometer away from the border of Germany. Dutch, however, is my native language.

I've come to understand that if you want to learn something badly enough, you'll find a way to make it happen. Having the will to search and succeed is very important.

Even though I had learned many languages, I still felt like there was something missing. As I approached my adolescence, I became more inquisitive. I knew about the great philosophers, the seers, traditions, cultures and esoteric disciplines, yet, something was still missing.

I believe an inquisitive mind always finds what it's looking for. It's the irrational curiosity that ultimately stumbles upon the answer.

I found my answer in December when I was seventeen. I was home thinking about this hole in myself when I suddenly noticed the snow outside. As the snowflakes began to cover the multicolored environment in a beautiful white blanket, a warm feeling washed over me.

I watched until the snow grew thick on the ground. I embraced the white desert as the snow began to fall harder. I needed to go out into it. So after I put on my shoes and a thick pullover jacket, I was off.

That crispy sound when walking over a new lair of snow filled my ears as the strange, but beautiful, white blanket changed the appearance of the land. There was intimacy and a sort of mysticism that filled the cool air. Nearby, a couple of kids were rolling around in the snow, wrestling with each other. This moment called me to reminisce about my past.

When the first snow fell three years prior to this experience, I had a similar urgency to go out into it. I took off my shoes and began walking around the nearby park with my wife and son.

After about an hour of walking around, Noah, my son, bent over to make a snowball. Noah finished his creation and we continued walking while he held it at his side. My wife and I laughed and talked as we admired the newly covered Amsterdam.

An hour later, we returned home. I went to take off my son's jacket when I realized that he was still holding the ball of snow in his hands! He told me he wanted to put it in the fridge and store it. Like most children, they want things to last forever. So, we let him cherish the memory by storing the snowball in the freezer.

I grew curious as to how he was able to hold onto the chilled ball for that long and not complain about the pain. I asked Noah to show me his hands so that I could see if there was any damage. To my surprise, his hands weren't cold at all. In fact, they were incredibly warm! I'll never forget my son's first experience with the cold.

Anyway, there I was in the snow-covered pasture, when I felt an irrational urge to take off my socks and shoes. Barefooted, I became strangely aware that it was not cold, just soft. There was an absence of pain. Instead, I felt a great feeling of joy and power. My conceptual being was flabbergasted. I wandered around in the snow for hours, taking in the vast whiteness. It inspired me.

Whenever something touches me in a way that makes me reflect, I don't feel like quitting; I don't feel limits, just a greater sense of being. That is the essence of meditation, where thoughts are no longer consciously driven.

That moment made a monumental impact in my life. The experience changed the way I thought about the cold. At the time, I couldn't understand how, but it changed the way I perceived it. It was my new friend.

To me, expanding consciousness is the path to true knowledge. The material you learn from books ultimately leads to an expanding consciousness. That experience finally quenched my thirst for knowledge. I now felt peace within and my mind was still.

Everyone will experience theses moments at some point in his or her life. I am convinced that these moments are meant to show us that there is more to life than satisfying our desires.

Sometime after this experience, I traveled 200 km up north to Amsterdam, the cosmopolitan city. I wanted to meet fresh, new minds. I had hoped to meet poets, writers, painters, Holland's best yoga teachers, karate experts, and more.

The thirst for knowledge continued to grow inside me and Amsterdam couldn't fix it. I was clueless as to how to quench that thirst. I quickly became lethargic. That's when I began to think about challenges. I wanted to conquer something that would make me feel more productive.

That's when the idea came to me. I would travel from Amsterdam to Dakar Senegal on bicycles with my brother, Andre. The idea had the potential to break the pattern, yet powerful enough to get me back on my feet. I had found hope.

CHAPTER 3:
THE ROAD TO DAKAR

Amsterdam is a city with a lot of channels. The city was built on a marsh 700 years ago, 25 kilometers from the North Sea. Since Amsterdam is adjacent to many bodies of water, we have a lot of rainy days. Our people are known for their tolerance to the near-constant rainfall.

Although Amsterdam is a nice and colorful city, it was too crowded for me. The center of Amsterdam was always clustered with cars and everything just seemed so… busy. After a while, I became fed up with it all.

The idea of traveling to Dakar Senegal quickly shifted from just an idea to a reality. Andre and I threw our old newspaper delivery bags onto the back of our bikes and set forth on an adventure.

In October, you can expect a lot of rainfall here in the Netherlands. The first few days of our travel were no different. When we arrived in Ardennes, Belgium, the air turned cold and the atmosphere had a chilling effect. We found shelter under a small overhang on the side of the road.

As cars passed by, they splashed water onto our bikes parked against the wall. We were extremely fatigued from pedaling through hilly regions and our stomachs were growling. I remember sitting there with Andre in the darkness, drenched and starving.

The only food we had to eat was dry cornflakes. We brought the food to our mouths and ate in silence. Usually, we're very talkative and enjoy conversing over a good meal; however, due to our immense exertion, we simply looked at the road and concentrated on savoring every bite of our food.

It was a cold night, but we traveled a bit more until we found shelter at a bus stop. With a full stomach and the comfort of each other's presence, we fell asleep. Our bodies may have been cold and wet, but we slept like rocks.

We went hard that day. The meal and the sleep were well deserved. Moments like those put my mind at ease. It's a resting place for my mind, so that I may feel accomplished, yet relaxed.

When we woke up, we shrugged off the fatigue, hopped on our bikes and took off at the break of dawn. It was a new day and the rain had finally stopped. We picked up a lot of distance while we biked over the hilly countryside.

The northern part of France was also chilly when we arrived, but luckily, there was no rain. We biked through the northern part of France in two days and arrived in Lyon. There was a noticeable change in the atmosphere. The houses were no longer made of bricks, but instead, replaced with stones and wooden beams.

The landscapes changed even more as we continued. There were different varieties of trees and flowers. We could tell that we were getting farther and farther into the southern part of Europe by the vastness of the Mediterranean Sea. There was an overabundance of colors as we passed palm trees, fig trees, bright sunshine, and good food.

As a Dutch guy who hadn't seen much of the outside world, cycling by the Mediterranean Sea opened my eyes. I was enjoying the breeze blowing through my hair, the rush of not knowing what would happen next, and embracing the differences of the new, but wonderful world outside of my home. I felt a change coming.

A lot of the world may view me as the one and only, Wim Hof, but that's not entirely true. Andre is my identical twin brother. We are genetically the same and look exactly alike. Because of the genetic similarities, we know each other extremely well. This drives our sharing for the love of plants, trees, rocks, the sun, and beautiful landscapes.

On our adventure, Andre and I spoke of a lot of things. One of the topics that we spoke of was a change we felt inside. We discussed the changes of mind, the mind itself, and enlightenment. While pondering the purpose of our trip, I felt something shift inside. I didn't know what it was, but it was powerful.

We continued on, pedaling through the majestic mountains of the Pyrenees, along the coast of Spain. Here, we met a German cyclist named Wolfgang. Wolfgang told us that he had ridden his bike through Africa. Our minds clicked as we shared inspirational stories.

He started by telling us a story of when he was traveling through the Nubian Desert. He was walking through the desert, with his bike by his side, when he noticed a lion lying behind the bush he had just passed. When he gazed into the lion's eyes, his body became paralyzed. After a couple minutes, the lion turned away and fled!

This story really impressed me and I was interested in learning more from the man I had just met. So, while biking along the coast of Spain, Wolfgang, Andre and myself discussed our interest in Zen. Specifically, we spoke of the spirit behind it and the different religions, cultures, and traditions it relates to. The discussions gave us understanding of what contemplation was all about.

Contemplation is the state of mind where your focus resides in the mind, moving your focus as you talk. It is a state of mind that exercises the real understanding of the self. If you exercise the mind by making sense of what is said, while contemplating your own thoughts, the mind becomes lighter and understanding is possible. A good point to get to is when the thinking process stops and energy dissipates consciously. This is known as "samadhi" in yoga.

We talked for days and contemplated even more. We tried to understand the meaning of life and the purpose of all of us traveling together. We had no books, no seers and no references. Luckily, I believe that true wisdom lies inside one's self. That evening we slept in a melon field near Valencia.

Consciousness is a physical state of being that is aware of one's self and one's own surroundings. If this state of mind is exercised, it becomes simpler to navigate, like a child gaining motor-skill experience by tinkering around with different ways of movement.

If you believe in an omnipresence, this is the way to make an ethereal connection. Similar to the way a GPS navigates the direct route to our destination, your mind can find the best way for you to connect with that omnipresence. To get to that point, one needs to go within and gather the energy to just do it. There is no false mysticism needed to explain what it's all about. If it's inside you, just do it!

If you want conviction, dig within yourself. If you want clarity, strive for understanding. If you want understanding, get wisdom and gain experience by just doing it!

You cannot bring yourself to understanding while you constantly worry. It happens when you are able to consciously let go. Don't think your goal is untouchable, something that has to be understood by science. It is very simple for those who want to make it a reality because once they find their path they will stay on it at all costs. I came to this realization during one of the days we were riding through the Spanish countryside.

By the time I had woken, Andre and Wolfgang had already left to grab a cup of coffee from a local cafe. I lay there for a while exploring the epiphany I had discovered the day before. It was the first time in my life that I realized, I was aware of *everything*.

Pure awareness is something to strive for. You will understand the meaning of this altered state if you choose to go for it. It is literally, an eye-opening experience. For those who adopt pure awareness, they believe it is the best experience able to be gained during their life. It is a simple, but unique experience. We are all unique.

Don't think it is difficult; it's just a different state of mind. Anyone is able to get it like the fruit from a tree once it's ripe. This true nature of perception is simple and has never left us. Just look within. Understand, contemplate and exercise this state of mind until it makes sense. Once the resource is tapped into, the wonders of life begin to appear to you.

Try it.

...

We went our separate ways when Wolfgang caught a boat transfer from Valencia to Tunisia. Andre and I continued traveling south through Spain and into Elche, which has the largest population of palm trees in Europe. We then decided to cycle to Almeria through the Sierra Nevada. When we were on the coast about 50 kilometers from Almeria, we stopped for a day to enjoy the beach.

"Andre the Practical", as I called him, made an oven from stones so we could bake our own bread. A Danish man saw us baking our bread on the beach and sat down to talk with us for a while. He told us that he had bought a place up the coast and that there were cheap properties nearby. *Splendid*, I thought.

Andre and I decided to purchase a property and live in the area for a bit. The place was ruined, but there were large amounts of banana trees, figs, crapes and cacti surrounding us. It was like our own botanical paradise!

We never did make it to Dakar, but we both had found our true paths: The way to the Self... and a botanical paradise.

CHAPTER 4:
A STATE OF MIND

*O*nce you know the way to your spiritual destiny, you can change.
Once you realize that there are no limits in your mind, you can change.
Once you realize there are no boundaries to what is possible, you can change.

Moving toward change is important. It will become evident once you begin to work for it. Achieving success is the result of the right practice (no matter what that may be), the right discipline, and the right road.

"Para mi solo recorrer los caminos que tienen corazón que alcanzar la iluminación."
This roughly translates to:
"The path my heart chooses will lead me to enlightenment."

It all depends on the path you choose and the decisions you make. In the end, it will all make sense. Until then, the heart is your guide. I trust this wisdom as truth in nature. It pushed me through every challenge, fear and obstacle.

Now, my final challenge is to go beyond and get in contact with my omnipresence, where we all live, but from which many are disconnected. I am not saying that I alone have the right to become connected. I believe anyone and everyone can do it!

CHAPTER 5:
GROWING UP

When I was younger, I didn't know what I wanted to do with my life. Honestly, I still don't have a plan; however, I feel that's what makes me who I am today. There are a lot of things that happened to me throughout the years that have shaped my perspective, character, and determination. I guess a good place to start would be my childhood.

I grew up with a normal family. My brother, Preston, and I were born in Miami, Florida. We moved to Pennsylvania after hurricane Andrew destroyed our home. Our first move was to Philadelphia, PA where my next brother, Julian, was born.

We stuck around in Philadelphia for about a year before moving across the state to Sharon, Pennsylvania. My mom and dad moved us to Sharon so that we could be closer to our grandparents. When I first arrived in Sharon, I was 5 years old.

A few years later, my parents had three more children. Their names were Brandon, Christian, and Natélie. I was the oldest and Natélie was the youngest. Everyone assumed that she would become spoiled with five older brothers, but they were wrong. She is now one of the most caring and considerate women I know and we're blessed to have her in our family.

It wasn't easy being the oldest. I always had to keep an eye on my siblings when all I wanted to do was play video games. As much as I wish I had been doing *anything* else, it taught me a lot. It gave me responsibility. I felt like it was my job to be a good example to my younger siblings. Although sometimes I made mistakes, my intentions were always pure.

Growing up in a household of five other kids can get pretty hectic, especially when living in our small ranch house in Sharon. When we first moved in, there were only five of us. Three kids later, we were short on bedrooms.

I learned how to be a very social person from always being sur-rounded by others. In the long run, it was worth all of the chaotic screaming and yelling from my siblings, as they'd play games to-gether. At the time, I couldn't understand how my parents put up with it.

My dad has been a car salesman for almost all of the years that I have lived in the house. Growing up, I felt like he blamed me for everything, like I was the only one to ever get in trouble. I remember him telling me on multiple occasions, "It's your responsibility to act mature. You should know better because you're older." A lot of the time, I would feel a lot of angst toward my father. I constantly told myself, "I never wanted to be like him". Actually, I may have told him that as well. Now, I realize that everyone has their own flaws and that my father's intentions were to give me responsibility to help me become successful.

I know I won't grow up to be like him because he's unique. He has raised six children and was willing to sacrifice all of his time to make sure that we were able to live life happily. We were nowhere close to wealthy, but we never would have survived if it weren't for my father's dedication.

During his many hours of driving back and forth to work, my father would listen to inspirational speakers like Tony Robbins and Jim Rohn. On Sundays, he would make us listen to several of their seminars. We *hated* it, but I now admire his perseverance and under-stand his purpose in doing all of that. He was trying to give us the knowledge that we needed to become successful if he should ever pass away. I now see it as the greatest gift he has ever given us.

Suffice to say, my dad didn't do it all alone. Throughout my life-time, my mother has always been there as my guardian angel. I be-lieve she is that way to all of us. During my earlier years, she was the typical stay-at-home mom. She picked out our clothes, tucked us in, said our prayers, and even made us whatever food we wanted because we were all so picky. She was always willing to go out of her way to make sure that we were happy.

When my parents lived in Miami, my mom worked as a nurse, but she gave it up to spend more time with the family when she became pregnant with me. Around the year 2000, my mom wanted to become active again. She wanted to help raise money for the fam-ily, but still be there for us. So, she decided to do something that the family could enjoy while still making money. She began her own business called Party Zone for Kids.

It all started with one moon bounce, also known as a "bouncer," that she rented out to families. As the business grew, she bought 14 more bouncers, cotton candy machines, popcorn machines, snow cone machines, and a facility to store the equipment and have parties at during the winter. Now, averaging over 300 parties a year, Party Zone for Kids is a stable business that provides for the community as well as our family.

My mother has always been our hero and the person we go to with our problems. I am really proud of my mom for putting up with everything we put her through. Now that the business is stable, she has returned to nursing school to become a Registered Nurse. We will always cherish the lessons she taught us. Even though she will one day pass on, the love she gave to us will never cease to reflect in our actions.

As you could probably tell, my parents had an incredible impact on my life. Although I never really had a set goal, I knew the *type* of person I wanted to become. Ever since I could remember, my mother would always tell me, "Anything is possible." She would also tell me that if I could simply *think* of an idea, then I would be able to find a way to make it a reality. Each night, before I fell asleep, my mother would whisper the following phrase into my ear.

"If you can learn how to use your mind, anything is possible." That phrase continues to resonate in my mind every second of every day.

CHAPTER 6:
THE SEARCH BACK TO MYSELF

January 1999

While reading the newspaper one day, I noticed one relatively short article. It was a column that included a photo of a person doing their job in the cold. Each day there was a new person in the paper doing a different job. Since it was the middle of winter, I'm sure the newspaper thought it would be nice to write about people who were willing to brave the cold for their jobs.

There were articles on merchants, window-washers, firefighters, farmers, and even prostitutes! I was initially interested in this section of the paper because I swim in ice water everyday. I thought that it would be a good idea to give the newspaper company a call and talk to them about my hobby. It turned out to be a great idea, as they were very interested to hear my story. One of their journalists scheduled an appointment to meet at the lake where I regularly partake in my activity.

When the journalist arrived, we headed out to the lake, so I could show him my hobby. Typically, when I go for these cold swims, I start by cutting a hole into the frozen ice and then submerse myself. After I completed this, the journalist took a couple pictures of me treading in the water. He then asked me some questions and I shared many stories of my experiences with the cold.

The next day, I was in the national newspaper! Wim Hof in the newspaper! It was awesome! What I was not aware of at the time, however, was the impact of the news on the media as a whole. Apparently, every television station had read the article.

Ten days after the article was released, television crews began to visit my daily swims and started filming my cold exercises. At least twice a day, television stations, magazines and newspapers were interviewing me; the media had entered my life.

I remember one specific interview quite vividly. During this particular interview, I was being filmed doing some swimming and yoga exercises. I began by cutting two holes out of the ice that were 7 meters apart. The exercise consisted of me entering the first hole, swimming underneath the frozen ice, and emerging from the other side. When I came out of the water, my body was steaming! Afterwards, I showed that I had remained completely flexible by doing yoga-flexibility exercises.

As the camera crew was packing up, I began to put on my clothes. I glanced out over the lake and saw a man walking in the middle of the ice. A moment later, the ice started to crack below his feet and he fell through! Since it was windy that day, a lot of the ice was not equally thick around the lake. Apparently, this man didn't know that.

Everyone around me just stood and watched; no one did anything to help. The man was struggling and couldn't get himself out of the hole. Every time he tried to pull himself out, the ice would break beneath him. Half-dressed, I sprinted toward the man in peril. He was about 100 meters out. As soon as I reached him, I offered my hand to help pull him out. Just as we grasped hands, the ice cracked beneath me and I too fell through.

It caught me off guard, but I did not panic. I wanted to remain calm in the presence of this anxious-looking man. I started talking to him in an attempt to calm him down. I thought this would help bring him back to his senses. I said, "I am going to push you up onto the ice, but you have to equally divide the weight of your body so the ice doesn't break again." He followed my instructions obediently as I pushed him onto the ice. When all was said and done, he ended up suffering from only a mild case of hypothermia, but at least he was safe and had done no serious damage.

In dangerous situations like these, you should always try to regain control and calm your senses. Most of the time, you can get yourself out of the dilemma by finding a logical solution.

Meanwhile, the cameras had been rolling for the entire event; it was all over the news that evening. The next day, I was in the paper and had even more media representatives visiting me. Many other articles were published and more of my yoga, ice climbing, swimming, and running experiences were spread throughout Europe. One of the articles even coined the name that most know me as today: "The Iceman."

Soon after, I, The Iceman, began to prepare for a high altitude run. I was going to attempt my first half marathon. The run would take place in Tibet, on the northern side of Everest, where I would run barefooted in the snow, wearing only shorts.

At 5,000 meters (16,500 feet), there is only half the amount of oxygen density in the air. We need oxygen for combustion to create warmth in the body. To be able to survive in higher altitudes, we need to acclimatize, a process whereby more red blood cells are produced in the body to allow for more oxygen to be carried by the blood. This will compensate for the lower amount of oxygen in the air at this level. At 7,200 meters (23,760 feet), the body reaches the threshold of its ability to adapt. It's known as the "death zone." At that altitude, the body begins to deteriorate.

During my preparation for the run, I met with a professor who had heard of my feats through recent publicity. He was connected to a research institute called TNO. He invited me to take part in an interesting experiment. I accepted his invitation because I was deeply interested in the research and the results it would produce. When I arrived at the research center to meet with the professor, he led me to the spot where the experiment would take place: the thermo-physiological area.

During our walk, the professor explained to me that his field was thermo-physiological sciences. Even though he had taught material on different temperatures and how the body reacts to them, he wasn't very fond of the cold. For the professor, like most other humans, the warmth is a comfort zone that he has problems stepping out of -- somewhat of a primordial nature. I told him that I liked the cold simply because it awakens all kinds of powerful feelings within me.

He then began to explain what would happen in his experiment. The name of it was "Cold-Induced Vasodilation (CIV)." As I was listening, I became more attentive and began to prepare myself to perform the best I could in the coming experiment.

Preparing oneself to perform well is typically a mental challenge that one must craft. You must make sure the body is focused 100% of the time. Where each limb moves, your mind must be there. Where you mind moves, your body must follow.

He then proceeded to show me the experiment itself. I was astonished at how intricate the layout looked. What was so interesting was that the experiment would only consist of the upper part of my index and middle fingers. I would need to place the two fingers inside of a little Perspex box filled with ice water.

He told me that people who work regularly in the cold, like fisher-men who need to work with their hands cleaning fish at sea, have incredible vasodilation in their hands. Vasodilation has to do with the opening of veins and arteries to help increase blood flow to cer-tain areas of the body. When exposed to the cold, there is a natural constriction of the veins in the extremities. It kicks in to protect and maintain the heat of the inner core temperature. The blood that cir-culates around the core is very important because it helps maintain functioning in the liver, heart, lungs and brain. Therefore, the core must remain around 37°C (98.6°F) for the body to function properly. If the core temperature raises or drops even two degrees, the body begins to malfunction.

When exposed to the cold, the blood's temperature can drop below 10°C (50°F), and the veins in the hand constrict. When the hand warms up, the veins open back up. Usually, it's an automatic physiological mechanism of the body that we are unable to influ-ence. By training through regular exposure, however, we are able to influence that mechanism dramatically. At first, that was merely my opinion. Later on, I would be backed up by several cold physiologi-cal experiments at Radboud University Hospital, but I will speak more about that later.

The professor then told me that the veins in the extremities of a person well conditioned to the cold, like those found in the hand of a fisherman, will open up after 2 minutes, on average. For someone that is somewhat able to withstand the cold, it could take up to 4 minutes. For a normal individual, it could take up to 8 minutes.

In my case, the professor was convinced that my veins were well conditioned. He knew I was someone who regularly exposed him-self to the extreme cold. He then sat me behind an iron table where the little Perspex box laid. I saw the ice water inside and a few ice cubes sitting on top of the box. He connected my index and middle finger to a couple of iron receptors that would be able to gauge the temperature of my fingers, as they were exposed to the ice water. He would be able to monitor the data on a nearby screen.

As soon as I placed my fingers into the ice water inside of the tiny Perspex box, the experiment began. The temperature in my fingers soon dropped to 10°C (50°F) and we waited. After 2 minutes, my veins didn't open. Not even after 4, 8, or even 10 minutes! The tem-perature continued to drop and there was no movement in my veins whatsoever. After 16 minutes with my veins closed, I fainted and fell to the ground.

…The experiment was over… *What happened?*

Results like this implied that the conditioning of my veins was not very good at all. After explaining my intention to run a half marathon, barefooted through the snow at an altitude of 5,000 meters (16,500 feet), the professor told me that I would have many difficulties with my veins not opening. If I were to do my run with my veins in this condition, I would be susceptible to severe cold injuries, especially because I would be exposing my body to freezing temperatures and high altitudes simultaneously.

I went home, extremely concerned and worried. The results made me feel a little hesitant about performing a new challenge, especially one that no one had attempted before. I was not sure whether or not I would be able to achieve success. What I did know, however, was that no matter what, I would always give my best, until it is impossible for me to proceed. Even though what had happened at the research center may have concerned me, I was not the kind of person to give up that easily. My heart is strong, but my mind is stronger.

Before all the research, I had believed I could do it. Call it intuition if you will. I've learned how to trust my mind in its direct contact with the nervous system, immune system, blood circulation and heart and this would be the key to my success for the upcoming challenge.

The time finally came for me to leave for my half marathon. With the research at TNO still on my mind, I surrendered my emotions and bent like a bow, to which my success would be the arrow released. I knew I could leave nothing behind and had to give it my all.

When we interact with nature, miraculous things can happen. Whenever you go beyond the rigid patterns of thinking, challenging yourself, you can receive a bounty of experience from hard nature.

With a camera team from a national television broadcaster, I flew from Amsterdam into Abu Dhabi, and then to Kathmandu. Kathmandu was a very beautiful place with a vivid society. In a town with little money in circulation and a small infrastructure, the townspeople seemed to be carefree. Like many other towns with little to no money, people are happy with less. Many of us take our belongings for granted, but these people survive with only the bare necessities, and that makes most of them content. It's a remarkable experience to see their smiling faces in an environment where most of us would feel uncomfortable living, without the access to normal technology (television, cell phones, video games, etc.).

From Kathmandu, we drove through Nepal and its hilly country-side full of banana trees. There were many colorful trees along the way and just as many flowers, dusty roads and rivers. I loved the beauty and exuberance of it all. I am always delighted to see how different things are in new places. If you're a sensitive individual, beautiful sights bring about extraordinary feelings. For me, this is typically true, but I reminded myself that I was there with a mission.

While we were driving through the countryside, the experiment at TNO crossed my mind a few more times. Even though I was ready to do my best, I was still wary of the possibility that things may go wrong.

We then stopped for a bit so the film crew could record me cross-ing a big river with a strong current. They thought it would be good footage for the television special. When we got to the Tibetan (Chi-na) border, we switched cars and went through the immigration process. A young Chinese translator and a large Tibetan driver ac-companied us to the Friendship Highway (also known as the "Gate to Hell").

We passed a lot of steep, curvy roads as we drove up from 1,200 to 3,800 meters (3,960 to 12,540 feet), to the Tibetan Plateau. As we drove into the largest village on the mountain, we were surrounded by a bunch of shacks, stony buildings and chilly weather.

The Himalaya Hotel, which is where we stayed that night, was nothing more than some dirty curtains, a few beds with blankets to keep out the cold, and warm tea. After eating dinner at a nearby restaurant, we returned to our beds and attempted to sleep.

I had never been at an altitude of such great heights before. I didn't know what to expect. I felt strange. My mouth was dry and tingling, I was lightheaded. Overall, I just felt off. The feeling only got worse as the night progressed; I had a splitting headache for the better portion of the evening. I cursed into the darkness yelling, "What the hell have I gotten myself into?"

Eventually, I drifted off into sleep and awoke the next morning feeling slightly better. My headache disappeared and I felt like I had found some newborn energy. It made me full of lust for the coming adventure. I ate my breakfast with vigor and joy. I was so excited that I couldn't keep my mouth shut. I spoke at breakfast about the challenge to come. Afterwards, we departed for La Lung La Pass at 5,060 meters (16,698 feet). We needed to meet with the translator and the driver again.

The rocky area of the Tibetan Plateau knows of little plants or trees. The higher the altitude, the more the vegetation diminishes. When you reach 5,000 meters (16,500 feet), there is no longer any vegetation. The only things that remain are rocks, dirt and you.

While driving up the mountain, we occasionally passed Tibetan houses. Most of them were colored purple or gray. It was an interesting sight when we would pass a Tibetan's house because each time, it would appear as if the wilderness had swallowed their homes.

Climbing along the curves and turns of the mountain, it began to snow. This made me excited. I felt like I was grabbing the bull by the horns and holding tightly. We reached the top and a rush of adrenaline raced through me. I jumped out of the car, took off my clothing and sandals, and began to run through the snow.

The snow felt good between my toes and the running was relatively easy to do. I was now fully confident in my ability to run through the snow. I believed that whatever happened in the experiment must have been a mistake. I ran for an hour while the film crew recorded. The day was a success, but more important, I had finally shaken my uncertainty!

Running at sea level is easy, but when you're running at high altitudes, the rules are different, especially when you aren't completely acclimatized. Usually, a person will get exhausted after running for just five minutes. I did surprisingly well and ran for a full hour and felt energetic the entire time.

After the run, however, the headache kicked in again. This time it stayed for days. It was absolutely terrible. I felt like my head was going to explode!

Just before reaching 5,000 meters (16,500 feet), we stopped at a little village to rest for the night. One of the crewmembers got sick from the high altitude and the team decided that it would be best to take her back to Kathmandu. The only person that stayed from their team was Jasper, the cameraman.

We stayed in the village for a couple more days to adjust. Each day we would climb a little bit higher to get used to the altitude, and then return to the village. Climbing each day got me used to the lack of oxygen. Finally, I was able to function normally and headache-free, making me confident that the run would be a breeze.

On a side note, I'd like to mention something that struck me as bizarre, yet very interesting, while in Tibet. I noticed a lot of the Tibetan children collecting cow dung in the fields that surrounded the village. They usually had a calm expression on their face while performing this task and gave off a sense of tranquility unlike any other place I've seen around the world. Though the Tibetans lead a completely different lifestyle, compared to people in the West, I had never before witnessed this kind of intrinsic peace that they were expressing. It was the most impressive thing that I have ever witnessed in Tibet. It's something that I try to achieve myself, each time I prepare for a challenge.

Meanwhile, the day finally came when I would run my half marathon. We drove up past the 5,000-meter mark (16,500 feet), over frozen dirt, snow and ice. Eventually, we came to a point in the road where it was impossible for us to drive anymore; there was too much snow. We stopped and began looking around for a starting point. We decided to put my clothes and other belongings behind a rock near the car so that I could run without carrying anything. We found a good spot and placed my things down. Here, I began my run, barefoot and in shorts, while Jasper was fully clothed holding his camera.

I felt remarkably good, gaining confidence as we moved forward. As we progressed through the snow and icy ground, I actually began to enjoy it all. While jogging along, I met a Tibetan woman singing on the slopes; her song sounded sacred and beautiful. I greeted her in a respectful way with wholehearted gestures and continued on.

After five hours of walking and jogging through the snow and ice, I realized that I was going to complete the challenge! I finished it with no problem whatsoever. Jasper said that all of the shots looked beautiful and the footage was all on tape; we were both content.

After the challenge, we drove back over the Friendship Highway through the Nepalese valleys and arrived at Kathmandu. We then drove out to the Stairway to Heaven. The Stairway to Heaven is at the banks of the Ganges, where they sacredly burn those who have passed away on a pile of firewood. I showed a couple yoga postures to some Sadhus who lived in the area and then we went on our way back to the Netherlands.

With the marathon completed and my confidence restored, all was well. I was ready for a new challenge

CHAPTER 7:
SUOMENLAINEN SISU - FINNISH POWER

March 2000: Kolari Lappish, Finland

A nationally distributed magazine contacted me with an interest in taking a couple photos and performing an interview. The article's content would discuss natural drugs, such as adrenaline, melatonin, endorphins, dopamine and more. I agreed, did the interview, and received a copy of the magazine later on. The article talked about adrenaline junkies, such as, skydivers, free climbers (rock climbers without safety gear), adventurists, and other people of this sort. The largest portion of the article covered my piece. It elaborated on many of my outdoor activities, such as running in the snow, swimming in ice water, and climbing snowy mountains, barefooted. The authors of the article believe that a high amount of dopamine and endorphins fuel my body for these cold-endurance challenges.

After the magazine was published, a lot of television stations became highly interested in me. They thought they could create a good television special by recording me perform the activities mentioned in the magazine article. Soon after, a television crew was sent to my front door.

Willibrord Frequin was one of these people that I had the pleasure to work with. Willibrord is a very well known television presenter. He does a lot of interviews and is famous for unmasking people. I was surprised to find Mr. Frequin standing in my doorway. I had recently seen him on television during his weekly program interviewing a cardinal of the Catholic Church. Frequin told the Cardinal, "You shit like everybody else, so what makes you so different?" Of course, Frequin said these words with respect, but he always digs deep for the truth. He does this to go beyond a person's appearance or status. I liked that quality about him, so I treated him with great respect.

Willibrord was a professional. He knew exactly how he wanted everything to look. He was very meticulous with his camera crew and he constantly tried to get perfect shots. He challenged me. I started the interview by doing my yoga postures; he was amazed. He had never seen a body bend and twist the way mine had. I then dove into the icy waters and swam to the middle of the lake. I even held my breath for a few minutes under the ice. He was thoroughly impressed. Mr. Frequin was also nice enough to let me talk about my new book for the television special. He had his shots and I got free advertising out of it. It was a fantastic experience. A couple of days later, the special aired and even more people became interested in my life.

About a month later, a team of people contacted me. They said they were highly interested in taking Willibrord and me to the northern part of Finland to swim under the ice. I was more than happy to go.

I had never swum large distances under the ice in the Netherlands, partly because the water isn't transparent. Also, swimming alone under the ice can be very dangerous and I never wanted to take any extreme risks. The crew, however, wanted me to swim 50 meters under a layer of ice one meter thick in Lapland.

When we finally left for our journey, I was excited. We arrived in Rovaniemi on the Polar Circle and there, I saw a lot of snow and ice. Actually, those were the only things that were visible. I really wanted to get out and enjoy the snow, but we still had to drive further north for another 200 kilometers (124 miles) to reach Pello.

Occupied by 10,000 people, Pello is a village beyond the Arctic Circle. When we arrived, the village was in the middle of an international ice-sculpting competition. The sculptures were beautiful. It's amazing what people can do with ice.

That night, from the room where I was sleeping, I saw thick snow falling with a silent presence. It was coming down harder than I had ever seen before. It made me ponder the event to come. According to our records, no one had ever swum 50 meters under ice water before, not even me. I would be the first to do it. Physically, I was prepared, but inside me, there was tension and fear.

The following day, we went to the lake to see where the event would take place. We found a nice spot next to a deserted mine. The layer of ice on top of the water was, indeed, almost one meter thick. The local diver's club happily dug us a 4x4 meter hole out of the ice. They then placed an old Russian tent over it to prevent the ice from freezing again.

Inside the tent, the hole looked like a blue diamond. The water was so clear that you could easily see the bottom of the lake 13 meters (39.6 feet) below. Even though it was beautiful, I was scared. I attempted to rid my fears by going into the water for a few minutes. I undressed, climbed down the steps that the divers had carved out of the ice, and submerged myself into the blue diamond.

It was a powerful experience. The thick ice that surrounded me was intimidating, yet inspiring. I had never seen ice that thick before. In the Netherlands, the ice was usually about 20 cm thick, possibly reaching 30 cm during the coldest winters. Even the water itself was somehow different than the water in Holland. I felt a sense of claustrophobia. It was an eerie feeling, so I just floated in the water and did not dive under.

For the next few days, I returned to the tent to better associate myself with the water. There was a void in the abyss that intimidated me.

During one of those days while I was sitting in the water, I decided to dip my head under and take a look around. The water was clear and beautiful. My stomach eased as I felt adrenaline pour through me; I felt alive.

It is moments like this that one needs to face his fears. The best way to have such a moment is to gradually confront the fear and approach it in a way that is both exciting and inspiring. You have to be decisive and physically prepared to do your best. After that, little by little, you will see progress.

The progress I made each day in understanding the water made me more prepared for my dive. My nervous system has learned how to change things on a cellular level. Your nervous system has the potential to do the same. When there is more activity in your cells, it can create a feeling of power and control. This feeling can supply confidence to help you reach your goal.

A couple of days after I had embraced my fears, the day came for me to go for a test swim. Nerves and determination were my silent allies. I remember beginning the day with a cup of coffee while I gazed out the window. We were to rehearse the record attempt with only a couple of people from the team. The goal was to see where all of the cameras should be set up, in order to get the best shot, and also for me to do a test swim. The crew's plan was to set up the cameras and then I would swim 25 meters. In my head, I was determined to do the 50 meters, but I didn't tell anyone.

Spontaneous events are puzzles in the mind that you have to figure out on the go. It's a part of living in the present. You have to be at your best and be alert to potential mistakes, because in that moment, the mind and its thinking process are one. You have to be ready to mold yourself to whatever life gives you. To be ready, you must be alert within.

When we arrived at the frozen lake, we discussed the way things were going to happen. Inside, I was plotting how I was going to achieve 50 meters on the practice swim, not just the 25. Nobody noticed that my mind was elsewhere; I kept to myself. A few minutes later, everyone was at their posts. The cameras were ready and it was almost time for me to attempt my dive. During my final moments of preparation, I went within. You cannot be more ready for a challenge than when you trust yourself and your actions... and I did.

I began my breathing exercises and drew more oxygen into myself. More oxygen in the muscles creates a form of insulation and an ability to exercise for longer periods of time. This would help in two ways. First, having more oxygen would allow me to be able to swim longer distances, and second, the insulation would be helpful for swimming in ice-cold water. With the sharp and beautiful diamond in the ice inviting me, I finished the final steps of my preparation and slowly entered the water with determination.

With my back against the ice wall, I took a few deep breaths to focus on my goal: 50 meters. I made sure to take careful breaths so I wouldn't disturb the oxygen saturating in my body. With one last inhalation, I let go and dove under.

I remember being glad that I had access to the ice water days before that rehearsal, because at that moment, I was completely comfortable and felt no cold whatsoever. The adrenaline had taken over my body and with each stroke, I felt more confident in my ability to succeed.

The water was refreshing. The crystal-clear lake offered a beautiful view. I started counting my strokes as I swam: *1, 2, 3*... A few moments later I passed the 25 meter hole and continued on like a torpedo: *28... 29*. It was at the 29th stroke where my vision began to get blurry.

From my experience with swimming, I knew that each one of my strokes represented one meter and 20 cm of distance. This meant that I was at about 35 meters when my vision became blurry. I didn't realize that the freezing water had the potential to damage my retina. With my vision foggy, I couldn't see where I was going, but I kept moving: *47...48.*

Wait a second... I realized that I had gone too far. 42 strokes represented 50 meters. I calculated this before my swim, but due to the unexpected blindness, I had lost my focus and passed the 50-meter hole. Now, I was at least 57 meters away from where I had started. There were only three holes cut out of the ice, which meant there were only three ways out: the starting point, the 25-meter mark, and the 50-meter mark; I was trapped.

I decided to make a 180° turn to put myself back in the direction of the 50-meter hole. I then swam 6 strokes in an attempt to get back to stroke 42. I felt all around the ice above me and couldn't find the hole. It was at this point that I realized the magnitude of the situation. Oddly enough, I felt no panic. I swam in different directions trying to find the hole, but all of my attempts were in vain.

My body began to feel light and I felt my mind slipping. The energy in my body diminished little by little as I swam around helplessly. As strange as it may sound, there was no pain whatsoever. I was swimming into unconsciousness when all of a sudden, I felt a hand grip me by the ankle and begin to pull me backwards. Jari, a member of the team, had saved my life and was dragging me back to the 50-meter hole. I went limp, relaxed, and about 30 seconds later we surfaced. Even though I was completely exhausted, I pulled myself out of the hole on my own.

I just sat there on the frozen lake for a while, playing over what had just happened in my head. My body felt no pain and no cold, just exhaustion. After a few good breaths, I eventually came back to my senses and the exhaustion faded away.

An annoyance built up inside of me and I yelled, "Damn you people! Where was the emergency diver? You had everything but my safety planned out."

Even though I was annoyed, there was a place in my mind where I was extremely happy. Not only did I swim the 50 meters that would break the record, I swam more than 80 meters trying to get out of that hole! I was now completely confident in my ability to perform the world record with ease. As I looked into the eyes of death, I had overcome my fear once again. I thought to myself, "Wow, what a powerful experience." We then packed our things into the car and made our way back to town.

...

The next morning when I woke up, I was completely at ease. Due to the events that had occurred the day before, I figured nothing else could go wrong. I had swum 80 meters before I began to pass out; 50

meters should be a piece of cake.

Everyone's attention was focused on making beautiful footage for the event. When I arrived at the site, they had a heated tent set up for me. The tent was more than I needed, as I prefer to do things my own way, so I just sat on the ground and took notice of everyone else around me.

The tension was high, like it usually is when there are expectations to fulfill. Everyone was working on something different. They were preparing the cameras, setting up the angles, and checking the water. They all were making preparations to make sure that the event ran smoothly, and so did I.

I stayed there on the ground for a bit, meditating and focusing on the event to come. After some last minute preparations by the crew, the time of action had arrived. The divers, who would be watching over my safety underwater, dove in. They opened the flap to the old Russian tent and told me they were ready to go.

During those last five minutes as I walked over to the tent and prepared myself, I could feel the tension around me. Everyone was focused on that moment and what could go wrong; I was completely focused on reaching the 50-meter hole.

When I reached the diamond shaped hole, I began to undress. The cameras were already rolling at this point so it was time to go. I joked with Willibrord once more as I walked down the steps and then brought my attention to the icy water. 50 meters would be no problem as long as I remained focused. I took a few more careful breaths and dove under.

I was under the ice again, with a conviction. This time, I felt no stress. There was no question as to whether or not it was possible. I swam freely, not really focusing much because I knew I could reach 50 meters with no problem.

At about the 40-meter mark, I realized something had changed. This swim felt completely different than the day before and I was already tired. What had changed? I soon realized my *focus* was the problem.

Focus is a delicate matter and it is very important when provoking the mind to stay alert. My nervous system, immune system and blood circulation need to all be working together in order to make my internal heating mechanisms function properly.

If I don't focus or give all my effort, everything will begin to unravel. This is what started to happen to me under the icy depths.

I finally made it to the 50-meter hole, but it was a lot harder compared to the 80 meters that I had completed the day before. As I emerged from the water, people on all sides congratulated me. Even though I ended up breaking the world record, I had learned an important lesson once again:

Do your best at all times!

CHAPTER 8:
SUPER POWERS

Every day, after my brothers and I arrived home from school, we would play video games. It was one of the ways we bonded together. We especially enjoyed games that were challenging and involved characters with special abilities. The idea of having super powers fascinated us. Often times we would use our imagination to pretend we were the characters in the video games.

I would assume that this is where my mother's philosophies fused with what I did in my spare time. *If someone is able to perform superhuman feats in a video game,* I thought, *shouldn't we be able to do the same in reality?* This idea began to give me some strange dreams.

At the time, there was this girl I liked. I was in 5th grade and the only time I would see her was during lunch period in the cafeteria. In one of my dreams, I was sitting in lunch and I wanted to do something spectacular to impress this girl. So, I stood on my seat, jumped in the air, and began flying around. Everyone clapped and cheered. "I didn't know he could fly," they said. As I landed next to the girl, she wrapped her arms around me and I woke up.

I had other strange dreams where I was able to move objects with my mind or was able to play back any piece of music after only listening to it once. I loved my dreams, they really inspired me, however, my parents emphasized that school was important and I needed to focus on my homework. So, I resorted to living vicariously through my video game characters.

A few months after my dreams began, my mother told me a story that she once heard over the radio. Apparently, a man froze to death after being locked inside a train with traveling cargo. As the story goes, the scientists concluded that the temperature couldn't have dropped below 60°F (15.5°C) that night. Yet somehow, this man froze to death.

The psychologists deduced that the man must have panicked and simply *thought* himself to death. I assumed this meant that his mind made him believe that it was colder than actually it was and his body responded accordingly. I imagined each organ slowly shutting down, as the man believed he was freezing to death. My mother told me that they found him curled up in a corner, his skin a deep shade of blue.

It was a sad story, but it really got me thinking. If a man could think himself to death by lowering his body temperature, could he do the opposite and warm himself up in a cold climate?

My mom and I spoke about it for a while and she suggested I try it out. "Imagine yourself sitting in front of a warm fireplace," she said, "or tanning at the beach." I tried it, but didn't feel any effects. So, I did what any other kid with a short attention span does at that age -- I gave up on the idea. Besides, "super humans" only existed in video games.

Even though my initial attempt failed, my mother's story remained engrained in my head. It just seemed possible to me. I couldn't figure out why I believed controlling your body's temperature was more possible than the other powers, but it stuck with me.

The idea returned to me from time to time, whenever I'd walk through winter's snow. I continually thought about how awesome it would be to walk outside without a jacket and create my own body heat. Little did I know that one day, I would meet a man who could do exactly this.

CHAPTER 9:
EL GLOCES - A CANYON IN THE SPANISH PYRENEES

Our bus had just departed from Leiden, a city famous for its old university. All around me filling the seats were 16 and 17-year-old students. I was sitting in the back of the bus, speaking to one of the professors about the book she had just published. I told her that I had also recently written and published a book of my own.

It was a long drive full of conversation and laughter. We drove through the southern part of Holland, Belgium, and most of France. As the night approached, everyone fell into a deep, peaceful sleep.

The following morning, when we had reached the southern part of France, we stopped at a rest stop for fifteen minutes, so that everyone could get out of their seats and use the restroom. While everyone did their own thing, I walked to the other side of the parking lot to stretch my legs. As I began my walk back, I saw the bus leaving without me!

I tried to get the attention of the bus driver by running and waving my hands violently, but my attempt failed. No one on the bus must have noticed that I was gone because it pulled away without me. I thought to myself, "They will notice that I am missing at some point and turn back for me." I waited and waited, but the bus didn't come back; it had left me behind.

Apparently, the professor, whom I had been previously speaking with, had gone to a different seat on the bus to sleep. She never realized my seat was left vacant after our restroom break. As for everyone else, they were too busy doing their own thing to realize my absence. It wasn't until they were about 400 kilometers from the rest stop when someone first recognized my absence.

Once I acknowledged the fact that they weren't coming back for me, I decided to hitchhike. Half an hour passed before a car finally stopped; my travels could finally continue. It went that way, from one car to another, until I finally reached the Pyrenees in Spain.

It was a strange way to travel, but it worked for me. I didn't even have my rucksack; it was still on the bus. The only thing I had on me was my passport. Yet somehow, things seemed to work out in my favor. A random stranger, once I told him of my predicament, offered to rent me a hotel room for the night and pay for my dinner! Wow!

The following day, I continued my hitchhiking in three different cars. I spoke enthusiastically with the drivers about all kinds of things: the weather, the mountains, the geological structure of the canyons, and even philosophy! After a long journey, I finally arrived in the Pyrenees. It was an unexpected, yet exciting adventure.

When I had finally arrived at the camping site in Spain, I met up with the group again. They were extremely surprised to see me. Reunited, we set out on our adventure. They were ready to embark on what we had traveled there to do: to rappel the canyons and see beautiful sights. Our first stop would be a canyon named, *El Gloces*.

El Gloces is a wet canyon in the Pyrenees. A lot of water passes through the canyon and people that venture through tend to get very wet. The water that flows down is typically cold because it drains from the high mountains. Therefore, wetsuits are used as a precaution when rappelling El Gloces.

With everyone prepared in their wetsuits, fashioned with rucksacks, belts and ropes, we made our way to the canyon. From there, we started abseiling our way through the labyrinth of rocks and water. The path inside the canyon was a narrow one with steep walls. It was extremely dark, but a beautiful sight. To get through the canyon, we had to jump into pools of water, swim, balance on boulders, cross large rocks and crevasses, jump gaps, and rappel into the abyss. Everyone had a lot of fun, despite the cold water that sprayed against us every step of the way.

After many thrilling hours of canyoning, we arrived at the bottom. From there, we had to walk for another hour, up the mountain, to get back to the parked bus. Everyone was exhausted, but our spirits were high. That night, we all went to a local pub to enjoy each other's company while we ate good food and drank good wine.

Everyone enjoyed the impression that nature had pressed upon us that day; even the professors had enjoyed themselves. While in the pub, a wave of excitement washed over me. I suggested that we go back to the canyon, right in that moment, and do it all again. This time, we would do it in the dark! Another adventure!

The students were overwhelmed with excitement and were ready to go; however, the professors shut down my offer. Since the teachers felt responsible for the students' safety, they did not want them to go on this risky adventure. Canyoning in the dark is extremely dangerous and could potentially have fatal consequences if one isn't careful. Fortunately for me, however, the idea was already locked into the mind of one of the gym teachers, who happily agreed to go with me.

Since the water in the canyon was going to be colder than it was earlier that day, the gym teacher completely covered himself up with his wetsuit. Only the front part of his face was exposed. I simply went in shorts. I was feeling great after the bottle of wine and within a couple hours, we were running over the stony path toward the canyon.

The canyon looked very different at night. The trees and rocks cast immense shadows against the earth. It wasn't intimidating, just different. As we arrived at the beginning of the canyon, we saw nothing but a black hole. There was no light in the canyon whatsoever, only darkness.

I told Tom, the gym teacher, that if we abseil the first rock, we're going to have to go all the way through; there would be no turning back. After a moment of hesitation, he replied, "Yeah, let's go!"

As we were descending into the black abyss, I felt different. It was a completely different experience than what we had encountered earlier that day. Specifically, my senses were very alert and I was aware of everything. Even though we were surrounded by darkness, I knew the canyon by heart and could visualize where each rock and crevasse was on the path.

Although we could not see, we listened very carefully to understand how the water stream was moving. We followed the current silently and only spoke to each other to detect the distance between our bodies. As our voices echoed against the rocks, we noted that it would be best to stray no more than two meters apart from each other.

It was a great experience being there in the dark with Tom. We, as humans, normally rely on our sight to guide us, but both Tom and I realized that instead, we could listen and feel our way through the canyon. We were tapping into and relying on a different part of our brain. Due to our new enhanced state of mind, we were able to make alterations to help us continue to stay alert. It all was natural.

A conditioned mind can cause narrowed perception, especially when you only focus on one sense and rarely use the others. Also, it's not about simply using them; it's about forming your entire perception through those other senses. Subsequently, you can begin to see the world in a different light.

Tom and I discovered this as we spoke during our progression through the canyon.

Everything was going smoothly and we were really enjoying ourselves. The water was no longer cold, as I had adapted by now, and my senses were sharp. As Tom and I followed the current, our surroundings emitted a tranquil feeling. We had just arrived at a crucial spot in the canyon and though we were in the dark, we were not blind. We found ourselves on a rock and the only way for us to get down was to jump. If we jumped too far, we would slam into boulders. Luckily, I knew exactly what to do. I made some calculations in my head and was ready to jump. Tom, on the other hand, wasn't as familiar with the terrain, so I thought it would be best to give him explicit instructions.

"Listen very carefully to where I enter the water. That way, you'll know how far and how hard you'll have to push off the wall when you do it yourself."

He nodded, with a little hesitation, but told me he understood. Since there was no light, he would have to listen very carefully to the sound of my feet as they entered the water. His hearing would have to be sharp and model that of a submarine's radar. He would have to trust me if it was going to work.

Without any further delay, I jumped. After a large splash and submerging a few feet under the water, I took two strokes to bring myself back to the surface. I looked up and said to Tom, who was still up on the slippery rock, "Tom, did you hear the distance?"

"Yes," he answered. I could still sense the hesitation in his voice, but he was now determined to jump; there was no other way. A few seconds later, I could hear him take a step and then leap into the darkness. He entered the water right next to me and surfaced a moment later.

"Is everything okay?" I asked.

"Yes," Tom said, with a relieved tone.

His trust in me, and the way he surrendered to the situation is what ultimately led him to success. He could not have done it otherwise. Letting go of his anxiety and freeing himself from hesitation was also extremely helpful.

Obstacles in life consume energy. Because Tom and I were able to overcome the obstacles in our way, we experienced a new type of energy. We felt powerful and full of vigor as we continued on. As we approached the final part of the canyon, moonlight began to peak through the rocky walls. It was a beautiful sight as we began to regain our vision and realize what we had just accomplished.

A few minutes later we were out of the canyon and stood motionless in the valley. Our minds were at peace and we felt immense joy. Tom and I embraced each other without saying a word. We had met a great challenge and conquered it.

By the time we reached where we were staying for the night, the students and the professors had already fallen asleep. I laid myself down in my bed, closed my eyes, and slept like a rock.

The next day, I took the group to another canyon in a warmer area. In the Pyrenees, the climate varies all over the place. It could be very wet and cold in one area, while very hot and dry in another. It all changes, so must one adapt to new surroundings, just as Tom and I had to adapt to master that canyon without light.

CHAPTER 10:
FEAR

I have the ability to climb steep rocks without gear and have no fear of falling because I am always prepared. Subconsciously, my mind clears itself in its sleep the night before. But, I wasn't always like this.

When I was younger, I suffered from nightmares. Climbing terrified me, but by persevering through my fears with training and meditation, I was able to make those nightmares disappear.

At first, it started as me finding a rock that I was afraid to climb. I would imagine myself climbing each step, grabbing each hold. Eventually, I would feel that I had climbed it multiple times and knew it like the back of my hand, even though I had never actually climbed it.

Don't get me wrong, that doesn't mean my fear completely disappeared, but after imagining it in my head, I began to see it from a different angle. No longer was I intimidated, but I felt like a child playing on a Jungle Gym. I was able to climb it with ease and my mind was finally free from the nightmare.

You might be asking yourself, how does this relate to the cold? Well, let me explain. The rocks can represent any challenge that appears in your life. It may appear impossible to overcome at first, but with a clear head and the will to press on, you will find a way to reach success. Sometimes it may be terrifying, but that is something you have to embrace. We are rarely tested when we are afraid of stepping outside of our comfort zones. That comfort zone can hold us back from doing something great. So, if you think it is possible, try it out. It's your mind; learn to take control of it.

In the Bhagavad Gita they say, "The mind under control is your best friend, the mind wandering about is your worst enemy."

Make it your best friend, to the point where you can rely on it.

Your mind makes you strong from within. It is your wise companion. The sacrifices you make will be rewarded.

Life doesn't change, but your perception does. It's all about what you focus on. Withdraw from the world's influence and no longer be controlled by your emotions. If you can grab the wheel of your mind, you can steer the direction of where your life will go.

Once you can feel the steadiness of the mind, it will convince you that it is the only way to live. Your spirit and willingness to do more with your life will become natural. Happiness and success doesn't come from years of thinking about trying it, it comes from taking action.

When you are "doing", each step you take will be a firm one. It doesn't matter if you don't succeed; confidence comes from experience. One of the easiest ways to gain confidence is by finding ways to get around obstacles. Failure is an option, but what makes you stronger is choosing not to accept it. Hesitation creates fear, increasing the likelihood that you won't follow through. So if you can, don't hesitate.

Becoming spiritual isn't about staring at a candle for hours or repeatedly saying asanas or mantras, it's how you express yourself. Believe in yourself and know you have what it takes. Let go of all doubt and anything in your life that is causing you stress.

At times, the feat may seem too impossible for you to reach. I guarantee you that this is not the case. It is a matter of finding a way to make it is possible. In the beginning, that is all that matters. All who are willing to seriously consider the possibility that there is more to life than what is already in the textbooks are capable of being the innovators that this generation will write about.

Cleansing yourself of your emotions can take time, so be patient. It may feel like you're losing a part of yourself in the process, but that's only temporary. In time, that feeling will turn into clarity. The people that I know that have experienced this change have never regretted their actions. They can now see the potential in their lives, whereas they could only see limits before. It is truly a magnificent transition.

I won't lie to you; it does take practice and perseverance. Make it simple for yourself by calming your mind from anger, understanding what makes you sad, and replicating the experiences that make you happy. If you want strength and success, just do it!

CHAPTER 11:
CAMP JUDSON

Although we never had a set denomination, my family raised me as a Christian. My parents were both raised catholic, but after a while they realized that they weren't comfortable with a few of the traditions. Therefore, they taught us about morality and explained religion just enough to give us a foundation. We say that we grew up in a Christian home, but they never really forced to adopt those beliefs; we had a choice.

For a long while, we only *occasionally* went to church. Our highest attendance rates were around Christmas Eve and Easter, however, we never went to the same church. We hopped around, never sticking to one place. My parents wanted to find a church where we could all feel comfortable, but by the time I had reached 9th grade, we still hadn't settled.

At that time, I was dating a girl named Whitney. She was an avid churchgoer and was there every Sunday. Her, and a lot of my other friends who attended that church, would always attend fun events in the evenings for their "Youth Group". I joined her a few times and found that I really enjoyed the environment. I brought Preston along a couple of times and he really enjoyed it as well.

We decided to start going to that church because we felt comfortable there. That summer, the church offered us an opportunity where they would pay to send us to "camp" for a week. My parents were extremely hesitant about letting us go to a place with people they didn't know, but after they became more informed, they embraced the opportunity and encouraged us to go.

A few weeks later, we were on the bus driving toward Camp Judson in Erie, Pennsylvania. The week was full of memorable experiences. I enjoyed it so much that I decided to volunteer as an assistant counselor a couple weeks later. The people there were really open and understanding. Plus, it was an opportunity for me to learn more about Christianity.

For the next four summers, I returned to Judson as a counselor. During that time, I made a lot of good friends and even more memories. Judson was a powerful motivator for me. I wanted to do more with my life and understand how people worked and functioned. That was about the time where I was really able to focus on my passion that developed as a child.

I still wanted to understand the mind and how it worked. Judson was a very inspiring place and it made me feel like I was capable of anything. While there, I was detached from all the video games, schoolwork, chores, and stupid things that I worried about in high school. I felt free, and that's when my mind began to wonder. It was one of the first few times in my life where I was able to think on my own. Petty things no longer influenced me. I wanted to change the world in a positive way. I wanted to help people.

At the beginning of my last year as a counselor at Judson, I met someone that changed the way I perceived the world. During staff training, I met a mysterious fellow named Jarrett. He always kept to himself and was very private, but when it came time for capture the flag or dodge ball, he was an obvious extrovert. When I had played against him in previous sport classes, I realized that despite how quiet he appeared to be, during any physical activity, he exploded with unbelievable amount of energy. In basketball, he was the quickest and most enthusiastic person in the game. In Ultimate Frisbee, he developed strategic plays while being a key part of the scoring process. He seemed like a good guy, but I really didn't know much about him, other than what I had observed.

For the 4 years that I was at Judson, I never spoke to Jarrett. Usually, Jarrett would sleep in the quarters above the office, but on one night in particular, Jarrett decided to join myself and a couple of other staff members in the counselor's cabin.

Sleeping in that cabin was Preston, Jarrett, myself, and two other staff members. After a couple minutes of talking about the day's events, the other two staff member fell asleep and began snoring. Jarrett, Preston, and myself continued conversing. We spoke about our majors and other interests in our lives. Then, the conversation moved to dreams and escalated to childhood passions. As the conversation continued, I realized that I wasn't finishing my sentences -- Jarrett was. Apparently, the way he processed information was very similar to mine. He was able to understand what I was saying without me actually saying it because he previously thought those things himself.

Actually, I found myself finishing his sentences as well. We clicked; there was something resonating inside both of us. It was as if my life and all of my thoughts as a child were building up to that moment. Jarrett and I realized that we had a lot of the same goals and we felt that it could prove beneficial if we worked together.

From that point on, my life would no longer include a one-time attempt at an idea, followed by nothingness. It would include the collaboration of someone who had as much belief in an idea as I did. We shared one mind and were willing to do anything to press forward. We understood each other, but more importantly, we had understood each other's core belief: *Anything is possible.*

CHAPTER 12:
HALF MARATHON IN LAPLAND

For a small portion of my life, I worked as a postman. It was my job to drive boxes, letters, parcels and advertisements to post offices so they could then be delivered to their specified locations. I worked alone during the nights. The solitude gave me time to reflect on past events and encouraged deeper thinking.

One day, while I was driving down the road, I received a phone call from a Canadian producer, representing the Discovery Channel. He asked me if I was interested in doing a challenge in the cold. I listened very attentively as he explained his proposition.

I held back my excitement and calmly told the gentleman, "Yes, I'd love to." He told me that he would send me an email soon and that I should reply at my convenience. I ended the call and continued my work as a postman. I was thrilled.

The excitement lasted all day. As soon as I got home, I turned on my computer and checked my email. The message was already sitting in my inbox. It explained that the challenge would be the center of attention for a documentary. The event would take place just beyond the Polar Circle.

At that time, it was November; the challenge was set to take place in January. The only thing we had left to figure out was the type of challenge I would pursue. I had already swam under ice and ran a half marathon on the slopes of Everest. However, my run was only filmed by Dutch television and wasn't internationally broadcasted. So, I sent an email back to the producer and explained that I could run a barefooted half marathon beyond the Polar Circle. It fit their expectations perfectly.

Weeks went by, December came, and I hadn't done any training whatsoever. As the date of the challenge approached, I became really tense, as I normally do. It's a natural reaction that occurs when the mind worries. To ease my mind, I decided it was time to start my training with a run. Since it was my first run in a long time, I only ran 1.5 kilometers (about .93 miles). It was just a quick jog around the neighborhood where I lived.

The following day, I went for a 7 kilometer (4.3 mile) run. I felt a little sore afterwards so I didn't run for the next two days. Instead, I went for a cold-water swim to relax and regain my energy.

The third time I ran, I ran barefooted next to a lake. I ran back and forth on a wooden boardwalk along the shore. It was cold and windy that day so no one was around when I did my run; it was nice to be able to run in peace. I didn't stop my run until blisters developed on the bottom of my feet. By that point, I had run a total of 22 kilometers (13.6 miles).

Over the next week, I simply continued my work as a postman. I would tend to my blisters from time to time and take care of them so that they would heal properly; it was a week of rejuvenation. After I healed, I returned to the place on the shore to run. Once again, it was cold and windy and the solitude was nice. I ran 24 kilometers (14.9 miles) barefooted and developed at least 20 new blisters. When I returned home, I was more than satisfied with my run and I knew that in time, my feet would heal.

Later that evening, my daughter stopped by my house and asked if I wanted to run a few laps with her around the park. I agreed and while we were running, I told her all about my new challenge. My legs were feeling great, so after two laps (8 kilometers/4.9 miles), I felt the urge to run faster. When we were finished, the run had made me so happy that I was extremely confident that the challenge would be a success. I was so overjoyed that I cried.

Challenges bring about the true nature within me. It alerts my body and mind, altering my state of being. It makes me feel so alive! It's like I always say, "We can do more than what we think." At those moments when I encounter a challenge, I become extremely aware of the deeper layers of my soul.

Since the challenge was quickly approaching, the camera team traveled to Amsterdam to take a few video shots of where I lived and record the activities that I do on a daily basis. There, we did an interview and took a few shots in a local abattoir (slaughter house). Afterward, the camera crew departed for Lapland, Finland where I would be joining them two days later.

Lapland can be a very, very cold place in the winter. The temperature can drop as low as -50° Celsius (-58° Fahrenheit). Even weak polar animals may die in temperatures this cold. It is really a survival of the fittest.

Two days after the crew visited my home, I had to meet them in Helsinki. We then took a flight to Oulu, about 800 kilometers north (497 miles). It was -20°C (-4°F) outside when our flight landed. While we were waiting for our ride to pick us up, I decided to take off my shoes and try running a kilometer in the snow. It felt great. The snow was in perfect condition for running. My little test made me even more confident for the challenge.

The next day, we went to the Finnish Institute of Occupational Health for a cold-water experiment. The experiment consisted of me sitting in a cold-water basin, which was set up inside of their laboratory. Professor Oksa, a world-renowned cold physiologist, was the man who performed the examination of my body. Oksa had a passion for the outdoors. Though it was not as extreme as mine, it was a pleasure meeting him and our discussions were rich and fulfilling.

Before we even started the experiment, Oksa first carried out a few baseline tests to get a general reading. He saw that I had a very small percentage of substance fat. He explained that it was an interesting discovery because without much fat, I don't have a lot of protection from the cold. He announced that he was excited to see how I would react when exposed to the cold-water basin.

To prepare for the experiment, the professor connected my body to many different machines. First, he connected me to an echocardiogram. He then gave me a pill to swallow, which would monitor my core body temperature. He also connected a blood pressure cuff to my arm and gave me a mask to measure the acidification of my exhaled breaths.

When the cold begins to impact the body, the extremities receive less oxygen and acidification begins. The more conditioned the body is to the cold, the less the body will be affected.

The vital organs need to have the body operating at 37°C (98.6°F) in order to function properly. If the temperature drops even a couple degrees below this, the body will begin to shiver and the blood will shunt from the extremities. That's when the core temperature really begins to be affected. The core temperature of the body shouldn't drop below 35°C, (95°F) otherwise the body will be more likely to suffer from hypothermia, which can damage the liver, lungs, heart and brain. When cold blood flows through the vital organs, the body slowly becomes dysfunctional. The heart beats irregularly, thinking processes and reflexes are slowed down, and breathing becomes more difficult.

When the blood temperature drops to about 30°C (86°F), the body begins to shut down. During this time, the vital organs could begin to fail, the heart could stop beating, and one would have the potential of falling into a coma. Ultimately, these final consequences could lead to death.

The specialists who research the cold say that sometimes, people can appear dead when they are pulled out of the water, while they really are in a comatose state. Sadly, sometimes people will attempt to warm up hypothermic victims too quickly and this alone can cause the person to go into shock and die.

We moved the experimentation process to the basin. I was seated on an motorized chair, which was controlled by a remote control in the hands of Professor Oksa. There, I would be lowered down into 8 °C (46.4 °F) water. When we finished up the connections, Dr. Oksa reviewed the monitors one last time and we were ready to go. He began lowering me into the water and the immersion began.

Dr. Oksa's first reaction was surprise. He was astonished that I had no gasping reflex when I first entered the water. It meant that the veins around my core had immediately closed and that they were conditioned very well. My adaptation to the cold water was excellent. Minutes past and my core temperature stayed the same. After ten minutes, Oksa noticed that my core temperature actually rose. He thought this was a remarkable change in my body. The powerful thing about the experience was that everything felt under control. I felt great.

My attention was positioned toward a point on the wall in front of me. It helped me stay focused in my mind so that I could stay warm. As a result, my core temperature remained stable despite the freezing cold water. Since I was feeling comfortable, I decided to enjoy it. I began asking the professor questions about his life and his hobbies. Later on, I realized that this caused me to lose my focus, which had been what was maintaining my core temperature. After 25 minutes, my core temperature had fallen .5 °C (.9 °F) and Dr. Oksa decided to end the experiment.

It was stupid of me to lose focus like that, but I now know that it's important to always pay attention and remain centered.

Cold water can be merciless and if you aren't paying attention, you can quickly lose control of the situation. Therefore, always remain focused and attentive.

After the experiment, the crew stayed to interview the professor. He stated his findings and said that he believed I would be able to successfully complete the half marathon due to the extraordinary control that I had demonstrated in the cold-water experiment. After we completed our mission in Oulu at the institute, we went back to the hotel and I enjoyed a nice, warm sauna.

The next day, we left for Kolari, where I would run the barefooted half marathon. The temperature had dropped to -30°C (-22°F). When we arrived, we stayed in a wooden lodge where we did a few shots of the arrival for the documentary. There were only two days left until the run, so we prepared the itinerary and scheduled the sleds that would carry the film crew.

Before we knew it, the day to run was upon us. Everything was set and ready to go. Both local and national journalists were present for the event. As everyone was preparing for the event to begin, I noticed the starting line was covered with reindeer skin. It appeared as if it were some sort of primordial spot, as if the skin was placed there in an attempt to bring back the prehistoric men. I stood at the starting line and gazed out into the horizon. It was time. I took a deep breath, let out an excited yell, and took off.

While running over the snow and ice, barefooted, and in such frigid temperatures, I honestly didn't know how it would end. My expectations were that I would complete the event with no problem, but I stayed very alert. I stayed in a place where I had heightened awareness. As I knocked away kilometer after kilometer, everything felt fine. Physiologically speaking, I was in control.

After 10 kilometers (6.2 miles), I checked myself over in my head. My mind was strong, limbs felt great, and my core was warm. There was nothing to be concerned about, so I just continued on. I even made jokes while I was jogging, sometimes speaking to the camera crew as they recorded me from the sled. I did this with caution though, so I could make this experience different from the laboratory and remain in constant control.

When you exert energy through talking, it's like opening a door and letting the cold air into a house. If you hold the door open for too long, the house will lose all of its heat. I made sure that I didn't leave that door open for too long so that I could remain focused on my body and succeed.

While I continued on, the chemistry in my body was working just fine. I had no problems whatsoever. The journalists were confident that I was going to make it!

That's when something began to change. I began to have difficulties in the front part of my left foot. I didn't know what was going on, but I could sense that something was wrong. It continued to get worse and worse until my whole foot resembled that of a wooden stick. I couldn't feel it anymore! This was all happening right as I passed the 18-kilometer mark (11.1 miles). There were only 3 more kilometers to go (1.8 miles).

I decided to just do it. Step after step, breath after breath, I made my way forward and eventually, I saw the finish line. It was another spot that was covered with reindeer skin, just like the beginning.

"I'm going to make it," I thought.

The last 200 meters of my run were beautiful. As I came closer, the sun broke through the trees and lit up the sky. It was a magical coincidence. While nearing the finish line, I gazed up at the sun. My gold medal hung in the air before me.

Despite the injury to my foot, I had decided to continue on until I crossed the finish line. At the time, I didn't realize what kind of a sacrifice I had made to finish the race, but it had opened the doors to a devastating problem -- a problem that would take me weeks to recover from.

After the race, we went directly to the local hospital. The dermatologist told me that I had third degree frostbite! I showed my foot to the cameras so that everyone could see what I had put my body through to complete the race. I returned to Holland on crutches...

CHAPTER 13:
FROSTBITE

Soon after the dermatologist told me that I had done irreparable damage to my foot, I was given a box full of medication. He had said that the damage was inflicted on the front part of my left foot and advised that I take the medication to keep it dry. He had also emphasized that it was very important to keep my foot from getting wet.

By the time I returned to Amsterdam, the color of my foot had turned to a dark, greenish-brown shade. It was a devastating sight. I couldn't sleep. I sat in my living room thinking about what could be done. I knew there had to be a solution to my problem. I wasn't going to just accept that my foot was irreparably damaged!

No! I'm not going to take it! I thought. I was so frustrated that it filled me with rage. Something inside of me began to fight from that moment on.

I was thinking about what the doctor had said about not getting my foot wet when a strange idea came over me. Cow balm! It's the grease that they apply to cure a cow's irritated udders.

Even though it is the opposite of what the dermatologist advised, I thought, *if it could help the irritated skin of a cow, it might be able to help my foot!*

It was at this point that my fight to heal began. With a newly found determination, I lay down in my bed, and slept like a rock.

The next morning, one of my friends went to the store and purchased the cow balm for me. I began to grease my foot and left no area dry. I felt that it was the right thing to do, despite the doctor's orders. I visualized myself getting better and stayed very attentive to my foot.

A couple of days later, television cameras came by to put The Iceman's terrible-looking foot on television. On the outside, it was green and black, but on the inside, the healing process was beginning!

While tending to my foot, I thought about what I had been able to achieve. With the help of the Discovery Channel, I was now known as "the guy who ran a half marathon beyond the Polar Circle, barefoot in the snow."

Looking back on my success that day, I am reminded of an old story I once heard:

The Story of Three Brothers:

Over a century ago, in the northern part of Finland, there lived three brothers. There was a sauna in a wooden hut near a large, frozen lake, ten kilometers from their village. Every day, the three brothers would travel out to the sauna and enjoy its warmth.

One day, a sudden rush of flames interrupted their relaxing sauna time. Something had caused a fire inside of the wooden hut! They looked around but couldn't find a way to extinguish the flames. The three brothers escaped from the wooden hut with only their lives. The fire had consumed their clothes and belongings.

It was a large fire that could be seen from afar. It was beautiful and warm, yet tragic and unexpected. Naked, the three brothers were forced to run ten kilometers through the snow, in the freezing cold of the night, to get home to their village.

The story of the three brothers shows that my marathon was nothing spectacular. The barefoot run was just my way of showing the world that we are all capable of doing more than what we had previously thought possible.

It is a memorable story and so is mine. News of my achievement spread all over the media. Despite my damaged foot, I was a real hero in the eyes of the public.

I didn't care about the media attention. My focus was on healing my foot as fast as possible. Back in December, right before I started training for the half marathon, I received a phone call from a man who was preparing for an expedition on Mount Everest. He was the team leader and wanted to know if I was interested in the ascent. Their idea was for me to climb Mount Everest wearing only shorts and sandals.

It was another opportunity to do a challenge that no one had ever done before. I was very interested and therefore, accepted his offer. What I didn't know at the time was that just a month later I would have "irreparable damage" done to my foot!

Initially, the sponsoring for the expedition wasn't going well.

Having just completed a world record and receiving a lot of media attention related to the frostbite, the money started flooding in from all directions. 50,000 euro here, 50,000 euro there. It was all flowing in and coming together. This, however, did not change the condition of my foot.

I had three months to recover. The dermatologist told me that there was no chance that I would be able to make that climb, or even have slightly recovered by that time. I decided to throw away all of the medication and increase my fighting spirit to heal. I started to grease up my foot on a daily basis. I remained optimistic that it would help my foot get better.

Despite everything the doctor said, a month later, my foot was healed! The dead, calloused skin had vanished and new, healthy skin turned my foot into a new one. It was like the injury had never happened!

To help promote the Everest expedition and the sponsors for the event, I stood in a box full of ice as a publicity stunt. My event appeared in newspapers, in magazines, on television, and even in the marketplace, where huge banners hung to advertise the expedition. It was all a part of the game and I was along for the ride. Eventually, the day to depart for Everest finally arrived.

CHAPTER 14:
WHO IS THE ICEMAN?

During the summer of 2009, I was not able to return to Camp Judson. I was forced to find a higher paying job to pay for my apartment, so I picked up a job as a dishwasher at The Deli, a local restaurant in State College. When the fall semester began, I kept my job to make some extra money on the side. I felt rejuvenated and ready for another school year. Jarrett and I spoke as often as we could, but because I always had a lot of homework, our conversations were usually cut short.

In one of our previous talks, I had mentioned to Jarrett that I thought it would be interesting to control body temperature. I told him the story of the man that died of hypothermia in a 60°F (15.5°C) climate. He enjoyed seeing the mind's potential just as much as me. Even though his major was Computer Science, he was very interested in learning everything that was Psychology related.

After my first week of classes, I received an email from Jarrett with a link to a YouTube video. The video was about a man they called, "The Iceman." It was a television special titled *Extraordinary People* featured on the Discovery Channel. The clip showed The Iceman running a half marathon barefoot through the snow, wearing only shorts; I was intrigued.

Here was a man running in temperatures below freezing, not 1 mile, not 5 miles, but 13 miles through the snow. I was extremely impressed by his stamina and how comfortable he looked while running. At one point in the clip, Wim, The Iceman's real name, explained that he controlled his internal thermostat using only his mind. This meant that it wasn't some genetic mutation or natural gift, but his conscious control.

My mind immediately filled with thoughts like, *"I knew it was possible!"* and *"Is this some sort of trick?"* I wanted to believe it was real, but I also wanted to view it from an objective perspective.

As I continued watching the video, I saw that Wim suffered from frostbite in his left foot.

"Okay," I thought, *"maybe it wasn't a trick if he actually got frostbite."*

When the video ended, I called Jarrett and expressed my excitement. We spoke of theories and how it could be possible. After ending the call, I went online and did some more research. I came across an ancient Tibetan technique called "Tummo," also known as "Inner Fire." This technique offered the Tibetan Monks the ability to withstand extreme cold and generate heat within their body, without any external force.

The most known story, passed along with the idea of Tummo, consists of Tibetan Monks sitting in the snow with cold, wet sheets draped over their backs. Allegedly, they would sit and mediate for hours, in order to generate heat. Their goal was to dry the wet sheets on their back, in the cold climate, using only the heat from their bodies.

This technique sounded awesome and I wanted to learn it as soon as possible. Winter would be around in a couple months and I was extremely interested in being able to keep myself warm, without the aid of layered clothing.

Now at the time, I was a huge fan of a book called *Way of the Peaceful Warrior* by Dan Millman and I really looked up to him as a role model. I followed a few of his seminars and read many of his other books. The concept in this particular book really inspired me to do more.

One day, I decided to email Mr. Millman, not really thinking he'd respond. To my surprise his secretary responded for him saying that Dan wasn't familiar with Tummo and suggested that I do some research on Wikipedia. So, I went to the webpage for *"Tummo"* and checked the reference section. There, I found a book called *The Bliss of Inner Fire*. The title intrigued me and I thought it was about time to take my research a little more seriously. I purchased the title and received the book a few days later.

When the book came, I put aside my homework and began reading. The text was kind of difficult to read because it used a unique set of vocabulary words that I didn't understand. I assumed it was common knowledge to most of the audience that followed yoga, but it was hard for me to comprehend. I went online to define some of the words I didn't know like *"prana"*, *"chakra"*, and *"kundalini"*.

I progressed through the book slowly and took my time to understand each chapter. The first few chapters expressed the background of Tummo and the opinions of the author. After a few days of sporadic reading, I finally came to the chapters explaining the technique. It focused on a lot of different breathing exercises and visualizations. It seemed strange, but I blamed my opinion on my ignorance.

After finishing the book, I didn't feel any closer to understanding how to control my body heat. I'm the type of person that likes to physically watch others and then ask questions. Therefore, I felt like the book was a dead end, so I threw it under my bed and pulled out my homework.

For the next few weeks, I focused on my classes and gave up on learning *Tummo*. I was disappointed, but I resolved my dissonance by watching videos of The Iceman on YouTube. One day, I was sitting in my 9:00 AM class listening to a professor speak on the subject of Personality Theory. As he prepared the next few slides, I decided to do a quick search on Tummo one more time before I gave up completely. I don't know why I felt compelled to do it right then in the middle of class, but I tend to have those spontaneous moments quite often.

I used Google's search engine to search for "Tummo" and the usual listings came up: a few websites with a definition, a forum site for those who study Buddhism, and a few images of monks sitting in the snow. I decided to revise my search and type in "Tummo seminar," just for the heck of it.

One new listing popped up that I hadn't seen before. It was a downloadable .*pdf* file containing a flyer. My professor began talking again; I ignored the last ten minutes of the lecture to investigate my new discovery. The flyer advertised a seminar to teach people the art of Tummo. The seminar was set to take place during the weekend, a month and a half later in Berkeley, California. The cost was about $250 and registration needed to be completed by the end of the month.

I was ecstatic! I had lost all my focus in class and all I wanted to do was tell Jarrett. For rest of the class period, I brainstormed ideas of how I could get to Berkeley, California in a month and make it to that seminar.

As I was leaving class, I told one of classmates and best friend, David Haneman, about my idea of going to California to study *Tummo*. He thought it was a cool idea, but impractical, especially because we were college kids with limited funds. Luckily, I had my job as a dishwasher. Although maybe not the most flattering job, dishwashing provided me with the funds I needed to perform research.

I called Jarrett on the way to my next class and told him about the opportunity. I had hoped he could go with me, but sadly he had an appointment in his hometown and was unable to reschedule. I would have to go to California alone... I never flew before, so the idea of flying alone across the country intimidated me. Regardless, I was determined to do whatever I needed to make it to that seminar.

Over the next couple weeks, I picked up a few extra shifts to cover the potential expenses of my trip. Each night, I'd come home from work with food caked under my fingernails. *It's worth it,* I'd repeatedly tell myself.

When my first check came in, I emailed the people who were holding the seminar in Berkeley and asked them if it was too late to sign up. They told me that there were still spots open and if I sent my $250 to them in the mail, they would send me the information I needed and place me on the roster.

The next day I sent out a check and went online to look for the price of plane tickets and hotels. The cheapest plane ticket I found was a $220 flight from Pittsburgh, PA to Oakland, CA. I called my parents and told them that I was about to lock myself into the trip. They didn't feel comfortable with the idea of me traveling to California, especially because I had never traveled alone before, let alone fly. After a long conversation over the phone, they agreed to let me go as long as I remained cautious and planned everything out. So, I went online and purchased airline tickets with the money I had earned from The Deli.

At that point, I didn't have enough money to pay for a hotel room, but I knew that they wouldn't give me the bill until I checked out. Therefore, I went online and searched for the closest hotel to the place where the seminar would be held. I found 5 hotels in a 5-mile radius of the building. I took the closest one with the easiest walking route to the seminar.

I had one concern. I knew that in some states, only people over the age of 21 could reserve and stay in hotel rooms. Sadly, I still had a few months until my 21st birthday. I called the hotel that I would be staying at and spoke with their manager. They assured me that it wouldn't be a problem; I was relieved. I then proceeded to go online and find out the distance from Oakland, CA to Berkeley, CA. Google Maps told me that it would be a 35-minute drive with traffic. With a taxi, it would be approximately $40 total, each way.

I looked at the map again and searched for nearby locations where I could buy food. Luckily, there was a Walgreens just up the block. After calling my manager to reserve that weekend off, I felt that I had done enough in one day and went to sleep.

For the next two weeks, I focused on my studies during the day and worked at The Deli during the night. My next paycheck gave me enough money to cover the cost of the two-night stay at the hotel, the taxi fair, and the potential cost of food. Three days before my flight left, I received a packet in the mail explaining the material that would be covered at the seminar. It also gave me the starting time and what to do when I had arrived.

Everything was set in place, and I was ready to take on my first big adventure. Other than my best friends, my family, and my manager at work, no one knew where I was going. I didn't even tell my girlfriend, Brooke Robinson, until the day before I left; I was afraid she'd think I was crazy. We had only been dating for a few weeks and I wanted to be really careful with who I told about my research because I didn't anyone to put me down, say it was ridiculous, or try to keep me from pursuing it.

Even though I wished Jarrett could have gone with me, I had to accept it and go on the behalf of both of us. I wanted to understand Tummo beyond what the Internet had to offer. Finally, I was going to have that chance.

CHAPTER 15:
EVEREST

On April 1, 2007, we left for Everest. We took a flight to Dubai and connected to Kathmandu. News of my approaching arrival was booming.

"Some guy from Holland is going to climb Everest in shorts!" The news was everywhere.

My philosophy was: *Hillary and Tenzin did it with clothes and oxygen. Messner did it without oxygen. I will try it without oxygen and without clothes.* It was a very controversial matter, but it spread throughout the news all over the world.

The journalists were waiting for us as we arrived at the airport in Kathmandu, Nepal. There I was, back in Nepal, with a new team. As we drove through the crazy traffic in the streets, cars honked all around us.

The expectations were high and this affected me, but I didn't let my feelings show. Instead, I held it inside, which only made me think of all the things that could go wrong. I reminded myself that the only thing I could do was to be ready and the rest would follow.

My main concern was my body. I needed to focus my nervous system, immune system, blood circulation, heart and mind to bring them all together. I also did a lot of my own personal research by speaking to the local Sherpas. They are very wise and know the mountains like the back of their hand. They told me, "We'll see how much you can do. Even though it will be a long hike, you seem fast and strong."

After they had witnessed me performing my technique during one of my training sessions, they approached me with questions. I decided to spend some time with the Sherpas until the day I left for Everest arrived.

The Chinese authorities greeted us as we passed the border. We then drove down the Friendship Highway toward the Tibetan Plateau. From there, it was only a 4,000-meter drive (2.5 miles).

We planned to stay in the village for a couple days so our bodies would be able to acclimatize. Along with buying large portions of food for the trip, we played football to help condition our bodies to the new climate. To further practice and prepare our bodies for the ascent, we also climbed nearby mountains. Before we knew it, the day was upon us when we would leave for the Everest base camp at 5,200 meters (17,060 feet).

We packed our jeeps and hit the road. Along the way, we passed all kinds of Tibetan villages and rocky pastures. After some time, we stopped at Rongbuk Monastery at 4,800 meters (15,748 feet). We filmed there for a bit, but didn't stay too long because we didn't want to intrude on the people that lived there. After an hour or so, we returned to our jeeps and continued our drive to the base camp.

Finally, we were there: the base camp of Mount Everest, Chomolungma (Chinese for *Everest*), Sagarmatha (Hindi for *Everest*). Here we would stay to acclimatize for a few days. Tents surrounded us. They weren't all just sleeping tents either. There was a huge kitchen tent where everyone cooked, a tent where people could purchase items and supplies, a showering tent, a tent to eat in, and an office tent where you could reserve your place on the grounds.

After we had found our spot and settled in, I went exploring in the adjacent mountains. Everything went well and I was excited for the things to come.

When I got back to camp, I started playing the blues on a guitar. Many people heard it and came over to listen. Afterwards, we played football again; though, with half as much oxygen in the air, it was hard to run for extended periods of time, so we didn't play for very long.

It is important for one to relearn his body's limits in a new environment.

When the team leader felt that the group was acclimatized enough, he decided that it was time to go to the Interim Camp at 5,800 meters (19,028 feet). I told the leader that we should look at the weather forecast before we left; I had a feeling that it was going to snow in the early afternoon. Since I was climbing the mountain in shorts, I wanted to make sure the weather conditions were perfect. This is where we hit our first snag.

In my opinion, I think the leader's decision to leave when we did wasn't a very good one. As we departed from base camp, the clouds began to cover the sky. The team leader told us to keep going while the clouds only became denser. When we arrived at 5,400 meters (17,716 feet), snow began to fall.

I told the group that the overall pace was too slow for me. I'm a lot faster when I'm in my rhythm and I needed to follow what my body was telling me. So, I continued on in shorts at my own pace, a fast pace. The head Sherpa tried to get a hold of me and slow me down, but I was ignited by my drive.

Finding a good pace can be the key to continuing strong. It's also important to watch how much oxygen you're consuming. You don't want to waste all of your energy and have to stop for breaths to recover. After a couple of times doing this myself, I realized it wasn't efficient. By monitoring your breathing and making sure you never push past your breaking point, you can continue on for hours at a steady, but strong pace.

The snow began to fall even harder and soon my visibility became limited. I couldn't see the path. It was my first time in shorts at an unknown height, in an unknown place, where blankets of snow covered the rocky terrain. Intuition and drive were my only companions. I felt surprisingly good, despite the situation, and continued my pace up the mountain trail. I was in the snow for hours. The limited visibility reminded me of my solitude, but I still felt remarkably well.

I looked ahead of me and saw the outline of an object through the snow. As I came closer, the shape widened out and I realized that it was a tent. When I was about a meter away, I saw a few Tibetans staring at me. They were astounded at the Caucasian man who had just emerged from the blizzard wearing only shorts. They invited me inside their tent, gave me some tea with sugar, and placed a blanket around my shoulder.

After three quarters of an hour, the head Sherpa arrived and looked in awe at me in total control of the situation. He was worried because he was responsible for everyone in his party; yet, I was absolutely content.

I felt that I had shaken hands with Everest's nature. I had connected with the mountain and its people. I overcame my fear of the unknown and my anxiety vanished. I also was able to see how fast I could move without acquiring any form of mountain sickness. The confidence I gained in my inner nature made me feel that I was on the path to accomplishing a lot more on that mountain. I had optimistic thoughts and felt fully capable. After eating in another tent across the riverbed, we returned to our sleeping quarters and fell asleep at our 5,800-meter mark (19,028 feet). I was ready to take on new steps for mankind.

The next day, our team leader had us acclimatize more by climbing in the neighboring areas. We climbed and walked over a small path toward 6,000 meters (19,685 feet). It was the highest point I had ever been on a mountain. It was also my personal record for highest altitude while wearing shorts. We then returned back to Interim Camp. The acclimatization process must have gone well for me because I felt great!

It was my personal goal to reach the highest point on Everest and for it to happen in only shorts. I wanted to show that being exposed, almost naked in nature, is the way it's supposed to be, even in the extremes. To me, clothing and artificial oxygen are like using a car to get from point A to point B. Unlike walking or riding a bike, you simply step on the gas, and go. Of course, it's still difficult to climb Everest even with auxiliary tools (oxygen and clothing), but doing it the natural way makes things a lot simpler.

The following day, we began our climb to 6,400 meters (20,997 feet). There, we would enter the Advanced Base Camp (ABC), where one can see the beautiful North Col at its height of 7,060 meters (23,162 feet). Tenzin (the head Sherpa) and I went ahead of the others because our rhythm and pace were much faster than the rest of the group. As we climbed up the slopes, the leader of the camera team filmed us. Tenzin told the camera that, despite being fully clothed, he was still freezing. He said that he was amazed at how I was still climbing in only shorts.

This is not something that I am able to do because I am fast and strong, but because I am able to fight through my fears and interact with the mountain. Instead, I am stronger and faster in a natural way, where I remain connected to the environment around me. My senses are more perceptive in the mountain climate where my body is exposed. My mind and body adjust naturally; it's reflexive.

We stayed a couple of days at the ABC camp and we were soon acclimatized. It's fairly easy to tell how well the body has adapted to the environment. All you need to do is monitor the oxygen saturation and heart rate. High oxygen saturation and a low heart rate are the ideal variables to be well conditioned in high altitudes. It seemed that I had both of these in my favor, as I had acclimatized extremely well. One of the days at the ABC, I was feeling so full of energy that I decided to climb the North Col. Driven, I threw on my shorts and jogged over to the base.

When I first arrived at North Col, the wind was really bad. The wind speed was over 100 kilometers per hour (62 mph). Of course, when you're wearing shorts in wind speeds that high, you can really feel it against the skin. I stayed there for about an hour, but decided that it wasn't wise to go up any further. I had no choice but to abort. I was disappointed, but I knew that I would be back soon to try again.

Later on, I returned to North Col with Tenzin. His pace was too fast and I was desperately trying to follow. *What happened?* I was faster than him when we first hiking to the Interim Camp, but now his speed had far exceeded my own. It soon was obvious who was more acclimatized in that terrain.

While trying to keep up with him during the ascent, I collapsed regularly while trying to catch my breath; I was exhausted. Slowly, but surely, I fought my way up until I reached the peak of North Col at 7,060 meters (23,162 feet). It was my new personal record in shorts!

At the peak, we set up flags around the area, including a flag of a poet, Rob Tuankotta, who is a dear friend of mine. Another flag we raised was the United World flag, which exemplified enlightened beings as the world's inhabitants. On the flag was a big sun with bright beams, symbolizing the equality of human beings. It was beautiful. Lastly, we took some pictures for our sponsors.

After we got a few good shots of the necessary material, we were content and headed back down to ABC. We passed the news over satellite telephone to inform the world of our recent achievement. We found out the next day that we had made international news! The headlines read, "Iceman reaches North Col" and "Who can stop the Iceman?" All was going well.

After several more ascents up North Col, I felt more acclimatized. Everyone was very impressed by my agility, speed and endurance. Also, the frequent checkups with the medical team showed that my oxygen saturation was high and my heart rate stayed low. *Perfect.*

One day, after returning from North Col, the team leader decided to go down a little to recover before the final ascent of Everest. It was a strategic way to ascend. We were so used to the thin air of the higher attitudes that at 4,600 meters (15,091 feet), the air felt thick. We stayed there for three beautiful days, barely eating anything. When you're in high altitudes, your appetite is limited. The higher you climb, the more your body shuts down the nonessential functions to preserve energy for the vital organs; it's a survival mode.

When we were completely recovered and felt refreshed, we went back to the ABC and then began travelling up to the 7,060-meter mark (23,162 feet) at North Col. We spent the night there and then left for the next marker. We made it up to the 7,200-meter mark (23,622 feet) and it was here that I had again accomplished a new personal record in shorts!

Finally, the day came for us to ascend up to the 7,800 and 8,300-meter marks (25,590 and 27,230 feet). Here, the Sherpas had set up a few tents for us. There were also oxygen bottles waiting for us, which we were to use when summiting.

That day, I felt great and went up the slope very fast. I ascended 200 meters in one hour with Tenzin! Then, I realized that something was wrong. I felt something going on inside of my left foot. The frostbite injury I had developed back in Finland was healed, but apparently the veins were not as conditioned as they used to be.

The entire circulation system, as well as the veins, has to be able to constrict and dilate to be able to adjust to the cold and altitude. Whenever there is less oxygen in the air, the veins in the extremities naturally close to reserve heat and redirect blood flow to the core to preserve the essential organs. Then, after adaptation, the veins open up again and the extremities are filled with warm blood. However, due to my recent cold injury, the veins in my left foot weren't opening.

There was a tight pressure and I began to feel pain. I could feel that the veins in my foot weren't going to open back up so I was forced to turn around. There wasn't a doubt in my mind that if I didn't turn back at that moment, I would lose my foot forever. I was not going make the same mistake twice. Even though the expedition cost 250,000 euro (about $340,000-$350,000) and completing this challenge would have brought me everlasting honor, being the only man to climb Everest in shorts, it was not worth losing my foot over. I decided to think rationally and listen to what my body was telling me.

I looked around on the roof of the world and felt satisfied with what I had accomplished. I had fought through my fears and set a new record height of 7,450 meters (24,442 feet) in only shorts.

The press brought the story and the pictures of the expedition to the entire world. I returned to Holland and prepared for my next attempt. In a month's time, I was going to attempt a Guinness World Record in a polar bear compound. By the time I got home, I felt completely rejuvenated and healthy in both body and mind. My foot thanked me for taking the time to heal altogether.

Remember, we can do more than we think, but only when we break through the inhibitions of fear and other obstacles. Rationality keeps us alive.

CHAPTER 16:
CALIFORNIA

Shortly after buying my plain ticket, I informed my professors that I would be flying to California for a few days. They were okay with me going as long as I made up the work, which I gratefully accepted. After getting my final things together and saying goodbye to my girlfriend, I jumped in the car and started driving home.

During the three-hour drive home from Penn State, I contemplated many things. First, I thought about everything that could go wrong, like missing a flight, getting lost, or even getting mugged. It took me a little while, but eventually I calmed myself down and tried to be a little more optimistic.

I told myself that what I was doing was important and helpful to my understanding of life. I felt mature traveling alone and taking an opportunity to improve my knowledge. To me, that was more important than my college classes. In the past, I had considered withdrawing from college to pursue knowledge on my own. Of course, there are plenty of benefits to attending a university, but I believe the structure is flawed. Regardless, I really enjoyed the idea of pursuing information that interested me. Not every class in college inspired me to do more and become better, but this opportunity did. I was ready to accept whatever came my way. I was ready to take on whatever challenge was ahead. More than anything else, I was ready to learn, to understand, and to hopefully gain wisdom.

My wandering thoughts on the three-hour drive made it feel more like thirty minutes. When I got home, it was almost midnight. My parents were happy to see me when I walked through the door. Even though I could see the fear in their eyes while they considered my safety, I told them I would be responsible and extremely cautious. "We're fine," they told me, but their body language said otherwise.

My flight was scheduled to leave the following morning at 8:56

AM from Pittsburgh International Airport. I was tired of driving and I wanted to get a good night's sleep. I said goodnight to my family and went to my room. After brushing my teeth, I fetched my laptop to check my email before going to bed. I searched through my backpack for my power cord to charge my laptop, but it wasn't there. *I must have forgotten it in my room at school*, I thought. Immediately, the list of everything that could go wrong flooded back into my head. My laptop was one resource I didn't want to be without.

I took my laptop, plugged it into my family's printer, and printed out everything I thought I would need: directions, flight itineraries, and a map of the area near my hotel. I returned to my bed and tried to fall asleep. I was worried about not being able to use my laptop in California. I soothed my worries by switching my perspective. Instead, I viewed it as a challenge. I would need to use my resources effectively and be prepared for the unexpected. After twenty minutes of thinking, I finally fell asleep.

The next morning, I woke up around 5:00 AM and left soon after; my father bought me breakfast on the way to the airport. I remember feeling nervous, yet excited. By the end of the day, I would be in a hotel room, by myself, thousands of miles away.

When we arrived at the airport, my dad hugged me goodbye and wished me well. Going through security made me nervous. For some reason, I was expecting airport security to arrest me. I don't know why, but I sort of expected something to go wrong; luckily, nothing did.

My first flight took off from Pittsburgh International Airport and arrived at Denver International. From there, I flew to Oakland International. By the time I touched down in Oakland, it was 5:00 PM (EST) and 2:00 PM (PST). It was strange being on the opposite side of the country; I was nervous, but excited at the same time. I was on my own.

I grabbed my luggage and jumped in a taxi. The driver told me it would be a $40 trip; I gave him the cash and the car started moving. I admired the scenery as we drove through the busy streets of California. Remembering that my parents wanted me to call them when I landed, I pulled out my phone and dialed their number. They told me that they were worried, but glad I was safe and on my way to the hotel. They asked me to call them when I arrived. By the time the phone call ended, we had just parked in front of the hotel.

I unloaded my bags and tipped the taxi driver. My heart beat with anticipation as I walked over to the office. Even though I had previously spoken to the manager on the phone, I was still afraid that they would turn me away because of my age. My worries were swept away when the receptionist smiled and handed me the key to my room. I gratefully thanked her and left the office.

The hotel was, by no means, extravagant. There was only one floor and about 30 rooms. The layout of the complex was in a giant 'U' shape. The building surrounded the parking lot where only a few cars were parked. I found my room in the corner of the parking lot. I opened the door and brought my luggage inside.

The room had a cozy, simple layout. There was a bed, TV, mini-fridge, table, lamps, sink, and two beds. I unpacked my clothes and placed them in the drawers beneath the television. After I got everything settled, I called my parents once more to tell them I was okay. I didn't stay on the phone too long because there was a few more things I needed to take care of before the sun set. I hung up the phone and collapsed on my bed.

In the room adjacent to mine, I could hear a man yelling angrily in a foreign language. I was really out of my comfort zone, but I was excited to have the opportunity to embrace it. All my expenses were paid for and my only priority was to attend the seminar. There would be no more worrying about making the trip possible; I was finally *on* the trip. The only thing I had left to do was enjoy it.

I rose back to my feet and pulled my laptop out of my backpack. I placed it on the table and turned it on. The hotel had free wireless Internet access. I quickly checked my email to see if anyone sent me anything about the seminar; there was nothing. My laptop only had about ten minutes left of battery. I shut it down to reserve the rest in case of an emergency.

After grabbing my wallet and room key, I walked out the door. I had a couple hours until sundown so I decided to buy groceries. I walked to the office to ask the receptionist if she knew of any places where I could buy food. My map told me where Walgreens was, but I wanted to make sure that it was still up to date. I didn't want to wonder around aimlessly looking for a building that was taken down years ago. Luckily, she confirmed that the Walgreens was still right down the street. I thanked her and went on my way.

It was a cloudy day and the air was chilly. The streets were busy with cars while children played on the sidewalks. It took me about ten minutes to walk to Walgreens. I bought a few microwaveable meals and a couple of fruits. I called Jarrett while I was shopping and updated him about what had happened thus far. On my way out, I found several "California" shirts on sale. I purchased two of them as souvenirs.

Across the street from Walgreens was an Office Depot. I stopped by to see if they sold laptop power cords. They had them in stock but the prices were outrageous. I decided to save my money and continue on without a laptop.

After walking back to my apartment and putting away the groceries, I changed into my running clothes. I wanted to check out the exact location where the seminar would be held later that evening. So I glanced over the map once more and tried to memorize the street names. When I felt comfortable enough, I grabbed my iPod and left.

I felt slightly intimidated as I jogged through the streets of Berkeley. I was worried that I would forget the directions, so I kept repeating them over and over again in my head. Eventually, I came to my first turn with no problem; before I knew it, I was standing in front of the building where the workshop would be held. It only took me about 11 minutes to jog from my hotel room to the building; I assumed that it would take me no more than a half hour if I walked.

The place was locked and the lights were out. I grabbed one of the pamphlets that were hanging outside on the wall. After catching my breath for five minutes, I turned around and started running back the way I came.

Knowing where I was supposed to go in a few hours made feel a lot more comfortable. It helped sooth my worries of possibly getting lost. When I got back into my hotel room, I threw my iPod on my bed and took a shower.

A few hours later, I returned to the building. It was a two-hour session where we were required to come in and finish our registration. They would also provide us with the information packet that we would be using over the next couple days. After we registered, a woman gave her testimony of how her life was personally affected by Tummo.

It was 9:00 PM (PST) by the time I got out. Back home it was 12:00 AM (EST). On the way back to my hotel room, I called my parents to tell them about my day and to wish them goodnight. I needed to be at the workshop the following morning by 9:00 AM, so as soon as I got back to my temporary home, I went to bed.

The next morning I woke up at 6:00 AM; the sun was just rising. I took a shower, ate breakfast, and began making my way to the workshop. The warmth of the sun's rays against my skin comforted me. The dark clouds from the day before seemed to be long gone. On my way over, I noticed a Popeye's Louisiana Kitchen. One of my best friends, at the time grew up in California and told me that Popeye's food was fantastic. I made a note of the restaurant's location and decided to stop by at some point during my trip.

A short while later, I stood in front of the familiar double doors leading to the workshop. I placed my iPod back into my backpack and followed a couple inside. Paintings of old people hung on the red walls. Statues of Buddha lined the hallways. I deduced that I was in some sort of Buddhist temple.

I began walking around, looking for the room listed on the information sheet. I found it at the end of a long hallway near a life-size statue of Buddha. I entered the room, gave them my name, and took my seat. Hundreds of people sat around me silently, all facing the stage, waiting for something to happen.

After half an hour of silence, a woman finally walked on to the stage and introduced the Tibetan Monk that would be teaching Tummo. He spoke for a couple hours about how Tummo is supposed to help us transcend, strengthen the kundalini, and unblock obstacles in our body. He then said something to the effect of, "Some enjoy Tummo because it produces a nice, warm heat in the stomach; however, the heat is only a side effect. The real power comes when you transcend."

After his speech, he had us perform breathing exercises. Apparently, this was the final session of a set of workshops that took place throughout the year. In their previous workshops, they had spent their time learning about Tummo's background, how it related to Buddhism, and other various breathing exercises. This session was the one where we were supposed to learn the actual *form* of Tummo. The breathing exercises were allegedly used in preparation for Tummo. The breathing exercises consisted of slow, focused breaths. Essentially, we were supposed to hold our breath for a minute, while sitting and doing some awkward movements with our arms.

After a quick lunch break, we came back and began learning Tummo. The form was not what I had expected. It didn't seem to be much different from the breathing exercises we had performed before lunch. Instead of only the arms moving, while holding our breath, we moved our upper torso as well. Our instructor also had us practice visualizing a fire in the center of our stomachs. With each breath, we were told to imagine the flame growing with intensity.

I was happy to learn the technique, but I didn't feel like I was getting any warmer. Also, I didn't feel comfortable with all of the beliefs that surrounded Tummo. I never studied Buddhism, but I understood the basic premises. They were saying that the only way you could perform Tummo was to follow their methods, exactly. I begged to differ.

From that point on, I began viewing the workshop from an objective point of view. I wanted to see if it was possible to perform Tummo without their set belief system. Sure, I did the visualizations of the little flame in my stomach, as well as the movements, but I remained detached from their views of transcendence.

As a result of shifting perspectives and viewing everything objectively, I found myself quickly growing bored. Of the 10 hours we spent there on Saturday, we practiced the breathing and Tummo exercises for only two hours each. For the other six hours we were there, the teacher elaborated on how Tummo affects the body and clears any obstructions in life. At one point, they asked us to imagine ourselves turning into some transcendent female being. I couldn't see how it could possibly relate to heating up the body.

When Saturday's workshop was over, I walked home. I was tempted to eat at Popeye's, but I decided to save the $15.00 I had left in my wallet for my final dinner in California. When I got back to the hotel room, I phoned my parents to tell them how my day went. I also reassured them of my safety. After hanging up, I tried looking over the instructional papers that they had given us on how to perform Tummo, but I found it hard to follow with all of their beliefs interlaced in the text. I decided that I would bring a notebook with me the following day, to objectively record the core concepts of Tummo.

When I woke up the next morning at 5:00 AM (PST), I realized that I was in the mood to go for a run. I used what was left of my laptop battery to find the directions to the University of Berkeley. The college was a mile and a half away from the hotel -- not too far for a run. After eating breakfast out of a complementary plastic cup, I grabbed my iPod and ran out the door.

Eventually, the campus was in sight. It took me about 20 minutes to get to the University of Berkeley. There was a lot of traffic on the road, making it hard to cross intersections quickly. I crossed the street and ran up toward the campus, alongside a wooden fence. As I turned a corner to continue jogging uphill, a speeding bicyclist struck me. Luckily, there was just enough time to lower my shoulder and brace for impact. A man flew through the air and yelled as his body skidded across the concrete; he grabbed his knee in pain.

He was screaming in some language I didn't understand. I repeatedly tried to offer my help but it appeared that the man didn't understand me. After I apologized over thirty times, the man rose to his feet, jumped on his bike, gave me a foul glare, and rode off.

For the next few minutes I stood there feeling guilty, contemplating if the man was seriously injured. As my iPod clicked and the next song began to play in my headphones, I snapped out of my daze and returned to my run. By the time I reached the campus, I had forgotten the incident.

In my opinion, the campus was much more beautiful than Penn

State's. There was luscious grass everywhere and little pathways that extended in every direction. I continued running uphill until I found myself in the middle of a park. Students were lying on benches and reading their textbooks. It seemed like a very lovely place to study.

Near the end of my loop around campus, I found myself running by the University of Berkeley's Gymnasium. I remembered it as the place where Dan Millman had trained in *Way of the Peaceful Warrior*. It was a surreal moment for me to be standing next to the gym where my favorite author had trained for many years.

I continued running home and arrived 20 minutes later. I took a shower, ate another quick breakfast, and then made my way back to the workshop. Mostly, the day consisted of more breathing exercises and Tummo practice. The teacher also taught us two more additional methods of Tummo, but allegedly, Tummo experts should only attempt them.

There is one moment in particular that I think is important to share with you. We had just finished the breathing exercises and began one of the Tummo forms. After about ten minutes of doing the form, my body felt warm. Ten more minutes went by and I found myself sweating. By the end of the exercise, my shirt and shorts were drenched with sweat. Somehow, I had managed to tap into the side effect of heat that comes with Tummo. I was ecstatic, yet strangely disappointed.

Ever since I had seen The Iceman on YouTube, I couldn't wait for the chance to consciously raise my body temperature. When it had finally happened, I expected more. I didn't like the idea that you had to be sitting down to properly perform Tummo. In the videos I had seen of The Iceman, he was running around barefoot in the snow, submerging himself in ice, and swimming around under ice water.

The only situation where I saw Tummo being useful to survive would be if someone were forced to be in extremely cold temperatures for an extended period of time. That's the only time where I could see sitting and warming yourself up as efficient. I now understood why the Tibetan Monks saw Tummo's main goal as transcendence, not heat.

When I exited the building where I spent most of my time over those last few days, part of me felt like the trip was worthless. The other part of me felt accomplished. *Well, now I know that there is at least one way to consciously warm up the body,* I thought.

On the way home, I stopped at Popeye's Louisiana Kitchen for my final dinner in California. Their chicken was delicious and I was extremely satisfied. After I got home, I decided to go for a walk around the city to help my stomach digest the food. I remembered seeing a sign for a pier on my way to the workshop, not too far off of the main street. I figured it was worth checking out.

It was a little intimidating walking through the streets of Berkeley at night. When I first diverged off the familiar path, I called Jarrett to tell him about my weekend. Having someone on the phone was also a way to calm my nerves from walking through unknown territory. I told him of my excitement that I had on the first day, but also told him how I was disappointed overall. In learning that the Tibetan way of Tummo involved only sitting, I explained that I wanted to learn more about how the The Iceman could do what he did.

I finished my conversation with Jarrett as I approached the Berkeley Marina Pier. To the side, there was a path that crossed a giant interstate. When I was on the bridge crossing the interstate, I realized that it was the very same highway that goes through my hometown. It was mind-blowing moment. Thousands of miles away from my home and college, I was standing on top of the interstate that leads directly to my house.

I continued crossing the bridge and found myself standing atop a hill facing a large body of water. At the time, I didn't know which body of water I was looking at. In the distance, I saw a long line of lights outlining the structure of a bridge. It was an utterly beautiful sight. I later came to learn that I was gazing at the infamous Golden Gate Bridge.

I returned to my hotel room around midnight and promptly fell asleep, but only after setting three alarms. The next morning, I was happy to have woken by my first alarm at 4:30 AM. I packed up my belongings, ate breakfast, and called a taxi.

The taxi arrived around 7:00 AM. The driver was a friendly fellow, very polite. While he helped me place my bags into the trunk, I noticed he had a twitch that shook his entire body. At first I thought my eyes were playing tricks on me, but after several more occurrences, I was convinced that the man must suffered from some form of Tourette's syndrome. I was worried about how it would affect his driving, but I climbed into the car anyway. A few minutes into the ride, I noticed the man jerk a few more times, but luckily, his movements didn't affect the momentum of the car. I safely made it to the Oakland Airport with two hours to spare.

During those two hours, I called my family and told them that I was coming home, safe. I also checked into my flight and ate a second breakfast. My first flight took me from Oakland, California to Seattle, Washington. From Seattle's airport, I flew to Chicago, Illinois. Finally, I left Chicago and arrived in Pittsburgh's airport in the early evening. In total, it took me almost 13 hours to finally reach my home in Sharon, Pennsylvania.

When I arrived home, I reflected on my trip as a whole. Although I hadn't learned what I was expecting, I had acquired a very useful experience and actually pursued understanding on my own. It was the first time in my life that I felt... fulfilled. As soon as I had known in my heart that I wanted to pursue knowledge, the opportunity opened up for me. All I had to do was follow the path. I was extremely grateful for my safety, yet even more thankful for the experience. It was the first leap in my quest toward understanding The Iceman.

CHAPTER 17:
USA

I first met Eric Mazer in Los Angeles when I was invited by a Guinness World Records show to break the existing ice-endurance record by half an hour. Eric was an independent documentary producer who did a lot of specials that aired on television. We had spoken a lot through email prior to meeting in person because he was interested in releasing a story on some exciting footage for *Ripley's Believe It Or Not*. The emails were always warm and friendly and when I arrived in LA, he offered to show me around the city.

While I was in LA, I broke the record by half an hour as I said I would, which brought the new world record to 1 hour and 34 seconds. Feeling great after my accomplishment, Eric took me out to sea to show me some great views. We saw Beverly Hills and talked about possibly working together in the future for one of his documentaries.

Years later, Eric hadn't forgotten about me. I received an email from him asking if I would be willing to come to New York City to break the existing Ice Endurance record. The event would take place in front of the Rubin Museum of Tibetan Art. He wanted me to be a part of a documentary that he was producing on The Iceman… Me!

After catching up, we began planning for New York. I had never been to New York City before so this would be my first time visiting the Big Apple. I was excited.

When I arrived in New York, I took note of the amazing architecture. New York City is a legendary place with impressive buildings that have astonishing detail. The decorations around the city were very beautiful and inspiring. I set my amazement aside and realized that I was there for a purpose: to break the existing Ice Endurance record in the streets of Manhattan. An entire Dutch television team accompanied me to NYC and together, both Eric's camera crew and the Dutch camera crew would be able to get a lot of great footage.

Before the event took place, I met with the director of the museum. I also had the opportunity to meet Dr. Kenneth Kamler and Professor William Bushell. The Rubin Museum of Art and The Today Show hired both individuals for special interviews. Together, they were going to enlighten the audience on my ability to withstand the extreme cold.

Ken Kamler, who had recently published a book entitled, *Surviving the Extremes*, was the main speaker during the world record attempt and would be helping to monitor my vitals. He would also be narrating the event to the people watching in the streets and at home in front of their televisions.

William Bushell, or Bill as I call him, is a well-established professor who received his PhD in anthropology. Through a lot of research, he remains connected to the Tibet House. He is most well known for his research on how esoteric eastern disciplines can benefit the western society. He is attempting to differentiate between the two societies with hopes to find insights that will benefit humanity. Very soon after meeting William, he gave me an extensive booklet exemplifying scientific data related to his research. I really felt honored. *Bill, if you're reading this, thanks!*

Two days after my arrival, I was asked to do a demonstration for The Today Show. Everything was set up in front of the studio. It was a cold morning in New York and there was quite a lot of wind in the streets. Before stepping into the Perspex box, I did an interview in my shorts. When I got into the box, they filled it up with 700 kilograms (1,543 pounds) of ice. Bystanders were in awe as they watched a normal guy subject himself to extremely cold temperatures.

After 40 minutes passed, they opened the box and frozen chunks of ice fell to the ground. I did one last interview with a man who claimed I was a "Human Popsicle" and then I went into a nearby building to take a nice, warm shower.

Later that day, we did more filming in Madison Square. After we finished filming, we all went for drink to warm ourselves up in a nearby Havana Bar. There, I saw myself televised on a big screen TV. I was famous in New York!

Since I would be attempting to break the world record at 2:00 PM sharp the following day, we all went back to the hotel and found our own rooms. I wanted to get a good night's sleep before the record attempt.

The next morning, we all had to wake up and go right to a meeting. The Dutch camera team and Eric's camera team were both present. To our surprise, a third camera team had shown up as well. It was a crew from ABC news wanting to do a documentary entitled, *Medical Mysteries*. As if three television teams weren't enough, 15 other stations ended up showing up at the Ice Endurance record attempt in Manhattan! There were people everywhere! Representatives from countries all over the world had been sent to film my event so that it could be internationally broadcasted.

Meanwhile, I just kept to myself and did what I always do; I prepared mentally and focused on the task at hand. In the final moments of preparation for the world record attempt, cameras surrounded the area and took their final positions.

I stepped into the Perspex box and I was ready to go. Dr. Kenneth Kamler's future girlfriend, Granis Stewart, hooked me up with some sensors, which would be monitoring my vitals. Soon enough, a team of people poured ice all around me. They poured the ice in until it reached up past my shoulders. It was at this point that they started the large digital clock, which would display the elapsed time.

Dr. Kamler and his assistant, Granis, checked my blood pressure every five minutes to monitor my vitals. They also checked my core temperature and my heartbeat. At one point, my core temperature decreased a little, but never to a dangerous extent. Things were under control. I didn't need the monitors to tell me how my body was doing. I could feel and understand everything that was happening. I know the dangers of hypothermia and I can control my body so that it doesn't reach that point.

The bystanders witnessed a man in control. The director of the museum explained, "This westerner is controlling his inner core temperature by using a Tibetan technique called *Tummo*. This is also known as *Inner Fire*."

To maintain control over the core temperature, you must influence the body by steering the hypothalamus; you can think of the hypothalamus as the thermostat in our brain. The veins around the core need to remain perfectly closed in order to maintain a 37°C (98.6°F) body temperature. The blood needs to stay at that temperature to prevent hypothermia and to keep the liver, lungs, heart and brain from shutting down. While the skin temperature may fall to 0°C (32°F), the core can maintain the proper blood temperature to stay alive. At this point, the body can generate heat three times as much as it does when in stasis.

Researchers have suggested that because of my cold training, I am able to control the autonomic nervous system to a certain degree.

Normally, people are unable to directly influence the autonomic nervous system, but with the proper training, it becomes possible. I am convinced that anybody can learn to do it. This is exactly what I did throughout the record attempt; I remained in control. At the 50-minute mark, I briefly sensed something strange going on in one of my kidneys; it felt cold. Focusing on that spot, I redirected blood flow to provide heat to my kidney. Within minutes, the sensors in that area detected a remarkable increase of 10°C (50°F)! Needless to say, it was warm again.

After that, Kamler watched a steady line as my core temperature stayed the same. He also watched as my heart rate went up a little. In order to maintain the blood's temperature, the heart rate *must* go up to warm the body. With that being said, the heart rate is something that should be carefully monitored to make sure that the situation doesn't become life threatening.

If my heart rate had exceeded 200 BPM (beats per minute), we would have stopped immediately the record attempt. Luckily, my heart rate never rose above 130 beats per minute. Even at 130 BPM's I was still able to generate enough heat and energy to circulate around my body to keep it warm.

I looked at the large digital clock to see how much time had elapsed. There was only one minute left until I would set the new record! As the last ten seconds approached, the crowd yelled in unison, "Ten... nine... eight... seven... six... five... four... three... two... one!" I broke out of the box and threw my arms up in triumph. I did it!

After a nice warm bath, I did an interview with Ken Kamler in front of the audience. It was quite the presentation. If you're interested in seeing the extensive interview, feel free to go online and watch it here:

http://www.thirteen.org/forum/topics/mystic-fire/38/

The news of my new record traveled quickly throughout the media, all around the world. That evening, people even recognized me as I was walking down the streets of New York!

It was a surreal feeling, being a celebrity. I had seen a lot of television programs in my life, but now, I felt like I was a part of it. I dared again and didn't meet failure; my confidence took a step forward and I was ready for more.

After my successful record, someone arranged a meeting for me to meet with Dr. Kevin Tracey of Feinstein Institute of Manhasset, New York. Apparently, Dr. Tracey was extremely interested in performing research to see if I could influence the immune system. I didn't know what to expect, but before I knew it, we were in a subway on our way to Manhasset. It was about 35 kilometers (27.9 miles) away.

On the ride over, I had a very interesting discussion with Professor Bushell, a modest gentleman who is extremely dedicated to science. Bill and I spoke of the potential benefits of cold exposure and how it could help individuals of the western civilization. Many diseases are caused by bad blood circulation, which can be extremely uncomfortable. We discussed many ways that the cold exposures could possibly help alleviate this problem.

Bill and I shared many similar beliefs and ways of thinking. It was a good conversation for the ride to Manhasset. After getting off the subway, we jumped on a bus, and before long, we arrived at the front gates of the Feinstein Institute.

As we were entering the institute, the employees informed us that it was prohibited to record anything during our visit. We said we understood and they led us to a large conference room where 12 individuals were seated around a large table.

After all of the introductions, I began telling the group about my vision of how using the cold correctly could greatly benefit humanity. They were all interested in what I had to say so they listened attentively.

From the conference room, we all went down to the testing room, where I sat in a cozy chair connected to a lung monitor and cardiogram. During the test, they actually had to switch out the lung monitor twice because they thought it wasn't working properly. When a lung monitor doesn't sense any air or breaths at all, it reads the person connected as dead, and I had went without breath for longer than two and a half minutes! After switching to the third monitor, I figured it would be best to stop my breathing exercises.

Dr. Tracey's team was also interested in watching my body work at the cellular level, so they extracted blood before, during, and after my experiment. The biochemical specialists planned to identify and compare 310 different blood values from the three samples.

After we finished the testing, we thanked Kevin Tracey and his team of specialists for the invitation. We made our way back to the entrance, where the bus was waiting for us. We said goodbye and returned to New York City.

Just as soon as we had returned to New York City, we had to leave again. We flew from the JFK Airport in Queens, to Saint Paul, Minnesota. As I mentioned a while ago, ABC news was shooting a documentary entitled, *Medical Mysteries*, and this was where the filming would be taking place.

When we touched down in Saint Paul, you could see just how cold it was outside by looking through the plane's windows. Everything looked icy and there was snow everywhere! The temperature read -30°C (22°F); it was like I was in Lapland again! It was so cold that the local elementary and high schools were cancelled because of the weather, as I overheard someone mention on the way to my hotel.

My hotel room was on the 26th floor, surrounded by skyscrapers; it was what you'd expect from a popular city. I got some sleep and the next morning, the camera crew knocked on my door and asked if I would mind if they did some filming.

I told them, "Of course not! That's why we're here, isn't it?"

The camera team started their filming by having me do a few meditative postures. I also did some breathing exercises and some physical exercises. They got some good footage and this also helped prepare me for the rest of the day.

Out of nowhere, Joe Anger, who was leading the team, sporadically had me go outside. He wanted me to mingle with the public out in the snowy weather, in my shorts, so he could record me asking people questions about the cold to gather their opinions. We recorded and interviewed with people all day long at the university, in the streets, and in the parks.

At the end of the day, we took a car to Duluth, Minnesota. There, we met up with two world-renowned medical professors. They wanted to perform a cold experiment to measure the physiological changes in my body.

When we arrived in Duluth, we checked in to a cozy hotel and found our rooms. At the hotel, we were greeted by one of the professors who would be performing the experiment. He seemed liked a nice guy and I was excited for the experiment to come.

After a good night's rest, we traveled to the medical school where the professors taught. We met in a laboratory that specifically studied the cold's effect on the body. In the lab, the camera crew poured some ice into a basin full of cold water. They hoped the ice would exaggerate how cold the water was so that the people at home would see that the water was truly freezing.

Filming can be a challenge sometimes. It really can test your patience with the amount of time it takes to set up the equipment, get the proper shots, and take down the equipment. Oh well, that's television!

Finally, the cold experiment was ready. They hooked me up to all kinds of wires in order to monitor my vitals in the cold water. Once again, while getting into the freezing water, I had no gasping reflex. As time progressed, my core temperature and my heart rate stayed the same. It looked like it would be another successful experiment!

When we finished the experiment, the researchers were more than happy with the results and indeed declared the experiment a success. We then flew back to New York, pleased with our accomplishment. After arriving, we went to the frozen shore off of the Hudson River to do a little more filming. We were happy with the footage we captured there, so we were able to relax for a bit. A strenuous week had gone by and we all had done extremely well.

When I got back from Minnesota, I was anxious to receive a call from Ken Kamler with the results from Dr. Kevin Tracey's experiments. Kamler finally called and informed me that even though Dr. Tracey was typically a very docile and calm man, he literally jumped in the air when he saw the results!

The results showed that I had suppressed the inflammatory marked bodies in the nervus vagus. This meant that I had consciously influenced my immune system, something widely seen as impossible. If one is able to influence the immune system by will, it could potentially have an enormous impact on humanity for the fight against disease.

From that point on, my new mission in life was to help people fight disease!

Half an hour later, after I had received the good news, I received a phone call from my wife with some very heartbreaking news. She informed me that my mother had just passed away. With this news, it took me back to the story of my birth.

Many years ago, when my mother was pregnant with my brother and I, the doctors actually had no idea that she was carrying twins. After my mother gave birth to my brother, Andre, the doctors took her to the recovery room, thinking she could relax. Once there though, she sensed that there was another baby on the way! The contractions were strong and my mother screamed for help. The nurse came to check on my mother and she too was convinced that another baby was on the way. The nurse ran to get the doctor as well as another nurse. All together they pushed the bed to the operating room where they would attempt to do a cesarean section. My mother was extremely hesitant of this kind of delivery due to some of the things she had heard about it in the past, but it was too late now. As a consistent churchgoer and a devoted catholic, she prayed that her child would make it out alive and eventually become a missionary. Before they could even get my mother on the operation table, she delivered the baby. By sheer will and strength, she was able to deliver her second twin, me. This is how I came into the world.

Now, my mother was gone. When I heard the sad news, it felt like someone had punched me in the stomach; I was breathless and there was a hole in my heart.

There are no coincidences; everything happens for a reason. It connects us to those we love, and can provide peace in our heart. In this sad moment, I tried to be strong and carry on with my new mission in life.

CHAPTER 18:
THE CABIN

After arriving back in State College, I returned to my normal schedule. I went to class, did my homework, worked in the research lab, and hung out with my friends. No one, except for a few of my close peers, knew about my trip to California. I acted as if nothing had ever happened, even though I felt completely different.

I was still interested in Tummo and hoped to pursue it more, but I didn't know what more there was for me to do. A few weekends after my trip, I showed Preston, my brother, what the form of Tummo looked like; he told me the motions looked ridiculous.

The following weekend, Jarrett and I went to his cabin to hang out and discuss my trip. While there, I decided to take advantage of the 32°F (0°C) weather and teach Jarrett the Tummo form I had learned in California. There was no heat source inside the cabin, so the temperature was the same as outside.

When Jarrett and I first sat on the floor in only our t-shirt and shorts, we felt relatively comfortable. We had just taken off our sweatshirts and sweatpants, so the cold temperature hadn't had a chance to affect our bodies yet. We started out with the breathing exercises, and then moved on to Tummo. My memory was a little foggy, so I referred to notes I took on the last day of the seminar.

After an hour of attempting the form, we didn't feel any different. Jarrett told me that he felt the same as he did when he first sat down. Disappointed, we stood up and began making lunch. After several minutes of moving around, Jarrett and I noticed something interesting. We suddenly felt really, really cold. It felt as if the temperature had dropped down to 10°F (-12.2°C). I suggested that we sit back down to see if the position we were sitting in was the reason for our original warmth. It wasn't. Sitting on the ground was even colder than standing up!

Jarrett and I were intrigued. We began performing Tummo again, to see if it had anything to do with the heat. We were amazed as we regained our warmth a half hour later. Soon after, Jarrett expressed the same disappointment that I had felt in California. Tummo was stationary; The Iceman wasn't. Even though Tummo seemed to give us heat, our main goal was to become like The Iceman.

After starting a fire in the fireplace, Jarrett and I discussed possible ways to transfer the effect of Tummo into a moveable form. We thought about changing our breathing patterns, visualizing a flame in our stomach while moving, and even trying some sort of hyperventilation technique. Even though we had a lot of different ideas, we didn't have the time to see them out. Jarrett and I were both very busy and had to return to college the following morning. That night, our excitement fizzled out with the fire as we fell asleep.

CHAPTER 19:
KILIMANJARO

Kilimanjaro, located in the middle of Africa, in the country of Tanzania, stands 5,895 meters (19,340 feet) tall. It is Africa's tallest mountain. Jereon, a Dutch cameraman and family friend, and I were on our way there for a climb. I had arranged a sponsorship deal with *Africa Safari* and *Natural Beauties* in Tanzania.

Jereon and I boarded a plane in Frankfurt, Germany and flew to Addis Abeba, the capital of Ethiopia. From there we took a connecting flight to the Kilimanjaro airport. As we made our descent into Tanzania, we saw Kilimanjaro to our right. It was easily viewable from the airplane windows and Jeroen was able to get a great shot for the footage.

Tanzania is a country with a lot of game reserves, Masaii, poverty and wildness. Even in rough times, most of the people in the area remain nice and have positive attitudes. Wherever we traveled, Tanzanians always greeted us with "Jambo," meaning "Hello," every time we passed them. This made me feel very welcomed.

My mission in Tanzania was to climb Kilimanjaro, the world's tallest volcano. It would be a lot different from any other mountain that I had climbed before because Kilimanjaro is not part of a mountain range; it is a freestanding, massive volcano that is almost 6 kilometers (3.7 miles) high.

Once we found ourselves in the right area, we were supplied with outdoor gear from a local outdoor shop and a camera from Nikon. Our shelter, which looked like it was left over from the colonial times, was in a secluded lodge. After settling into our rooms, we met our guide for the mountain, John Minja. From a porter, to a cook, to our transportation, John was in charge of everything. I was able to see the type of person he was from the moment I met him. I was excited to see what was to come in the next few days.

Before long, the day to climb was upon us. We were charged with energy and ready to begin. I became very anxious and excited, as I don't like the waiting before an upcoming challenge.

My excitement and anxiety cause a drive to succeed within me. This part of me always takes control when I am climbing. I may not know what will happen next, but I am always determined to succeed.

The drive to Kilimanjaro National Park only took us about two hours and thirty minutes, but it felt longer than that. When we finally arrived at the front gates, some last minute preparations were made. We had to organize permits, divide our supplies, and make our payments.

When we passed through the gates, a tropical forest with large trees and a wide variety of flowers suddenly surrounded us. There were monkeys in the trees and birds in the sky. Everywhere I looked it was a beautiful sight. I was most impressed by the large tree ferns that reached 20 meters (65.6 feet) high; they were enormous!

That day, we climbed from an altitude of 1,300 meters (4,265 feet) up to 3,200 meters (10,498 feet). As we progressed up the mountain, we took notice of how the vegetation changed. Instead of the large ferns and booming wildlife, small trees and bushes surrounded us.

The African crew that guided us up the mountain took very good care of us along our journey. Our stomachs were full and our minds were content, as we got ready to rest for the night. I am always eager to climb as fast as possible, but I know that it is not good to push an entire crew just to satisfy my desire, so I cooled myself down. We all slept peacefully that night.

The following day, we climbed up to 4,200 meters (13,779 feet) and collected stamps along the way at the checkpoints. At 4,200 meters, the vegetation changed even more drastically. Smaller bushes, different flowers, and strange succulents surrounded us.

As we traveled, John, our guide, made our journey extremely interesting along the way. He knew all the plants and trees by name in English, Latin, and Swahili. He was also very intelligent about the wildlife we saw as well. He knew the behavior of all of the birds and animals, including what they ate, and how strong and intelligent they were. We all learned a great deal from John on our trip.

As we continued making our ascent, it began to rain. The rocks and ground quickly became slippery. Due to the rain, our progression slowed and we were soon completely soaked and exhausted from the frictionless ground.

Since we were all wet and tired, we headed back to our camp at

4,200 meters and set up our tents. As soon as the rain stopped, we were able to take some beautiful pictures of the Kilimanjaro summit and Mt. Kenya. The visibility was great with no plants or trees to block our view.

Meanwhile, in my mind, I was concerned about the slow pace that we were using to ascend the mountain. I spoke with John about the slowness of the expedition. He saw my determination and desire for speed, so he told me that he and I could ascend up the mountain together at 2:00 AM, while the others were asleep.

I informed Jeroen of my plans to summit with John. Jeroen, who has a completely different drive and personality than I do, was confused by our drastic change of plans. I explained to him that I wasn't capable of going at such a slow pace and how doing so took me away from the rhythm I needed to succeed. I was a man on a mission with a powerful drive. Therefore, I was happy that John was willing to help me reach my goal.

We barely got any sleep that night before 2:00 AM came around. Luckily, everyone was in a deep sleep as we tiptoed quietly out of the tent toward our unknown adventure.

The moon lit up our path surprisingly well. The drowsiness that was with us when we first awoke was gone now that we were using an energetic pace.

I must admit, I felt better being apart from the group. I was excited to progress at a pace more to my liking.

The mysteriousness of the mountain engulfed us as we approached the western bridge. The western bridge begins at 4,600 meters (15,091 feet). It is a quick, but steep part of the Kilimanjaro trail. It was covered in snow and very slick. I began to feel the lack of oxygen; my body felt heavier. I had to force myself to focus on the present and not think about how much more of the journey was left. Will power and determination pushed me through every step.

As we were climbing, I had only one word on my mind: *summit*. Since there were no real paths up the mountain, we had to find our own way up the steep side of Kilimanjaro. The climbing seemed to go on forever; it was endless.

Dawn came upon us rather quickly and the massive mountain became much more visible with the light from the sun. However, since we were on the opposite side of the mountain, in reference to the sun, the warmth of its rays couldn't touch us.

We pressed on, but without proper acclimatization, it was a lot harder to climb than we had initially anticipated. Even though John regularly climbed the mountain as a profession, he was having a very difficult time. To reach my goals, I pushed myself to the limit with an incredible drive. John was forced to keep up with my provoked speed.

As we were nearing the summit, right before entering a huge crater, we encountered a difficult spot where the rocks and ground are completely covered in ice and snow. Despite its danger, it is a place that provides a marvelous view over Africa. The view provided me with some unexpected joy, despite the throbbing in my head from the lack of oxygen. I did my best to ignore the pain and pressed on as we reached the 5,600-meter mark (18,372 feet). We were approaching the summit, but it was proving to be an incredible battle. Our bodies were starving for oxygen and were quickly becoming fatigued. Little by little we ascended up the steep hill toward the summit.

Finally, through many breaths and streams of sweat, we reached the Uhuru peak; we had won the fight! Somehow, we had generated enough energy to push us to the top, despite our deprivation of oxygen.

At the top, John and I embraced each other, feeling extremely connected now that we had succeeded together. He had seen me at my weakest and I had seen him at his. This journey was a struggle of two men: John and the "Manaume Barafu" ("Iceman" in Swahili).

For many years, I had an irrational hunger to climb Kilimanjaro, always hearing about people who have climbed it. I had wanted to become one of them and now I was. Even though it was a lot harder than any other challenge that I had attempted thus far, we had succeeded. Our adventure had turned out with a completely different outcome than we had planned; however, it seems that many of my adventures turn out this way.

Be expectant of this when you are on your own: expect the unexpected!

The final steps of our adventure were hard and I could've fallen unconscious many times, but sheer will and determination had been my companions. Due to this, I received great respect from many porters on the path along the way. Together, they sang, "Iceman, Iceman," as well as many other songs. I even memorized one of the more famous songs that most porters and guides know. It went like this:

"Jambo, jambo bwana
Habarigani, ni suri sana

Wakeeni magaribishua
Kilimanjaro, Hakuna matata"

This song tells the story of a stranger who is welcomed. It tells the stranger to do their very best and take life as it comes on the strange Kilimanjaro. I enjoyed the meaning of this song and it made me think about all that I had accomplished.

After we took some pictures on the peak, John and I went down the long trail to the other side, passing an enormous glacier on the way. Tired and relieved, we continued our way down. I could feel the oxygen in the air increasing more and more as we descended the mountain. I had finally won the battle for oxygen; I could breathe comfortably again.

Since we had been out all day, I got some pretty bad sunburn on my face. As we arrived back into camp, Jeroen was really shocked seeing me in that shape; he seemed worried. After explaining our adventure to the others, we gathered up all the rest of our things and descended the mountain together.

The next day, we arrived at the South Gate of the Kilimanjaro National Park. When we got there, a Tanzanian film crew was waiting for us. They had heard that the Iceman climbed Kilimanjaro in shorts in only two days and wanted to hear more about it!

When I got back to the Netherlands, there were a lot of television appearances waiting for me. News of the Iceman doing something extraordinary had spread quickly; my story was at a high demand.

Soon after my return, the BBC called me, asking if I was interested in doing a challenge in the cold. I suggested a full marathon, in shorts, in Lapland, Finland. This adventure on Kilimanjaro had given me a lot of confidence and though I had never attempted a full marathon in shorts, I was ready to challenge myself. It would all be mind over matter.

CHAPTER 20:
HELLO ICEMAN

During my last couple years at Penn State University, I worked in a research lab that focused on facial expressions and human emotion. As a research assistant, my job was to run participants through experiments. On December 2, 2009 in between running participants, I re-watched old YouTube videos of The Iceman. Eventually, I came across a strange video that consisted of a slideshow of pictures that were taken using an infrared camera. The video was short and only had a few pictures of The Iceman stretching in front of a large group of people. I could tell from the white color emanating from his body that he was generating a lot of heat.

I had seen the video before, but I had only watched the first ten seconds of it. This time, I decided to let it play all the way through. During the last five seconds of the video, The Iceman's website flashed across the screen [www.innerfire.nl]. I didn't know that he had a website. I became very intrigued.

I checked out the website and found a small section with contact information. Listed in the contacts was Wim's email address; I was ecstatic! I had always wanted the opportunity to talk to The Iceman and now it was possible. Of course, I was extremely doubtful that he would reply. I thought he would never get back to me, being that he was a really famous individual and probably very busy.

Even though I was extremely doubtful, I had a lot of faith. I believed that if I were meant to speak to The Iceman, he would get my email and send me one back. If nothing happened and my email was left unread, I would move on from Tummo forever. I felt that this was my last chance to learn how to do it properly, to understand what it was like to be able to control my body temperature -- like The Iceman.

Here is what I sent him:

"Hello Mr. Hof,

My name is Justin Rosales. I am a student at Penn State University (Pennsylvania) and, well I really don't know how to make this formal, but it's an interesting topic and I'd like to be as open as possible. My friend and I have been researching g tum-mo (Tummo) for a while and I personally traveled to Berkeley, California to find out more information about Tummo to try to discover more about this "inner fire". I found a workshop. The man that led the workshop goes by the name of: Tenzin Wangyal Rinpoche. It was a weekend seminar that lasted about four days. However, they met several times during the year to try to teach this art. Personally, I only made it to the last session because I was unaware of this seminar until a few weeks before.

Anyways, they went over the 9 breathing techniques, the warm ups for the chakras, the Tsa Lung, the Bar Lung, and the Drak Lung. I feel that there are different ways to perform Tummo. I have already read a book called "Inner Fire." The techniques were a bit different from the ones taught at the workshop.

Mr. Hof, I am very interested in mastering the art of Tummo. Of course my friend and I are westerners, and based on the research that I've done, the Tibetans aren't really friendly when it comes to sharing Tummo with people in the Western culture. I have heard they say "They put everything in the wrong context." "They have no imagination" and "It will not work." But to be honest sir, my friend and I are veryyyy determined and open-minded. We are really interested in this idea and REALLY want to try to make this work, for ourselves.

The reason I am emailing you sir, is that you can do something that I haven't seen in the Tibetan research that I have performed… Despite all of the articles that I have come across, I have yet to see anyone stand up, or even run while performing g tum-mo, other than you.

So I was wondering if you were planning on doing any workshops any time soon to teach your methods of Tummo. My friend and I would love to find a way to meet up with you to learn. We are more than interested in your work, your way of life, and everything. We wouldn't document this in any papers or anything like that; we aren't with the news. We are two students that are very interested in bettering ourselves to learn, understand, and gain knowledge. We just want to improve. Sir, we'd really appreciate any response to this email, even being turned down. We admire that you are someone that isn't with Tibetan culture that has mastered this art of Tummo. Thank you very much.

-Justin Rosales
Penn State University"

After sending the email, I returned to my lab work. My friends in the lab knew about my research in California. They also knew about my interest in The Iceman. I told Anthony, the graduate student I work for, that I sent The Iceman an email. I also mentioned my doubt of not getting a response.

Ten minutes after sending the email, I received this:

"Dear Justin

There are no secrets.
Everyone, every mind, can understand the concepts. Especially, when it is taken in with an open heart. I will get back to you.
In the meantime, try to learn by listening to the lecture that I did in New York after performing in the streets of Manhattan. Search for the Google video, "mystic fire".

Greetings,
Wim Hof"

After reading this email, I said in a loud, enthusiastic voice, "YES!" Anthony looked up from his desk and asked me, "What happened?" I told him The Iceman had just responded. I was clueless as to which video Wim was talking about; I thought I already seen them all. I also didn't know what "mystic fire" was. So I used Google to search the words: "mystic fire," "iceman," and "wim hof." A new result popped up, one that I hadn't seen before. Here is a link to the video that I had found:

http://www.thirteen.org/forum/topics/mystic-fire/38/

The video starts out with a man named Kenneth Kamler, describing what typically happens to someone's body when they are exposed to the cold. In his presentation, he transitions to how Wim's body reacts differently to the cold. He then offers his theories of how it is possible. Afterward, Wim is called on stage and asked to speak.

Wim begins by telling the audience, "Science can only go so far. We are humans, and humans can go beyond science." Wim then goes into a long explanation of what he's done in the past and what he plans to do in the future.

Near the end of the video, Wim says that he has a different philosophy now. He mentions that he has done a considerable amount of record breaking and achieved many goals. Now, he wants to teach others what he has learned. He wants to help the unwise understand what he experienced so that they can experience it too. His new goal was to begin sharing the opportunity to become The Iceman with the world.

After seeing this video of Wim, I felt that I understood him on a deeper level. I saw who he was, beyond the celebrity that television made him out to be. I saw him as someone who was willing to do whatever it takes to change the world. He was a future version of who Jarrett and I had hoped we would become. Wim achieved the impossible and was actively looking to do more.

I emailed the link to Jarrett and asked him to call me after he watched it. The new information re-inspired me to continue my quest for knowledge and understanding. My laptop told me the temperature outside was currently 32°F (0°C). I wanted to immerse myself in my research and begin to gain experience with the cold. So I took off my jacket, packed up my things, and walked outside.

It was a twenty-minute walk to my apartment from where I was and my t-shirt didn't do much to protect me from the cold. A few seconds after walking outside, I could feel the goose bumps popping up all over my body. Shivers rolled up my spine and I could see my breath each time I exhaled. It was cold, and the 15 mph (24.1 kph) winds weren't helping. With each gust, I felt as if someone or something was sucking the heat from my body. After ten minutes of walking outside, I lost all feeling in my fingertips. My fingers felt like rocks when they rubbed together as I formed fists. I was afraid that I was doing serious damage to my body and I would have to deal with consequences later.

As I continued my walk home, I received a lot of attention from people. There were a lot of glares, raised eyebrows and open mouths; almost everyone stared. At first, I was really self-conscious, but then I understood that what I was doing was going to be bizarre to most people. This is why Wim is so famous. Most people view what he does as a circus act because they can't imagine doing it themselves.

When I finally reached my house, I slowly managed to pull my keys out of my pocket. It was incredibly hard to unlock the door as I fumbled through each key with numbed hands. Eventually, the lock turned and I pushed the door open.

As I walked in, the hot air from my home engulfed my frozen hands; they began to sting. It felt as if the tips of several hundred knives were positioned around my hands and someone was applying pressure to all of them at once. It was unbearable.

I felt dizzy, so I went to my bedroom and lay down. I closed my eyes and tried to think the pain away. It wasn't until twenty minutes later when I started to feel some relief. Eventually, the pain dulled and faded away completely. Luckily, it appeared as if no permanent damage was done to my hands. My fear of frostbite had left me once I regained the feeling back in my fingertips.

That night, I received a call from Jarrett. We talked about how awesome the video was and he told me that he had enjoyed seeing the different side of Wim. Where the Discovery Channel's video of Wim running the half marathon made him seem superhuman, Wim's interview made him look more normal. You could easily tell he was a regular guy that just wanted to help people. That's what Jarrett and I loved about Wim, that he was willing to make sacrifices to show people their true potential.

At one point during our conversation, Jarrett and I agreed that Wim was taking the world in a new direction. He was looking for ways to help people live more efficiently. Most of all, Wim was selfless, humble, and more than willing to teach people his technique.

I described to Jarrett my walk home earlier that day and how painful it had been. I told him that I thought the key to unlocking The Iceman's ability was by conditioning our bodies through direct exposure; I assumed that over time our bodies would adapt to the harsh conditions.

Speaking of pain, I decided not to try any more cold exposures until I spoke with Wim again. I didn't want to do any damage to my body and ruin my chances of ever learning to control its temperature.

The following day, I received an email from Wim explaining how "the cold is a hard, but righteous teacher." He told me that we, as humans, lost our natural ability to adapt to the cold over time. To get it back, we needed to naturally adapt through progressive exposure.

In response, I sent him the following with my frigid walk home in mind:

"Thank you Wim,

All of your thoughts are very enlightening and good to hear. It makes sense and does feel natural. My one question is... as I expose myself, how do I know when to stop. I can accept the cold, and my body feels fine, however, when outside in a t-shirt and shorts... my fingers start to hurt... then burn... and eventually lose feeling. At what point should I stop? Or should I just wear gloves. Though, if I do wear gloves, does it take away my ability to adjust?

I am sorry for my misunderstanding, but I'm trying to do it as accurately as possible so I do not hurt myself. Thank you for your continual support and advice!!! My friend and I are happy to be learning and regaining the natural mechanisms!

-Justin Rosales"

To which, he replied:

"Hi Justin

In the beginning you will feel the cold, your fingers and toes will react. I am a rock climber who climbs without gear. I need to have good control and good blood circulation in my fingertips to hold on.
Here is what helped me train my hands. Try it out yourself:
Find a rock or cold item, touch it and let the fingers react until it does not feel good anymore.
Then remove yourself from the cold and wait a couple of minutes. This is when the veins in your hands are opening up again, the natural way, and make it possible, in my case, to climb for hours on ice-cold rocks; it feels great!
Once again it is all natural, but you have to find out through experience.
I helped many people heal their feet's reaction to the cold by having them walk barefoot in the snow for a quarter of a mile, with the right mental attitude. After that, they didn't have any more problems with cold feet.
The secret is that their veins were too small, restricting blood flow. With exposure, you can condition the veins to become larger and allow more warm blood to reach your extremities. It is not hocus-pocus.
You can condition the veins by exposing them to extreme colds. When you first enter the cold, the veins and arteries will constrict, restricting blood flow immensely.
After they're conditioned, the veins and arteries open back up again, while in the cold, and they can continue to pump warm blood to exposed parts of your feet. This increases the circumference of the walls of both the veins and arteries... It's all natural.

Simple,
Wim"

This was the first time it was beginning to make sense to me. Understanding that there was some science behind the ability made it seem more achievable. I viewed it as if I was going to train a muscle or run a race, each time pushing progressively farther.

I didn't have any cold slabs of rock available, so I would have to be creative. Regardless, I was ready to start training.

CHAPTER 21:
MARATHON BEYOND THE POLAR CIRCLE

Two weeks after Kilimanjaro, I was on my way to Lapland, Finland. After coordinating with an English production company, we came up with the idea to drive from Amsterdam to Lapland for a marathon. Along the way, we drove through Germany, Denmark, Sweden, Finland, and then finally Lapland. Each country became colder as we traveled farther north.

When we reached the southern part of Sweden, the snow began to fall. Slippery roads and very cold temperatures greeted us, yet we still had another 1,500 kilometers (932 miles) to travel before reaching the Polar Circle!

Eventually, we reached our final destination: a very small resort in Lapland. The place was made out of wood, but it kept us very warm. Outside, wild reindeer frolicked in the thick snow that surrounded us; it felt like a scene right out of a Christmas tale. When the temperature dropped down to -20°C (-4°F), the condensed air froze, making the snow look like beautiful, sharp diamonds.

Shortly after our arrival, we met a local fixer. A fixer, as most television personnel call it, is a person who arranges and plans out many different camera angles at the location of the shoot. While the fixer was attending to the angles, the rest of the crew needed to find a way to make a track for the marathon in the nearby hills. They had to figure out what exactly had to happen, and where it would all take place, so it was good that they were very keen on the details. As I watched everyone working, I began to feel very anxious and alert. This is how I always feel before a challenge. It's a natural way to prepare the mind.

The next day, we went to a reindeer farm and spoke with the herder. He was dressed in reindeer skin and lived in a typical, Lappish nomad tent. It looked very similar to that of a tipi, very Indian-like.

The Lappish nomads are also very similar to the North American Indians.

The herder told us stories about their traditions, fire rituals, as well as their life and respect for nature and reindeer. The nomads in the area were diminishing quickly, as snow scooters removed the necessity of transport by reindeer, leaving them with no income. I honestly feel that it is a pity to see modern times take over regions like this.

One of the stories the herder told us explained how the Lappish people, also known as the Sami, had developed telepathy to speak to their far away neighbors. However, once the telephones were invented, the telepathy disappeared with time. Another pitiful loss.

The day before the run, we went to the track and did some pick up shots. Pick up shots are the shots that you can't actually shoot when the run is live because the angle is too difficult. So, I took the opportunity to get a good work out in, and ran for a bit through the snow, just in my shorts.

The snow was neither hard, nor soft. It was a different texture than what I had been used to, but I ran for a while through the white, covered wilderness. As I was running, the snow covered the ground in a way that made it hard to see what kind of surface I was stepping on. Everything seemed fine, when all of a sudden I stepped on some uneven ground and heard a "Krrrrrrik!!!"

My right ankle twisted and it began throbbing with pain. The next day was the day I was supposed to run my first full marathon ever and I had just severely sprained my ankle! My confidence was shattered. *Would I be able to do the marathon?* I thought.

I was overwhelmed with insecurities and doubts, but the only thing I could do was continue on with determination; mind over matter. I told the crew that we had to change the track on which I would be performing my run. I explained to them that I had sprained my ankle because the snow was too deep and it would be impossible to run through. They agreed to survey the surrounding areas and look at some different trails with hardened snow layers. I didn't sleep very well that night, but I was determined, and that gave me energy.

The following morning, before my run, I had to undergo a medical checkup. The professionals told me that my physiology was much healthier than an average young man. They told me that my resting heart rate was extremely low, at 38 beats per minute, with good blood pressure. Then... they saw my ankle. Their suggestion to me was that I should not run the marathon; of course, I disagreed. They saw my determination and told me that if I chose to run, it would be at my own risk. So, after taping my ankle, the medical professionals wished me luck and sent me on my way.

The newspaper and television reporters were present when I arrived at the starting spot of the newly plotted course. I mentally prepared myself one last time before getting out of the car. When I was ready, I went outside, had a piss, and started running! I began my run so rapidly that it threw everyone off guard. No one had expected me to begin like that, so everyone had to quickly pack their bags and follow me in a hurry to catch up.

The crew all sat in the back of the car with the rear door propped open so they could film me as I ran. They were driving a little bit ahead of me at a slow pace, so they could get some good shots. They filmed my feet from close up, far away, from the side, with wide angles, and close angles. Everything was going extremely well.

Kilometers passed and there were still no problems whatsoever, so I kept on running. With everything going so well, my worrying had stopped and I was able to enjoy the environment; my regained confidence helped me relax and enjoy the nature that was in front of me.

Ten kilometers went by… 20 kilometers… and I still had no problems. However, when I ran over the 25-kilometer mark (15 miles), the cold began to have an influence on my muscles. The acid that accumulated in my legs was really slowing me down. This is where the determined mind began to play its role. My mental preparation began to pay off, as the run became a challenge of will power.

I pulled myself together and focused on every numbed step through the snow; I would not succumb to fatigue.

Remaining focused can pull you through almost anything; it alerts the adrenaline in the nervous system to kick in.

This run was a fight I needed to win, just like Kilimanjaro. On Kilimanjaro, my fight was with the lack of air, but there in Lapland, it was the cold and my unprepared physical state.

Months before this run, I had prepared myself by sitting in a horse stance, with my knees bent over for a half hour, to practice getting rid of acid build up. It took focus, but it worked. This is the kind of focus I had to attain during my run. Despite the heavy feeling that I still had in my legs, I made it past the 32-kilometer mark (19.8 miles). I stayed in my trance, traveling the long distance through the woods.

By the time I reached the last two kilometers, I was almost walking. As my eyes fell upon the finish line, I regained some of my energy. The final stretch was adorned with cheering people and torches. My goal was now in my reach. When I crossed the finish line, I was engulfed in praise; I had done it!

After my first full marathon was successfully completed, I was guided into a wooden hut where my family was waiting; they cheered for me when I entered. They sat me down by the fireside and handed me a beer and cigarette.

"Like the Indians", I said, "A cigarette smoke is for peace and accomplishment." Everyone around me was flabbergasted when they realized that I was a smoker and a drinker. Athletes don't typically have these habits. They were shocked at what I was able to achieve, despite my vices.

The reporters continued to ask me questions while the film crew reviewed their footage. The run was complete, and I was more than satisfied. I had just taken another pioneering step deeper into my mind. Once again, I was also able to overcome my fears and insecurities. That night when I was relaxing by the television, my run came on the news. It was a beautiful thing to see.

The following day, my legs were incredibly sore; I could barely walk. The following three-day car ride was enough time for my legs to completely recover. During the car ride home, I came up with a new challenge that I would like to someday fulfill: to run 50 kilometers (31 miles) in the Sahara Desert without drinking any water. I hope to accomplish this goal sometime in the future.

CHAPTER 22:
HM… HOW CAN I TRAIN?

*A*fter a few more exchanges of email with Wim, I decided to construct my own training program. Wim emphasized that any exposure to the cold leads to improvement. So, I came up with the idea to make miniature ice baths for extremity immersions. I looked around my apartment for something small that could hold water, ice, and one of my extremities.

Eventually, I decided to use a one-gallon plastic garbage can that was stashed in my closet. I placed it in my bathtub and filled it up with cold water. I then went to my kitchen, grabbed two ice trays, a towel, and a container of salt. I brought everything into my bedroom and closed the door. After changing into shorts, I dumped the two trays of ice into the water and added salt. I had heard in the past that salt was used to lower the freezing point of water; I didn't know if it was true, but I wanted to do everything I could to make the water as cold as possible. At the time, I didn't have any thermometers to check the temperature of the water, so I made a mental note to order one online when the experiment was over.

After letting the ice and salt chill the water for a couple minutes, I touched it with the tip of my finger to see if it was ready. Immediately, I could feel the blood rushing away from where my finger entered the water. I was hesitant, but still excited to see what would happen. After taking a few deep breaths to calm my nerves, I started the timer on my stopwatch and dove my right hand into the ice water.

The pain was immediate and intense. It felt as if someone was cutting off my hand in multiple sections. My body became extremely warm and I soon felt lightheaded. I didn't know what was happening. I was afraid, but I left my hand in the water anyway. I kept waiting for the pain to dissipate, but even after 60 seconds, it still remained.

During the time that my hand was in the water, a lot of things flooded through my mind. At first, my entire body was telling me to pull my hand out… immediately. I tried talking myself through it and telling myself that I would be fine, but everything inside of me was screaming in agony. I was afraid I was going to do damage, but then I remembered that I had never heard of someone losing his or her fingers after a couple minutes of cold-water exposure; I doubted I would be the first. So, I continued to fight through the pain.

Eventually, around 90 seconds after I had first placed my hand in the water, the pain began to dull, and then numb. My mind eased, but I questioned the phenomena. *Can I not feel anything because I damaged my nerves? Is the water just warmer now?*

I checked the water with my left fingertip; it was still freezing. Then, I tried moving my fingers; they were slow, but still moved nonetheless. Not more than two seconds after I moved my fingers, my fingers began to burn again, just like when I had first put my hand in. It seemed that any movement of my immersed limb would take away the numbness and bring me the immense pressure.

I stopped moving my hand and tried to reach the numbing phase again. After another 20 seconds of biting my lip, the pressure finally eased away, but about a minute later, something else happened. I began to feel tingling at my fingertips. It didn't feel like pain; it was just unpleasant. I guess you could say the feeling was comparable to when your hand or foot falls asleep.

This sensation frightened me. I hadn't gone into detail with Wim about what I was supposed to experience, so I pulled my hand out. For my first exposure, my hand was immersed for 3 minutes and 7 seconds. It seemed like a long time, but I had nothing to compare it to.

After drying off my right hand, I sunk my left hand into the water. The same thing happened as before. The pain came, then the numbness, and then the tingling. I pulled my left hand out at 1 minute and 30 seconds. I blamed my inability to keep my left hand in as long as my right hand on my right-handedness. I assumed the vascular system in my right hand was stronger since I had used it more.

When I had finished putting away all of the things I used for my test run, I got online and ordered two thermometers. The first one I ordered was a digital cooking thermometer that measured temperatures from 10°F-250°F (-12.2°C-121.1°C) using a metal rod. The second was an infrared thermometer that could measure the air and skin temperature. I figured if I was going to be serious about training, I might as well document my experiments and watch my data change over time. For that reason, I placed my extremity immersions on hold until my thermometers arrived.

A few days later, the first snow of the season fell. We received several inches and it whited out the State College area. Ever since I had watched Wim's interview video, I had started trying to implement one of Wim's philosophies into my life.

"If you want to withstand the cold, you must to learn to enjoy it. Learn to like the cold. We have taught our bodies to avoid the cold and to put on a jacket when we feel uncomfortable. We are taught that the cold can get us sick, so we try to evade it at all costs. It's important to do away with this habitual aversion and learn to enjoy it. With this state of mind, you can begin to benefit from the cold and enjoy adapting to it."

When I first woke up and saw the snow outside, I came up with the idea to go out during the evening and walk barefooted through the snow in a nearby park. Before I did so, I wanted to ask Wim for his advice. Before leaving for class that morning, I sent Wim the following email:

"Hello Wim,

As I train more and more, I find myself questioning the best way to possibly go about it. Later on tonight, I plan on going for a walk in the snow. We just had snow fall for the first time this season, so I plan on walking to a nearby park in sandals, a t-shirt, and shorts. Once I get there, I am going to take off my sandals and walk barefooted through the snow. One of my questions is would it be better to walk around with a shirt on or off?

In a lot of your videos, you're only wearing shorts. Should I do the same? I'll probably wear a hat because I have short hair and I lose a lot of heat through my head, but should I go without a shirt?

-Justin
Ps. Sorry to bother you again"

Wim's response was sitting in my inbox by the time I got home from class:

"Hi Justin

First of all, you are not bothering me. By the time I was 17, I had been attracted to esoteric disciplines for years.
When the first snow fell, I went out with new energy. It was childish

simplicity; my mind was empty. The snow showed itself to be strong and good enough to run in, wearing only shorts. I ran around in the un-trod-den snow in a wide circle for over an hour. It looked and felt like magic; there was no pain in my extremities whatsoever, but when I got back into the house where the heat was, I feet began to feel immense pain!

The veins had adapted themselves to the cold, soft surface outside. Once inside, they had a hard time readapting to the heat. That pain is caused when blood is forced through the closed veins.

Your body and mind will learn how to overcome it. Your determination and conviction should be positive and strong. Never force your body to go past its pain threshold. Listen to what your body is telling you; it is your teacher and guide. It's an intrinsic function, so use it.

When you go out, go without a t-shirt and at least partially barefooted.

Greetings,
Wim"

I decided to wait for the sun to set before beginning my adven-ture; I didn't want to draw any attention to myself. Before leaving the house, I grabbed my backpack and began putting things inside. I packed a towel, two pairs of socks, a hoodie, my wallet, and my phone. My attire consisted of shorts, socks, sandals, sweatpants, a long-sleeved shirt, and a hat.

My computer told me that the temperature outside was 29°F (-1.67°C). The snow was still falling when I left my home. The side-walks and roads were covered as the white powder stuck to the ground. In an attempt to stay warm, I immediately began jogging as soon as I stepped off my front porch. After five minutes of trotting through the snow, I realized that my feet might be in danger. The socks and sandals weren't doing much to protect my feet from the chilling cold. I began to worry.

My feet were already burning and I hadn't even run barefoot yet! With each step, it felt like I was walking on needles. When I got to the park, I ran to the closest bench and sat down. I took off my socks and pressed my feet between my hands in an attempt to warm them. It didn't do much, so I pulled off my wet socks, opened my bag, withdrew my other two pairs of dry socks, and put them on. But even that didn't help! My feet were still freezing.

Being in the middle of a secluded park with was no one around, I felt helpless. I considered calling one of my friends to pick me up, but I didn't want him to find me like that and ask questions. My mind started to race. I imagined getting frostbite on my feet and having to amputate my toes. I was beginning to think I would never become like The Iceman.

Despite the new pairs of dry socks, I began to lose the feeling in my toes. In my last attempt to warm up my feet, I pulled out my towel and wrapped it around them. Suddenly, I noticed a light shining from somewhere below and quickly realized it was my phone! It must have fallen out when I pulled my towel out of backpack. I reached down and tried to get all of the snow out of the buttons. It was soaked and the power wouldn't turn on.

Great, I thought, *now even if I needed to get a hold of someone to come and pick me up, I couldn't because my phone is broken.*

At this point, all I wanted to do was get back to my house and warm my feet up. The only choice I had was to run back through all of the snow, in my sandals and socks, and hope that I could make it home before my feet froze off. I packed up my towel, put on my sandals, and started jogging.

Twenty minutes had passed from the time I had first entered the park. In that amount of time, another half an inch of snow had fallen onto the ground. I was hoping to run in the footsteps I had made on the jog up, but they were already refilling with snow. Also, since I was running downhill this time, my stride wasn't the same. Every few steps, I would slide, shoving the snow into my sandals.

After five minutes of running, I realized a new sensation in my feet. For the past half hour, I hadn't felt anything; they were numb. Now, there was a sharp, burning sensation spreading across the soles of my feet. Assuming that they were on the verge of frostbite, I concluded that I needed to find a place to warm them up, immediately. Luckily, there was a Burger King a couple hundred yards ahead. I pressed harder, motivated to escape the frigid weather as fast as possible. Within a couple minutes, I finally entered the heated Burger King.

In different circumstances, I would have been self-conscious about wearing socks and sandals in the middle of a Burger King during a snow storm, but do to the my presumed dire circumstances, I didn't care what people though of me. Many stared, but I ignored their looks and found a quiet place in the corner to sit down. However, I did feel bad using the warmth of Burger King without purchasing any food, so I stood back up and ordered a coffee from the cashier.

When the coffee was ready, I returned to my table where I could be left alone and take the weight off my feet. I pulled off my soaked socks and placed them on the bench beside me. I pressed my feet together, trying to warm them back up. The burning sensation was consistent until that point, but after pressing my feet together the burning sensation spread and grew more intense. They felt like they were exploding from the inside out. The pain lasted for minutes, making it extremely hard for me to maintain my focus. I gritted my teeth and attempted to look normal so the people around me wouldn't notice my pain, but there's nothing normal about a bare-footed man in a restaurant, in the middle of winter.

I felt dizzy and wanted to put my head down, however, I was worried that the restaurant would call the police if they thought I was sleeping. So, I kept my head up and fought through the nau-sea. A lot of things were going through my mind while I waited for the pain to dissipate. Most of it was imagining what it would be like to live a life without feet. I also considered how upset my parents would be if they knew what I had done. My most promi-nent thought, however, was how I had failed to do what The Iceman considered as easy. My feet hadn't adapted to the cold at all; they suffered consistently.

After 45 minutes of sitting in the corner of Burger King, I began to feel extremely awkward. The pain was finally beginning to lessen in intensity. I decided to suck it up and try to make it the remainder of the way home. It was a seven-minute jog from Burger King to my house and it looked like another inch had fallen since I had first walked in. I was worried and hesitant, but I continued to tell my-self that it was almost over. Soon, I would be out of the cold for the night.

I took a deep breath, tightened the straps on my backpack, pushed the front door of Burger King open and began sprinting. I felt the fa-miliar chill at my feet as I pressed through the snow. It was slippery and extremely hard to keep my balance. Several times, I slipped and landed on my hands and knees. My body was covered in snow and my feet burned; I just wanted to escape it all.

Out of breath and discouraged, I finally made it to my house. I threw my backpack on the couch, stripped off my socks, and stag-gered into the bathroom. After turning on the lukewarm water, I stepped into the tub and waited. When the water touched my feet, searing pain surged through my legs. I held on to the shower door to prevent my knees from collapsed. Somehow, even though the water was only lukewarm, it felt like it was boiling my feet. Once again, I took a few deep breaths, and fought through the pain.

My feet were yelling at me to get out, but I waited. Eventually, the pain dissipated and my muscles began to relax. After my nerves settled, I lay in my bed and contemplated giving up my goal of be-coming The Iceman. It was going to be really hard to "like the cold" after that episode. Still, I did not want to be like everyone else who had one bad experience and then turned their backs forever. I decided to stick with it. The least I could do was give it one more try.

Not wanting to end the night with a failure, I rose from my bed and went outside to the front porch. I was wearing two pairs of socks and a several layers of clothing. Disappointed that I hadn't been able to get any *real* training in the cold, I tried to find a cold rock near my porch. I planned to attempt the exercise that Wim had explained in his email earlier that day. Sadly, there weren't any rocks near my porch, but then I noticed the large metal poles, supporting the roof. I lightly touched the pole with my index finger; it was *freezing*.

Excited, I turned on my stopwatch and gripped the pole with both hands. Immediately, I could feel the blood rushing away from my fingertips and move toward my chest. If my fingers could scream, they would have. Because of my experience with ice-water immersion a few days earlier, I knew there would be a point where my hands would adjust, so I continued to fight through the cold. After three minutes of aggravating pain, it finally eased away -- first in my right hand, then my left. I left them there, waiting for the pain to come back. As soon as they began to ache two minutes later, I pulled them of the pole. The pain stopped almost simultaneously.

Now that my feet were somewhat healed, I wanted to train them too. With my stumbling fingers, I took off both my socks, pushed the button on my stopwatch, and stepped off my porch into the snow. For the first two seconds, I felt fine, but then the pain began to pour in. I buckled to my knees as imaginary daggers stabbed the bottom of my feet. Despite what I had just experienced in the cold, this felt much worse. It wasn't a dull, numbing pain; it was sharp and unbearable.

I couldn't take it anymore; I stopped my watch and stepped out. Frantically I fumbled with putting my socks back on. I only lasted 7 seconds! *What?* It felt like at least 30 seconds. Apparently the pain had altered my perception of time.

I went back inside and laid down in my bed, reflecting on the night's events. My dangerous encounter with the cold had taught me a valuable lesson: To always train in conditions that I could control. I never again wanted to willingly experience being alone, in danger, and helpless in the cold. From then on, I vowed to be extremely careful with everything I did in relation to the cold. I would always make sure I only performed tasks that I was confident I could complete. If I wasn't confident, I would train at a lesser intensity, or train a different part of my body until I *was* confident.

Strangely enough, this experience didn't tear me away from the cold, but instead made me much more interested. I really wanted to

CHAPTER 23:
CONTROLLED TRAINING

*A*fter my cold episode in the park near Burger King, I decided I should be more careful during my training exercises. I planned to control the conditions as much as possible so that I could focus on progress, rather than survival. Therefore, I came up with as few ideas that, hopefully, I would be safe doing.

Even though I told myself I wouldn't do any more submerging of my extremities in cold water until my thermometers arrived, I wanted to try again. Instead of doing my hands, I was interested in finding out what it would be like to put my feet in. Now, at the time, my feet were really sensitive and had no training whatsoever. I rarely wore sandals because socks and shoes always felt more comfortable to me. Therefore, I thought it would be extremely painful if I started by submerging my feet in ice water. Instead, I decided to take it easy and start with only cold water, no added ice.

Despite my lack of thermometers, I still wanted to document my exercises. I grabbed my stopwatch and opened a blank Word document on my computer, that way I could at least view my records in the future.

December 5, 2009 was the first time I put my feet into cold water. At first, I was a little intimidated, but then I just wanted to get it over with. Being that my feet were extremely sensitive, I had a feeling they were going to "burn" more than when I had put my hands in. I set up my timer and placed my right foot into the one-gallon bucket of cold water.

At first I felt nothing. Then, after about 2 seconds, the pain started to creep up my foot into my knee. It felt like it was exploding from the inside. My entire body heated up and I felt lightheaded. I couldn't sit still; my body was twitching. I tried rubbing my knees to ease the pain. Eventually, the pain subsided. I noticed that the "numbness phase" began at 1 minute and 23 seconds and wrote it down in my notes.

During the time that my foot was numb, I tried to keep it very still. I recalled from the first time that moving any part of the exposed limb would, essentially, "reset" the cold. It was a strange phenomenon, but it remained to be true. The pain was absent until I reached 40 minutes and 30 seconds. Only then did I begin to feel the cold tingle in my toes. I was afraid that this meant I was doing damage to my foot. Instead of pulling out, I tested my theory by leaving my foot in the water a little longer until the cold, tingling feeling spread.

I withdrew my foot when the tingling feeling had reached my ankle. The foot was bright red and stiff when I removed it from the water. I tested the flexibility by bending my toes. They moved slowly, but seemed to be just fine. I dried off my foot with a nearby towel and placed it into a sock to warm up.

I proceeded to prepare my left foot for the cold water. Despite the pain in my right foot, I considered what it would be like to put my left foot in ice water. I knew it would probably hurt a lot more, but I had hope that I would be able to fight through the pain. I filled the bucket with a tray of ice cubes and dove my foot into the water. Immediately, nausea overwhelmed me. I rubbed my knees, trying to take my mind off of the pain.

After three minutes of agony, my body and mind finally settled. Seven minutes later, the cold seeped in and I felt the familiar tingling. I took my foot out after 11 minutes of exposure. It may not have lasted as long as my right foot, but the end result was the same: stiff and red. I dried off my foot off with another towel and placed it in a sock to warm it up.

The next day, I repeated the same process. This time, I exposed both of my feet to the ice water. It took my right foot 3 minutes and 50 seconds to adjust to the freezing temperature while my left foot took 4 minutes. When I say, "adjust", I am referring to the amount of time it takes my extremity to become numb, at which point there is no longer any pain or pressure. It can also be referred to as the point in time when the exercise becomes bearable.

After exposing both of my feet to the ice water, I did it again, one after the other. For both feet, the improvement in my ability to adapt to the water was much more apparent. Although it took an average of four minutes for each foot to adjust, the pain was only mild. This made it extremely difficult for me to tell the exact point when the water became bearable, because after the initial shock, the pain just slowly faded away.

For each of my second attempts, I timed how long it took for my feet to feel normal again. I defined "normal" to be the point when my foot regains maximum flexibility and doesn't feel slow anymore. It took 46 minutes for my left foot to completely return to normal and 42 minutes and 48 seconds for my right foot.

The next day, I gave my feet a break and submerged my hands instead. I found a giant metal bowl in the kitchen and made my usual concoction: salt, cold water, and ice. With the bowl sitting on my lap, I submerged both my hands into the water at 6:35 PM. My hands seemed to become bearable at 2 minutes and 6 seconds. At 19 minutes, I took my hands out due to the appearance of the tingling sensation.

After I took my hands out and dried them off on the towel, a burning sensation spread across my fingertips. Yet, even though my hands were "warming up," cold sensations crept up my forearms; it was really confusing. They felt colder outside the water than they had inside the water. Furthermore, my motor skills had significantly slowed down. I put on gloves in an attempt to warm my hands; instead, the opposite occurred. The gloves had made my hands feel significantly colder! I ignored the strange sensations and continued to wear the gloves until my hands warmed up 45 minutes later.

The following day, December 8, 2009, my thermometers finally arrived. I set up my equipment, let the ice sit in the water for a bit, and then took the temperature. The water was 45.4°F (7.4°C). When I put my right foot into the water, I was surprised to find that I had received no initial shock; I just went into the adapting phase. It only took my foot one minute to completely adjust to the water. I was amazed. After only a few days of training, I had made enormous progress.

After 12 minutes of exposure, I began to feel the slight tingle in my toes. I was confident in my ability to last longer, so I pressed on. I noticed that the water felt colder than when I had first put it in, so I took the temperature again. At the 22-minute mark, the temperature on the thermometer read 35°F (1.67°C). It had dropped over 10°F (5°C)!

Three minutes later I took my foot out; I didn't want to force my body to do something it couldn't handle. The total time my right foot was in the water was 25 minutes, which was 6 minutes longer than the first time I had ever submerged my foot in ice water. I was excited to see progress, especially because the immersions weren't as painful as when I had first begun the experiments. It took my right foot 29 minutes to return to normal after withdrawing from exposure. That's about 13 minutes less than the last time I had exposed my foot to ice water! The results astounded me.

I didn't have any more ice in my freezer to resupply the bucket for my left foot. I measured the temperature of the cold water to be 44.5°F (6.9°C). When I had first put my foot in, I was somewhat disappointed that there was an initial shock, unlike my right foot. Despite the pain in the beginning, my left foot only took 2 minutes to completely adjust to the cold water. The slight tingle in my toes began to creep up on me at the 11-minute mark. I withdrew my left foot when it began to ache at the 20-minute mark. It took my left foot 34 minutes and 13 seconds to return to normal. That's 12 minutes less than the last trial I had for that foot.

Authors Note:

Instead of explaining every piece of the results, I have decided to exclude my quantified data from this point on. I apologize for any inconvenience this may have caused you. If you are interested in seeing this data, please refer to www.becomingtheiceman.com

...

A few weeks after my dangerous experience in the park, the snow began to melt. It seemed like an opportune time to try running under the conditions that Wim had suggested. I called up my friend, Dave Haneman, and asked if he wanted to go on a run with me. Dave agreed to come along. He had just bought new running shoes and was interested in trying them out.

The weather said it was 39°F (3.89°C) outside with no wind. Sadly, there was no way for me to run with my feet partly exposed, like Wim had suggested. Either I could run barefoot, which wasn't really any option due to a lot of broken glass in the streets, or I could run with shoes. I picked the shoes.

When Dave arrived at my house, I informed him that I would be running in only shorts and shoes. "You're crazy," he told me, "but do whatever makes you happy. Just make sure you're ten feet behind me at al times; I don't want people to think I know you." He smiled.

The cold air brushed across my chest as we started running. It only took about 30 seconds for my body to adjust to the cold. For my first time ever running bare chested, I was relatively comfortable. Even though I could feel my hands slowly losing heat, the rest of my body felt perfectly fine. I was amazed at how easy it was.

After several minutes of running, I began to have difficulty breathing. My mouth was dry and my throat was sore. Normally a mouth breather, I tried switching to my nose. A few attempts at sucking air through a runny nose proved to be rather uncomfortable. I decided to switch back to my mouth and deal with the consequences.

Fifteen minutes into our run, my body succumbed to the cold. My hands were numb and my chest was burning. I was unable to keep up with Dave's pace because the muscles in my leg were tightening. The cold feeling, originally only in my hands, had spread to my entire body. I was quickly losing the battle to stay warm.

After twenty minutes from first leaving my apartment, Dave and I separated. I felt that if we stopped to say goodbye, I would not be able to make it home, so I settled for a "see you later" and continued running. I tried to increase my speed to get home faster, but my legs were already pushing their limits.

After twenty-five minutes of running, I finally escaped the freezing cold and entered my apartment. Surprisingly, the only pain I received when readjusting to the temperature was a slight burning sensation -- nothing more. After using the restroom, I noticed my skin's color in the bathroom mirror; it was bright red. Unsure of whether or not this was a good sign I put on a hoodie and pants, and waited for my body to warm up.

When the clothing touched my skin, I started to feel colder. Confused and shivering, I tried to get warmer by lying in my bed under the blankets. After 20 minutes of constant shivering, I finally felt warm again. The cool tingling that had coursed through my body had dissipated.

Even though running in the cold was an exhilarating experience, I felt like I wasn't getting the full Iceman training. It was mid-January and there was little snow on the ground; most of it had melted. I wondered what it would be like to run through a snowstorm wearing only shorts and shoes. Several days later, I got my chance.

That weekend, Preston and I hung out at my apartment. He played video games while I did a bit of reading for class. After finishing the chapter around 11:00 PM, I looked out the windows and noticed it was snowing! I smiled to myself and was overwhelmed with the idea to go for a run. I checked online to look up the State College temperature and saw that it was 31°F (-.5°C) outside. I wouldn't be able to focus on my homework; the snow was to calling me.

I expressed my excitement to Preston and told him I was going to go run downtown in the snow. At this point in time, Preston didn't know much about my Iceman research. He only knew that I went to California for a workshop and occasionally performed a few cold exercises. Naturally, when I told him about my plan, he looked at me as if I were insane. After several seconds had passed, his face relaxed and turned into a smile. I assumed my cold interests had temporarily slipped his mind.

A few minutes later, I stood at my back door wearing only shorts and tennis shoes. With my hand on the knob, I took a couple deep breaths, turned the handle, and ran out into the snowy abyss. "Good luck!" Preston called to me from behind. I started running down the street toward the luminous, downtown sidewalks.

The conditions outside were *perfect*. I had never seen State College so beautiful. The snow was falling in clumps and there was no wind. My view resembled that of a television station skewed by the static of bad reception. My body screamed at me as it adjusted to the cold, but after a minute of exposure, it relaxed. There was no more shock or "cold feeling." I was comfortable. The snow melting on my skin, felt like a cool refreshing blanket. As my feet crunched over the snowy sidewalks, they produced a lovely rhythm. *Thick-thunk-thick-thunk-thick-thunk.* It felt like a dream. The world seemed too beautiful to be real.

The sight of people brought me back to reality. There were women dressed in mini-skirts being escorted by their boyfriends. They were desperately trying to keep their balance through the untouched snow, but it proved to be an impossible task. Numerous times, I saw couples slip and fall onto the concrete sidewalks. The men would try to help the women off the ground, only to lose their footing and fall right beside them. It reminded me that I needed to pay closer attention to my steps.

After running by the falling couples, I realized that breathing in the cold, dry air through my mouth, was extremely uncomfortable, so I tried something different. I kept my mouth shut and breathed solely through my nose. I also slowed my pace down to the point where I didn't feel like I was pushing myself and needed extra oxygen. Doing this made me feel ten times better. Not only did I not have to worry anymore about getting a sore throat from running in the cold, but I also realized that it made me warmer.

As I approached the middle of the downtown area, about 6 or 7 minutes into my run, I noticed a sudden change in volume. There was loud music blaring from the apartments on both sides of the street. The towering buildings on each side resembled the skyscrapers found in miniature snow globes. What set apart these buildings from the ones that were in snow globes were the drunken students partying on the balconies. Several screamed profanity at me as I ran by. Some even made snowballs from the snow that accumulated on their porch and aimed for me as their target. Luckily, none of them hit my exposed flesh.

The streets were now filled with people going to and from the bars. Almost every person I ran by had something to say.

"Are you crazy?"

"Put a shirt on, you won't get girls that way!"

"Somebody lost a bet… Naked lap!"

"You wanna fight?!"

Apparently, my bare-chested running threatened some guys to the point of confrontation. I simply ignored them and continued running.

When I reached the loop to turn around to come back toward my house, I looked over my shoulder and noticed a man chasing me. I had no idea who this person was or what he wanted, but for the next three minutes he chased me. As he ran by women on the streets, he would ask for high-fives and encourage them to cheer me on. I couldn't tell if he was being sarcastic of if he was extremely intoxicated. Eventually, his footsteps faded away and I was alone again.

By the 12th minute, I could feel my fingers begin to tingle. It wasn't painful, just noticeable. The rest of my body felt completely fine; actually, I felt extremely warm. This realization encouraged me to increase my speed for the rest of the run home.

I arrived back in the comfort of my home after twenty minutes of being exposed to the cold. After a few seconds of being inside, I felt the desire to go back out again, not because I wanted to go for another run, but to expose my feet to the fresh snow.

I took off my shoes and went out into my front yard. My feet were hot and sweaty from running in socks and shoes, so the first few seconds of standing in the snow felt refreshing. After thirty seconds had past, I was still comfortable. My body wasn't sending me any signals to get out; I was content. When a few minutes more had past, the sweat on my exposed chest began to chill and I started to feel cold. A few seconds later, my feet began to feel the effect as well. Feeling like they were on fire, I pulled out and jogged barefooted into my house.

The pain alleviated as soon as I stepped into my warm home.

"How'd your run go?" Preston asked from the bedroom.

"Awesome," I replied. "I'd say it was a success!" I walked into my bedroom and noticed he was still playing video games. As I entered the room, he paused the game and turned to face me.

"Wow!" he said. "Your chest is bright red! Are you okay?"

"Yeah, I feel great! My chest is tingling, but I still feel really, really warm."

"Cool, glad to hear it, Just."

I threw on a pair of sweatpants and a hoodie in an attempt to warm my body quicker. The warm material against my skin made me feel colder. I was thoroughly confused.

What's happening to me? I thought. *I'm supposed to feel cold and shiver when I'm outside, not when I'm inside wearing warm clothes.*

Soon after my cold episode ended, Preston finished playing his game and we said goodbye. I sat in my room for the next few hours, too excited to sleep. The night's experience had given me a sense of accomplishment. I had found a fun, yet safe way to train my body in the cold. Finally, I felt like I was doing *real* Iceman training.

...

The next few days were consumed by dishwashing and school-work. There was hardly any time for me to do any of my new cold exercises. Therefore, I found another way to train. Whenever I'd leave my house, walking to work or class, I would only wear shorts and a t-shirt. No matter how cold the temperature was, I stayed consistent. Some days, I would leave for class around 8:00 AM or 9:00 AM and not return home until 10:00 PM. Those were the days I dreaded the most.

Even though I was extremely busy, I was still determined to become the Iceman. I put up with the long cold days in hopes that one day, my body would be able to stay warm despite the freezing temperatures. It was hard at first, but I stuck with it. I was given plenty of looks, where I could tell people doubted my sanity, but I didn't let their skepticism stop me.

During my time walking around Penn State's campus wearing limited clothing, I noticed only one weakness. Sure, my body would get cold for the first five minutes of exposure, but it always adjusted to the outside temperature. The weakness was in my hands. Within a few minutes of adjusting, my hands would begin to tingle, then hurt, then ache, then throb. When I couldn't endure the pain any longer, I would find the closest building and go inside until my hands warmed up. My hands were the only reason why I would ever seek shelter.

While the rest of my body remained warm, my hands screamed in agony. Eventually, I had enough. I knew that if I wanted to last longer in the cold, I would need to dedicate more time to cold exercises.

Over the next few days, I brainstormed ways to increase the intensity of my training. During one of my dishwashing shifts, I came up with the idea to use a metal bowl instead of a plastic garbage can for the cold-water container. I theorized that the metal would be able to retain the cold longer than the plastic.

After my dishwashing shift, I went home and grabbed a metal bowl from my kitchen. I filled it up the same way I had normally filled up my plastic garbage cans -- with salt and cold water. I then added two trays of ice with hopes of dropping the temperature a bit more. The temperature of the water in the metal container was measured to be 43.3°F (6.3°C), which was lower than the temperature I had previously measured in the plastic can when I had first received the thermometers.

I realized that due to the wide mouth of the metal bowl, I would be able to fit both of my hands into the water comfortably. I put a towel between my legs, placed the bowl on the towel, and sat comfortably on the couch. Being that both my hands would be underwater simultaneously, I would be unable to record the data during the exercise. Therefore, I decided use the time to focus on the exercise and pay close attention to the changes in my hands.

I took a few deep breaths, closed my eyes, and placed both of my hands into the water. With my eyes closed, I could focus on every sensation. A second or so after immersing my hands, they began to sting. The pain grew more intense as the seconds passed. Several times, thoughts came screaming into my head.

"You're going to hurt yourself"

"Get out now!"

I tried to calm my mind and ignore the pain, telling myself that it would soon be over. Eventually, the pain subsided and I was able to sit comfortably. I named the timeframe from when I first put my hand into the water to the point when the pain went away as "the adaptation phase," hereby known as: *Stage 1*.

After the pain faded, I felt nothing else. My body was relaxed and at ease. I repositioned my hands in the bowl and immediately, the cold shock flooded in. Pain surged back to my fingertips. After a few seconds of tensing my muscles, the pain eased away. I recognized the absence of pain and overall tranquility after the initial shock as "the relaxation phase," hereby known as: *Stage 2*.

Several minutes passed since the beginning of *Stage 2*. Slowly, a tingling sensation appeared in my fingertips. It was similar to the feeling of a hand or foot falling asleep. Steadily, the tingling increased. Worried thoughts filled my head.

Pull it out, Justin. You're doing damage to your body. This isn't good.

Curious as to what would happen, I ignored my thoughts and forced myself to stay in the water.

Over the next minute or so, the tingling spread from my fingertips, up to my knuckles, and then to my wrist. My thoughts became overbearing.

What are you doing? Take it out now!

I felt like my body was literally screaming at me to remove myself from the cold substance. Afraid, I listened to my body and pulled out my hands. I deemed the first signs of a tingling sensation and worrisome thoughts as: *Stage 3*.

After drying off my hands on the towel beneath the blanket, they began to burn. The pain was unbearable. Once again, they felt like they were exploding. I took the bowl off of my lap and placed it on the ground incase my writhing body knocked it over. I shoved both of my hands inside my shirt and placed them under my armpits. I jumped as my cold hands touched my warm skin. Within seconds, the pain intensified. The heat from my body had raised the pain level to "excruciating". My first thought was to pull away, but I gritted my teeth and fought through it.

Several minutes passed before the pain finally dissipated. I realized that I had made a grave mistake; I never should have pushed myself that far into *Stage 3*. I made a note to always remove myself from the cold at the first sign of *Stage 3* (i.e. tingling and worrisome thoughts).

I considered what would have happened if I had forced myself to stay in longer, but I knew that there would be dire consequences for fulfilling my curiosity. Therefore, I deemed anything more than the noted symptoms of *Stage 3* to be considered as *Stage 4*. I could only assume that prolonged exposure to *Stage 3*, or the onset of *Stage 4*, would inevitably lead to permanent damage, something I had hoped I would never have to experience.

Sadly, that was the last exercise I performed during the fall semester. Finals were a few days away and I desperately needed to do some studying. Therefore, all of my time was devoted to studying, finishing projects, and working dishwashing shifts.

After finals, I had a little more time, but not a lot. With the semester over, most of the students employed at The Deli were home for the holiday season. As much as I wanted the time off to see my family, I needed the money to pay for my rent. I also saw it as an opportunity. Staying in State College over winter break would give me ample time for cold training.

On December 23 at 12:05 AM, I returned home after a long shift at work. I had spent the last few days recouping after my extensive studying for finals, but I was now ready to get back to training. After showering, I lay down on the couch in my living room and stared at the ceiling. While brainstorming new ways to train my body, my mind stumbled upon the idea of full-body immersions.

I remembered Wim saying he took daily swims in a frozen lake for exercise. Sadly, there was no place around my apartment where I could freely swim in the winter. I convinced myself that this was a good thing. I would rather be in a controlled environment than subjected to unforeseeable circumstances. I didn't want a repeat of the night when my feet were freezing in the park. Eventually, I settled on the idea of using my bathtub as my controlled environment.

While trying to figure out the details of how I could use the bathtub to simulate a frozen lake, my friend, Danielle Cardell, texted me. Danielle, or Dani as I usually call her, was one of the few people that knew about my trip to California and my research on the Iceman. In our texts, we were discussing the exercises I had used thus far to train my body (i.e. cold runs and hand/foot immersions).

When I finalized the details of how I would go about the full-body immersion in the bathtub, I asked Dani if she would like to come over, supervise, and perhaps participate. She said she didn't know if she was going to participate, but she would be willing to come over and supervise to make sure that I would be okay. I was worried that something may go wrong and if it did, at least she would be there to call 911.

...

The clock read 1:08 AM on my car's dashboard as I sat in Dani's driveway. I was listening to an audiobook of C.S. Lewis's *Mere Christianity* while waiting for her to come outside. If Dani decided to try the full-body immersion after I did, it would be the first time anyone, other than myself, willingly agreed to participate in my cold exercises. The idea of sharing Wim's teachings with someone else excited me. I didn't know how others would react to the cold, but I was interested in finding out.

When we got back to my house, Dani and I talked for a good half hour. We hadn't seen each other in a couple weeks, so we caught up on each other's lives. Eventually, the discussion switched to the topic of the cold. I gave her a few in-depth explanations about the methods I used to train and then I proceeded to show her the buckets I used for my extremity immersions.

She was still unsure about whether or not she wanted to try the full-body immersion, so I suggested trying a different cold exercise first. I filled up one of my plastic trashcans with cold tap water, salt, and twelve ice cubes. After letting it chill for a bit, I placed the contents in front of Dani. I didn't bother taking the temperature of the water. It was simply a demonstration of what she would feel upon entering the bathtub. I explained my perception of the four stages and told her what to expect. She was eager to try it out.

After taking a few seconds to prepare herself, she plunged her right hand into the cold water. Within a few seconds, the shock became evident on her face. She squinted her eyes, bit her lip, and took noticeably larger breaths. I began to tell her things like, "Don't worry, the pain will go away soon" and "just try to relax, it'll make it easier to adjust."

Soon enough, the tightness of the muscles in her face relaxed and she finally appeared comfortable. She smiled and told me that the pain was gone.

Instead of pulling her hand out, I asked Dani to keep it in until she reached the beginning of Stage 3, where the tingling would set in. I figured that it would be beneficial for her to recognize that moment, so she'd know when to pull herself out of the water if she ended up doing the full-body immersion.

Eventually, Stage 3 set in. Dani removed her hand, and I dried it off with a towel. She walked me through her experience in detail, from the beginning of the shock, to the tingling in the fingertips. She was still unsure about the bathtub, but she agreed to watch me do it first and then decide afterward.

I left Dani in the living room and went into the bathroom to turn on the cold water. We didn't have a drain stopper, so I plugged the hole with a rag that I found under my kitchen sink. After placing five trays of ice cubes and a container of salt in the bathroom, I changed into my bathing suit. After the water filled the tub, I poured in the ice cubes and salt and let it sit.

I figured ten minutes was a sufficient amount of time to let the water chill. When I took the temperature, it read 42.6°F (6.8°C). Somehow, the water was colder than any of the extremity immersions I had previously performed. Then again, I never used five ice trays to fill up the plastic garbage can. After calling Dani into the bathroom, I pushed the timer on my stopwatch and tried to get into the water as fast as possible to avoid any moments of hesitation.

I was used to the cold water on my feet, so stepping in wasn't so bad; the shock came when I sat down and submerged my lower body. Something in my head began to scream at me. *GET OUT! This is freezing! What are you doing?* Despite my powerful thoughts of aversion, I shifted my weight and sank lower into the tub.

As the water crept up my stomach and washed over my chest, something snapped. I lost all control over my breaths and I began gasping for air. I shut my eyes tight and sunk the rest of the way into the tub until my shoulders were completely immersed. The parts of me sticking out of the water were my head and my two kneecaps. Apparently, I was too tall for the tub and was incapable of fitting my entire body underwater.

My body felt rigid and I had developed uncontrollable shivers. I desperately tried to calm myself down and regain control of my breathing. I tried slow breaths, deep breaths, and even holding my breath; none of it worked. Instead, I tried focusing on relaxing every muscle in my body.

At the one-minute mark, my body was beginning to relax and the shivers were fading away. By 1 minute and 30 seconds, I had completely adapted and regained control over my breathing. That's when I realized a peculiar sensation. Only a few seconds earlier, I had been unbelievably cold, but now, the water felt warm. In fact, all of my body felt warm. I was comfortable.

It felt like a game, and I was winning. The only thing I had to focus on was relaxing and taking slow, deep breaths. It no longer was a struggle between my conscious thoughts and my reflexive actions. For that moment, I had complete control over my body.

At three minutes, I began to lose control; the convulsions returned. The shivers were much harder to control and I was becoming very anxious. So, for the next 5 minutes, I struggled with regaining control. I attempted to suppress the shivers, but only succeeded a few times. Even then, I was still only for a few seconds. I didn't know where the shivering played into the four stages, but I relied on the signs from my previous experiences.

Finally, at 8 minutes and 26 seconds, I felt the tingling sensation in my toes and fingertips. Being that it was my first time in a full-body immersion exercise, I didn't want to push myself more than necessary. I found comfort in the idea that I could set up the bathtub again and try any time I pleased. Therefore, I stopped my stopwatch and stood up from the water.

The air felt warm on my body and my skin tingled. I looked down and noticed my skin color was a deep shade of crimson. I resembled someone who had been lying in the sun for hours without the aid of sunscreen. When reaching for my towel, I realized my movements were incredibly slow. It was strange. I had to consciously focus on the action of grasping each finger around the towel. Usually, I am very good at multitasking, but in this situation, each movement required my full attention.

I began drying myself off and immediately noticed something was wrong. I couldn't feel the spot where my towel had touched my skin. Several more times, I poked the skin on my arms and couldn't feel a thing. I proceeded to dry myself off using a dabbing motion.

I would put it on one place, let it soak up the water, and then move on to another area.

When I tried drying off my feet, I lost my balance and grabbed the shower door to prevent my fall. Unbeknown to me at the time, I had gripped a very sharp metal edge. I couldn't feel anything. I didn't notice the large gash in my hand until the blood marks appeared on my white towel. I had acquired a 2 to 3-inch slice on my left hand. The accident encouraged me to be more careful with my movements.

Despite the slowed motor functions and the lack of feeling in my skin, I felt great. I was really comfortable. After getting out of the bathtub, I went into my room and changed from my bathing suit to a long sleeve shirt, sweat pants, and socks. I then proceeded to go into the living room and discuss my experience with Dani.

Soon after sitting in the living room, a strange feeling came over me. I suddenly felt *extremely* cold. I was beginning to regain my sense of touch back, so I touched my arm to feel the temperature; it was warm. Just then, I began to shake violently, succumbing to uncontrollable shivers. Confused, I stopped talking and told Dani to give me a few minutes so I could try to regain control over my body.

Oddly enough, I suddenly had a strong urge to take off my clothes. On the surface of my body, I felt like I was overheating. On the inside, I could feel the cold blood coursing through my veins. It didn't make any sense.

Fighting the urge to take my clothes off, I began jumping around in an attempt to get my blood pumping and adrenaline flowing. It made me feel lightheaded, so I sat back down. I tried explaining to Dani what was going on inside me, but every time I spoke, my body would shake and my teeth would chatter. It was ridiculous. This lasted for the next 45 minutes.

Eventually, my shivers stopped and I felt like I had regained control. Somehow, my unexpected cold episode didn't faze Dani. Instead, it seemed to inspire her. Her eyes lit up when I asked if she wanted to try it.

"Sure," she said. "Why not?"

Since she had left her bathing suit at home, I gave her a pair of my shorts and a t-shirt to change into.

A few minutes later, Dani and I were standing in my bathroom. She seemed extremely anxious as I checked the water temperature. The thermometer read 46.8°F (8.2°C). The temperature must not have fazed her because she soon replied with, "Welp, here I go!" and lowered herself into the water. Immediately, she began gasping for air.

"Try to relax Dani," I said. "What you're feeling will be over soon."

After 1 minutes and 20 seconds of going through the initial shock, her body became less rigid and she was able to finally relax. Even though she suffered from an occasional shiver here and there, she was in control.

In an attempt to help Dani remain in control, I asked her to not talk unless she was updating me about her body. Not seeing anyone, other than myself, perform these exercises before, I was worried for Dani's wellbeing. I sat by the tub and gave her my full attention the entire time.

When she began to feel the tingling in her toes (*Stage 3*), 7 minutes and 42 seconds had passed. I stopped the stopwatch and helped her out of the tub. I reminded her to move slowly when drying herself off.

A few minutes later, she had changed and we were now sitting in my living room. As she described her experience, she kept emphasizing how easy it was after the initial shock (*Stage 1*) had passed. While in Stage 2, she had felt comfortable and warm. She shivered as she explained all of this to me, but she didn't seem to be as bad as I was. She was able to complete her sentences without interruption.

Danielle was the first person to ever join me for a cold exercise. I will forever remain grateful to Dani because her experience showed me that the patterns I had recognized weren't in my head, but were a part of reality. Danielle was easily able to identify when her body transitioned from one stage to the next. Seeing the same changes happen in someone else excited me.

Before the full-body immersions and the snow runs, I was still somewhat skeptical about Wim's abilities, but after seeing Danielle's performance and hearing her detailed account, my doubts vanished completely. From that point on, I believed that *anyone* could train to become like the Iceman.

CHAPTER 24:
RESEARCH

Recently, many articles have been published about "The Ice-man." The most important discovery that I think is worth talking about is that I am capable of consciously influencing my immune system. It has been proven at the Feinstein Institute in Manhasset, New York and now at the Hospital in Nijmegen, Netherlands.

As you may recall, a few years ago In Manhasset, I performed a meditation experiment at a biochemical research institute. They asked me to meditate at room temperature. The doctors connected me to a lung-monitoring system as well as a cardiograph. They stuck a needle into my left arm and withdrew blood before, during, and after the meditation. I had to wait a week before hearing those results.

When I received that call from Dr. Kenneth Kamler, I was ecstatic. They found that I was able to suppress the inflammatory bodies influencing the vagus nerve. This means that they found proof that I could directly influence the autonomic nervous system. With this great news, a new fire had started within me.

This means that my technique can be a viable way to help cure diseases. The immune system is the power source that deals with what makes us sick. If I can do it, so can everyone else. It is just training.

Last year, I was invited to the most famous theatre hall in Holland by the Circus der gedachten. They're a platform for innovative thoughts and ideas. They had read one of the articles about my passion to become a dedicated contributor in helping to prevent disease in the world.

When I went, I spoke about my interest in finding cures for diseases. The director of the circus had a degree in medicine. After hearing my speech, we got in contact with the renowned Radboud

Hospital in Nijmegen, Netherlands.

They organized a meeting with a physiologist named Professor Hopman. Hopman and her team were very interested in performing an experiment on me. So, I went with the executives of the circus and drove to Nijmegen.

When we arrived at the hospital, I was introduced to many people, including a pleasant Professor Hopman. She escorted me to the laboratory and showed me around. She then introduced me to each member of her research team.

Soon after, the tests began. My heart, blood, and veins were all monitored. They also monitored the cold's temperature, as well as my core temperature, lungs, and more. I tried my hardest to give the best possible results.

I had wires connected all over my body. Willingly, I entered a Perspex box that they then proceeded to pour ice cubes into! As soon as the ice was up to my neck, the timer began.

They checked on me every five minutes. Every fifteen minutes, the doctors extracted blood from my veins. The monitors were active, and so was I. Everyone was busy with their particular job, yet everyone was watching me. It felt like I was at the circus again!

They all seemed very excited to be experimenting on me. The Iceman was sitting in a Perspex box filled with 700 kilograms of ice! It was a different experience for them compared to any other dull experiment. They were monitoring an adult male in one of the most extreme situations imaginable.

After an hour and a half in the ice, I had no problem whatsoever. I was charged up when I came into the laboratory and it carried on to the end. I gave it my best and I hoped the results would agree.

When I was getting out of the icebox, I was struck with regret! I had forgotten to use my breathing technique in the ice. It would've made the results much more significant, but it was too late. So I let it go and hoped that my performance had been enough.

Everyone was excited. The room was fuller than when I had first entered. Many more professors and doctors from the university must have came in to witness the event.

They sat me down in a chair and the afterdrop began to kick in. They noticed my shivering and asked what I was feeling.

I then told them that I am like everyone. I can sense both the cold and the heat. The only difference between myself and everyone else is that when I focus, I can withstand the cold much more than the average person. After warming up, they let me return to my home to await the results.

A week later, we were back at Radboud sitting in the Professor

Hopman's office. Seated around a large table, we were given sheets that explained the results. Hopman sounded excited.

"It seems," she said, " that you can influence the autonomic nervous system. You were able to maintain your core body temperature at 37.1°C (98.78°F). You were able to do this while immersed in the ice for an hour and a half. This has never been done before."

She continued while pointing at the large collection of books behind her, "We can rewrite all of these books in my office, and tell that the autonomic nervous system can be influenced by human will!"

After catching my breath at hearing the astounding results, I told them that I had always believed it was possible. Despite the disbelief of others, I had always known. There was no longer any speculation; the results were sitting in my hand.

I then proceeded to look over the results in full detail. The first thing I noticed was that my blood pressure remained normal the entire time. Normally, when someone is exposed to extremely cold temperatures, the blood pressure dramatically increases to warm up the body. You can call it the "survival mode."

My pulse also stayed relatively the same. When exposed to cold, the pulse has been known to double, or even triple the normal resting rate.

While I was submerged in ice, I was able to triple the oxygen density in my body by 300%. By simply standing there, without shivering, I was producing 3x more oxygen to warm up the exposed parts of my body. This is not a "typical" physiological reaction.

They found that the activity in each individual cell in my body became hyperactive after immersing in ice. Even a week after they took my blood, they were still able to see the activity in my cells.

One of the most significant pieces of data was my skin temperature compared to my core temperature. My skin, which was measured by 16 sensors placed at different spots on my body, showed a dramatic decrease in temperature to almost 0°C (32°F). Despite the decrease in skin temperature, the core temperature, which normally decreases with the skin, remained at the same temperature, 37.1°C (98.78°F).

The carotid artery, which is one of the major arteries that provides blood flow to the head, showed another remarkable result. Typically, when immersed in the cold, the carotid artery's most important job is to provide blood flow to the brain. Apparently, from the observations made in the experiment, I was able to reverse the blood flowing to my head.

A likely hypothesis is that since my head wasn't immersed in the cold water, it didn't need to be warmed up. So by telling my warm blood where to go, I was able to direct the blood flow to the core parts of my body that needed it the most.

...

Shortly after the results came in, I came in contact with a man by the name of Professor Mihai Netea, an immunologist. Normally a very peaceful and calm man, when Professor Netea heard the results of the experiment, his body leaked with excitement.

He then proposed a new type of experiment to me. He told me that there was a method to show how effective immune systems are by injecting the blood with endotoxin. This endotoxin causes the body to react as if it were poison. This "poison" provokes the immune system to react violently by releasing cytokines into the bloodstream. Usually, someone injected with endotoxin suffers from nausea, fever, headaches, and an overall flu-like state. This experiment is known as the Endotoxin Experiment.

If I can influence the immune system, everybody can; that is my goal. It could change how things work in terms of healthcare for people all around the world.

Apart from the talk of the endotoxin experiment, immunologists had already begun subjecting me to other kinds of studies.

While lying on a bed, connected to all kinds of monitors to watch for heat, blood pressure, and cellular activity, researchers withdrew blood from me 18 times! After an hour and a half of doing nothing, they had me do another hour and a half of my breathing exercises, inducing my meditative state.

They sent the withdrawn blood to 6 different laboratories to measure different things. One of the labs that received the blood was the endotoxin department, however, they were unable to release the results until the Endotoxin Experiment took place. They didn't want to influence my state of mind.

However, there was a slight problem with the Endotoxin Experiment. The doctors wanted to inject me with endotoxin, but the ages that are allowed to participate in this experiment have to be between 18-35; I am in my early 50's!

Even though I am as strong as an ox, I could not get past this age barrier. The doctors who previously saw the results were anxious to prove that the immune system could be consciously influenced. There was a lot of frustration, but we remained patient and persevered.

For what felt like ages, we waited. The ethical commission administration needed to clear me before I could participate in the experiment. Finally, after many days, I received a call that would change the world forever.

CHAPTER 25:
THE INVITATION

Wim and I sent a lot of emails to each other over the course of winter break. We would speak to each other two to three times a day. Despite the frequent conversations that Wim and I had, I was unable to push myself to develop the technique further. I felt like I had encountered an obstacle that was too hard for me to climb over by myself.

For the longer part of the winter months, my days were dedicated to working in the day and hanging out with my friends in the night. Of course, there were a few times where I would feel inspired and do a few Iceman exercises with my friends, but to them, it just seemed like a cool party trick.

"I bet you can't stand in the snow for [X] minutes," they would say.

I wanted to push myself but I lacked the motivation. My job consumed my days and by the time I got home from work, I was too exhausted to do anything. I would take a nap only to be woken up by my friends' calls, asking me to come hang out with them. Since most college students were home for break, my coworkers were my only friends in town.

I remember feeling extremely guilty every time I walked home from their houses. The air was always cold and it reminded me of my desire to train. Even though I had an incredible connection to one of the greatest cold experts in the world, I was squandering my opportunity to learn. The constant guilt was draining me.

That's when I received this email:

Date: January 16, 2009
"Hi Justin

This year in spring I will give a workshop in Poland on our farm in nature. You should attend.

Keep on,
Wim"

I was ecstatic. It was the opportunity that I had been waiting for all along. I immediately called Jarrett and read the email to him. He was just as excited as I was. It was the next step in taking the cold training more seriously; however, there was one small problem. Jarrett and I were both currently scheduled to take classes during the spring. If we were going to attend the workshop, then we would need to make sure that we were both available.

Therefore, I sent Wim the following:

"I am wondering if you happen to know when your workshop will be in the spring. Jarrett and I are wondering because we'd have to make arrangements. Any information would be very much appreciated. Thanks!!!
-Justin"

He quickly replied with:

"Hi Justin

It is going to happen in the very beginning of May. May 1st - May 7th. I hope to see you and you have to consider the price. What is your financial position?

Many greetings,
Wim"

I texted Jarrett the date and we both checked our schedules. We soon realized that we had a major conflict. May 1-7 was the week of our final exams. It also happened to be Jarrett's last semester of college. It was essential for him to be there during that last week, so he would not be able to attend the workshop. I could sense his disappointment. If I went, I could still share the technique with him upon my return. Therefore, I vowed to myself that I would attend the workshop at all costs.

During the next several exchanges of emails with Wim, I found out that the total price of the workshop would be 500 euros, which was about 720 US dollars at the time. That's a lot of money for a college student to fork over on a *"whim."* Aside from the cost of the workshop, I would still need to pay for a round-trip plane ticket and get myself a passport.

Not more than a few hours after first hearing of the workshop in Poland, I devised a plan to make the trip possible. When I called my parents to tell them about my trip to Poland, they were not happy. The conversation went something like this:

Me: "Hi Mom!"

Mom: "Hi Sweetie."

Me: "So, remember when I told you that I was talking to the one guy I saw on TV, The Iceman?"

Mom: "Yes… why?"

Me: "Well, he has been training me for the past few months to become like him. Actually, I just received an email from him, inviting me to come participate in his workshop during the first week of May."

Mom: "…Where?"

Me: "Um… Poland."

Mom: "I don't know if I feel comfortable with that. You have never met this person in real life. How do you even know if you're talking to guy you think you are?"

Me: "I don't know. He has told me things that lead me to believe it's him, like things he's going to do before it's even released in the media. He's also given me a lot of information about the cold that few people would know anything about. Honestly, I believe it's him."

Mom: "Well, your dad probably won't be happy about you going to Poland, especially because we wanted to take you on vacation. What are you going to do about your job?"

Me: "I guess I'll put in my two weeks notice before I leave. To me it was a means to an end. Now, I have a reason to leave. Although, I still need to put in a lot of hours before I go, so that I can afford it. In total, it looks like the trip is going to cost me about $1,700."

Mom: "Yeah, as much as your father and I would love to give you money, we really don't have it. Don't be using your loans for this either; that money is for school."

Me: "Don't worry, Mom. I understand that if I want to do this, I will have to raise the money on my own. I also need to get a passport."

Mom: "I really have a bad feeling about this. I don't feel comfortable with you going. It's not that I don't trust you, I just don't trust the people you're talking to; I don't know them."

Me: "I know, but I am also confident that I'll make it there and back just fine. My biggest challenge will be raising the money, but I think it'll be worth it. This is a once in a lifetime opportunity. I don't know if he'll ever offer again. I have to try."

Mom: "Okay, just make sure your grades don't suffer and that you're able to pay for food and rent this semester."

Me: "All right. I'll do what I can. Thanks. Love you."

Mom: "Love you too, bye."

After I got off the phone with my mother, I started thinking of ways to make more money. I remembered that there was a place downtown where I could give plasma twice a week, averaging a total of $50 extra a week. I called in and scheduled an appointment to begin donating.

It seemed like everything would be okay, but I also knew that my schedule was about to get a lot more hectic. Not only would I be working part-time at The Deli, but also my classes would be starting up the following week and they would require a lot of my time and focus. I also had responsibilities in my research lab.

My time was going to be cut short and I quickly realized that I would need to make sacrifices. No longer would I be able to spend late nights hanging out with friends, but I would need to remain focused, otherwise I could kiss the workshop in Poland goodbye.

In an attempt to keep things organized, I devised a list of things to do to make the trip possible:

· Get a passport

· Raise +$1,700 to cover the total and unexpected expenses

· Make enough money so that I can also cover the cost of food and my rent ($475 a month)

· Rearrange my schedule and talk to my professors to take my finals early

· Maintain good grades so my mother doesn't have a reason to keep me from going to Poland

Normally, if I were told that I would have to raise $1,700 at a part-time job, while enrolled as a full-time student, I would freak. Actually, I came pretty close to freaking out numerous times, but the idea of doing something meaningful with my life outweighed all of the sacrifices and possible consequences. I was ready to accept everything I had to do to make the trip happen. Instead of my goals being "go to college and work to pay it off," it became "go to college, work, and make enough money to do something that could improve my life."

To me, Poland wasn't an option... It was an obligation. It was what I needed to do to *live*. I accepted the steps necessary and made sure that it was a lifestyle I could accept. Beyond that, nothing else mattered.

This shift in perspective totally changed the way I lived my life. Over the next several days, my classes began. Already, I felt different. Normally, I would go to class, sit there, and stare off into the distance until it was time to leave, but now, I listened attentively. Why? Because I had a purpose. I needed to learn the information so I could make time for myself to learn what was actually important to me. My psychology classes were too slow and were layered with information. As informative as they were, they didn't grab my attention, but life experience did. I wanted to see what was possible in the world and I had finally found a way to pursue it.

At work I became extremely efficient and motivated. I did the best job I could because I wanted to feel like I deserved that money. With each paycheck, I felt like the value of my life was increasing. I always knew that something could possibly go wrong and that the Poland opportunity may disappear, but I made sure that I did everything in my power to ensure that I could afford the trip when the time came.

Everything I did, I did for Poland. I wanted to know if Wim could actually control his body temperature and withstand extreme colds. Seeing something on the Internet doesn't mean it is true; I needed to find out for myself. If it was real, then I wanted to see if it could be a skill that could be developed in everyone.

I felt like my hopes of understanding would be lost if I didn't train with Wim, in person. I didn't care about the information that college had to offer; I cared about the human potential. I saw more potential in Wim's ability than I ever had in a college degree. When I came to that realization, my original path of getting a job and settling down had vanished. A new road was being paved for the direction of my life and *I* was in control.

CHAPTER 26:
WORKSHOPS

During my free time, when I'm not attempting new challenges or being tested for research, I give workshops and lectures. I typically give my workshops like I give my speeches. I don't have a program; however, I do know the message I want to convey.

My techniques, exercises, and methods are the product of many years of experience in hard nature. I present them in a way that is relatively easy to adopt and understand.

It takes more than being able to understanding something to experience it for yourself. Therefore, I tell everyone that they need personal commitment, dedication, and perseverance before attempting any of my cold training.

Despite the hundreds of workshops I give each year, I am still learning ways to improve my method of teaching. Sometimes, it can be hard to give people knowledge; therefore, I attempt to teach people how to *experience* it.

Of course, most of the people are excited at first, but excitement fades. My goal is to make an impression in their mind that lasts a lifetime. So I search for various methods to help convey knowledge, making that impression.

In my search to learn how to teach, I have found two words that truly envelop all of what I believe: trust and conviction. If you don't trust yourself or your body, it's hard to move forward to take risks. If you aren't willing to commit and stick with it, even if you don't encounter failure, your chances are slim if you want to reach your goals.

Therefore, I tell you that it is possible to reach the immune system and influence the cardiovascular system as well as the mind. The mind is our seat in which gives us control over the body. Once we learn how to take that seat, we can control the body instead of being subjected to its automatic changes.

It's a great feeling when you can consciously experience all of your body's functions working efficiently. We are wholesome beings that strive to feel good and connected. As we are connected to our peers and family, it's just as important to remain connected to ourselves. If your body reacts a certain way, figure out why. Try to understand it.

Meditation is also a great way of doing this. It finely tunes your ability to listen to things outside of your worrisome thoughts. To do what Justin and I have done, you need to have will power, faith, conviction, and deep trust in yourself. If you're willing to expose yourself to nature gradually, you will gain the understanding in time.

Disease surrounds us in today's society. It is everywhere. There are too many negative feelings in the world. It is easy to fall victim to living each day blindly, expecting that one-day, everything will become better. Believing that somehow, the world will magically be at peace and you will be happy. You have to take action to see changes. One idea can change the lifestyle of the masses.

Even though you may completely understand, it needs to be understood by your body as well. It is a machine that works efficiently when your body and mind are unified and resonate together.

If I want to climb vertically up a mountain with no gear, then I need to go deep within myself and make sure that both my body and mind are ready. I need to trust my body in that it won't defy what I ask of it. I also need to trust my mind so that it doesn't bring up negative thoughts. It's about connecting the subconscious and the consciousness of oneself. If a rock slips and I am in danger, I need to be able to react without thinking.

When I climbed Mount Everest in shorts, my faith and trust were with me the entire time. Despite how insane I looked climbing in a blizzard wearing only shorts, I *knew* I wasn't crazy because my mind was focused and attentive. Yours can be that way too.

I am not that different from everyone else. The only thing that sets me apart is that I choose to embrace the cold while others choose to avoid it. Sometimes, when it's cold outside and I'm emotionally exhausted or physically drained, I don't want to embrace the cold. I just want to wear a jacket and be warm. It's not that I don't feel the cold, because that's not true; I simply choose to accept it and trust that my body will do its best to adapt.

"We can do more than what we think." It's a belief system that I have adopted and it has become my motto. There is more than meets the eye and unless you are willing to experience new things, you'll never realize your full potential.

To experience what the world has to offer, you have to learn from the greatest teacher on earth: *nature*.

There is an inscription at the local zoo near my house that says, "Natura Artis Magistra." It means, "Nature is the true artist of life."

Do you experience that? Ask yourself, "Have I ever experienced the wonders of life?" Meditate about it. Meditation helps your spirit bloom like a beautiful flower. The experience can be beautiful and great.

Poetry is the language of the soul. So listen…

"Life is like a dewdrop on a grass leaf. When is slips away, it's gone forever."

This is why we must challenge ourselves to become better and open our minds. We have amazing opportunities to bloom. Understanding can bring us happiness if we are just willing to experience life.

My techniques, methods, and exercises have helped people reconnect to their inner nature. It's helped them regain control of their bodily functions and know when there is a problem.

My message to the world is this: "We have the power to prevent disease. Utilize that ability."

Perhaps this illustration will help convey my point.

Imagine that there is a big building wherein lays a security guard. Let's say this building represents your body and the immune system is the security guard that protects it. Meanwhile, there is a pyromaniac who is interested in burning down the building. He think's it is a beautiful site, but he loves to see destruction. Well, if the security guard falls asleep, the pyromaniac has an opportunity to get in. It only takes one small flame to begin the devastation. If the security guard is alert and doesn't need to sleep… then he can constantly protect his property. Only then will this little flame be prevented.

The immune system has the potential to constantly be alert. It can notice when an intruder enters and instantly send out the forces needed to eliminate the disease. It just takes a bit of training and will power, but I think it is worth it. It's our body!

We have moved too far away from nature and we can't guarantee health. I define being healthy as a wholesome being whose bodily functions run efficiently and keep you happy.

To reach this potential, we must be like a hard working electrician who notices when the power goes out and instantly knows what to do to fix it.

My workshops are about challenging your beliefs and building foundations that will help you take care of your body. The cold can do amazing things if you are willing to trust yourself, show conviction, and have faith. When you can reach that point where you are stronger than the cold, you will realize an internal peace because you will then understand the power of nature.

One more point that I would like to make is this: *Do not overthink things.*

It is good to use our mind when we need it, but it needs its rest too. We can get sick when we don't rest our mind. Psychosomatic things can happen. One of the amazing things about the cold training is that in that moment when you are exposed, you are forced to only think about the present. All of your worrying, all of your stress, all of your problems disappear. If you try to think about other things, the cold brings you back and says, "Hey! I'm still here."

Letting go of your mind, like you have to do in the cold, is a technique that I try to teach. Your happiness resides in a quiet mind.

Sometimes during my workshops, a rush of energy courses through my body. I've been told that people can visibly see when I am excited because I become very open. I want to help people experience the energy that is in all of us. It is the source of a free mind, courage, will power, and faith.

The truth is not shallow. The truth goes deep and can penetrate the heart and mind and calm it. Like a pond where the ripples have ceased and the water is still, only then will you see the beautiful treasures below. Like a hint of daylight in a cave, it can generate hope.

To be happy, the method and exercise doesn't matter because it is never the same for anyone. For wood carpenters, mechanics, parents or teachers, they find the love in what they do and it makes them happy. However you may find clarity, as long as it makes you happy, do it.

Therefore, do everything with conviction. Believe and trust in yourself. But most of all…

Be happy.

CHAPTER 27:
PATIENCE

A few days after I had received Wim's invitation, my excitement wore off. At first, four months seemed like plenty of time to complete my to-do list; I was wrong.

When I first received the invitation email from Wim, I had forgotten about the whopping 19 credits I had scheduled for that semester. This severely limited the amount of time I could spend outside of class. Homework and dishwashing at The Deli took up any free time I had left.

Classes moved slowly for the first few weeks. Luckily, my professors were kind enough to let me reschedule my finals. As long as I provided proof of a plane ticket, they would approve my excuse.

Most of my mornings and afternoons consisted of me going to class and working at The Deli during the evenings. After I'd get out soaking wet from working in the dish room, I would walk home and take a shower. When I was clean, I'd pack up some food and walk 30 minutes to my research lab to work on my homework for a few hours. On multiple occasions, I found myself pulling all-nighters to complete an assignment that was due the next day.

It was a hard time for me, but I accepted the sacrifices. I'm usually a very social person who loves to hang out with as many people as possible, but there wasn't enough time anymore. I lost most of my friends that semester. They knew that if I wasn't working at The Deli, I was either in class or doing homework in the Moore building, which was where my research lab was located. The only people I talked to were my family, my co-workers, Jarrett, my girlfriend (Brooke), and Dave Haneman.

Luckily, Dave and I were in the same major and therefore, took a lot of the same classes together. There were a few nights where I would travel to Moore and Dave would come along. We didn't talk much because we usually had a lot of work to do, but it was nice to have his company. Some days, his presence was the only thing that got me through the night.

One day in the middle of February, I suddenly got a burst of inspiration. Because I couldn't decrease the amount of time it took me to receive paychecks, I decided to tackle another item on my to-do list: my passport.

After a phone call to my mother, I learned that I would have to pick up an application from the local post office, so that's what I did. After examining the application, I noticed that I needed to include two 2x2 inch photographs of my face. I didn't know how to get those done myself, so I called the post office and tried to figure out where I could go to get my picture taken. They explained to me that I could take my picture at their facility as long as I made an appointment. They then transferred me to another line where I was greeted by someone's voicemail. I left my name and phone number and asked whoever received the message to return my call at their convenience.

Well, they never returned my call. I even called back 10 more times over the next few weeks, but I never heard back. Frustrated at how difficult it was proving to be to get my picture taken, I decided to try it myself. It couldn't be that hard, right? Wrong.

I took several pictures of my face using my laptop computer and cropped them suitable to the government's guidelines. I then proceeded to take them to local printing stations in stores around town, but none of them printed in 2x2 inch dimensions. I felt hopeless. So, I did what any other college student does when they run out of options: I asked my parents for help.

When I spoke to my father over the phone and explained my dilemma to him, he told me that it was an easy problem to solve. He told me that the Rite Aid in my hometown took passport photos at a very low cost.

Awesome, I thought sarcastically. *Now I just have to find the time to drive three hours to my hometown, get the picture taken and drive three hours back. How am I going to do that when I already don't have time to spare?*

I had to wait another two weeks before I could find the time to drive to Sharon. It was my first day off in a while and I skipped my last class of the day so I could make it home.

The actual process of getting my picture taken turned out to be much easier than I had expected. It only took ten minutes and a few bucks to finish something it had taken me weeks to accomplish. I dropped the pictures and my application off at the post office in my hometown and made my way back to school.

I returned to State College with a heavy workload waiting for me. Apparently, putting off one day of homework is enough to leave me struggling to play catch up for days. When I finally accomplished enough to feel like I could breathe again, I began thinking about the workshop in Poland.

I had never traveled outside of the country before; I didn't know what to expect. The scariest thought that came to my mind wasn't, *Will I get lost?* It was, *What if I lose the money before I meet Wim and don't have a way to pay for the workshop?*

Over the next few days, I looked into methods that I could use to get the money to Wim before I got there. I eventually decided on trying a wire transfer. Wire transfers have acquired a lot of bad press due to the amount of email scamming that goes on nowadays, but after looking into it, it seemed safe enough. My parents didn't seem to think so, nor did any of my friends for that matter. Everyone always said the same thing.

"That sounds shady. I wouldn't do that if I were you."

Well, after Wim sent me his bank information via email, I started to believe them. The information looked really sketchy. It was written in a language that I didn't understand and none of the provided numbers were labeled. I prayed that printing the information and giving it to the bank would be enough to make a successful transfer.

I drove to the bank in-between classes, thinking that it wouldn't take too long; once again, I was wrong. The woman helping me with the transaction was completely oblivious as to what the numbers meant. It was her first time doing a wire transfer as well.

Talk about nervous, I was terrified! There was a lot of, "I guess it could be this…" or "Maybe this goes here" going around. When I left the bank, I didn't even care that I had spend the last 2.5 hours there and missed my class; I was worried that I had just lost the $720 that I had worked so hard to acquire. By this point, I was praying that everything would work out. I felt like I had no control over anything and I knew that if that money disappeared, there wouldn't be enough time to make enough to cover the costs of the trip.

I sent Wim an email when I got home, begging him to send me an email when he received the money. I told him that the bank and I were really confused and we didn't know if we did it right.

It was March 16, 2010 when I sent Wim the money via wire transfer. One week later, there still had been no indication that he had received the money. I was convinced that my money was gone. I believed that my dreams of becoming like The Iceman were lost forever. I started to believe the "what ifs" that my parents had suggested.

"**What if** he's not who he says he is?"

"**What if** he just takes your money and doesn't talk to you ever again?"

"**What if** something goes wrong?"

On March 31 at 1:00 AM, before I went to bed, I sent Wim one last hopeful email:

"Wim,

Did you receive the money?

Greetings,
Justin."

In the morning I woke up to this (March 31 - 3:20 AM):

"Sorry Justin

Yes I did
Busy
We will have a great week

Greetings,
Wim"

My heart soared and my dreams were rekindled. I quickly forgot about my worries and imagined myself swimming in a sea of ice. I was back on track!

CHAPTER 28:
TEXEL

I awoke this morning to the sound of whistling birds outside my window, singing a beautiful sonnet comprised of their own *chirps* and *tweets*. The time was 4:00 AM. It was a windy day in March, but the skies remained clear.

I started the day off with my normal breathing exercises, followed by a period of meditation. As I went through my normal routine, I became filled with vigor.

Life is wonderful, I thought, *when you are disconnected from stress and emotion.*

Today, Manely, Marnix, one of his cameramen, and myself took a ferry to the island of Texel. I was in Texel last year to do a workshop and they asked me to return to do a follow up.

Texel is an island just north of den Helder. It's a marine base that's located at the shore's end of Holland. The workshop took place in a non-heated stable. The location was empty, save for the participants and the sheep as our witnesses. Jaap, the organizer of the workshop, opened the session by welcoming everyone.

After a short speech, he passed the torch off to me. It was my turn.

"The cold has the potential to boost your energy levels," I said. "It can give you a certain type of energy that can fill your body and make you whole."

The group formed a circle around me and I became the center of attention. I then explained my breathing exercises and the possibilities that they can open up.

"You are an open book. Begin to experience the content of the story and try to understand where your life is and where it's going. Each day is a new chapter with new opportunities awaiting you."

The stable was really chilly. I could tell that the 15 people surrounding me would begin to suffer if we did not do something soon. So, to conserve everyone's energy, I led them outside and began exercising.

The grass was soft and the wind was blowing cool air. Soon after we started exercising, I asked them to sit down on the mats that they had brought with them and begin the breathing exercises.

After several minutes of breathing exercises, I asked them to perform pushups. First, I had them try doing pushups while retaining air in their lungs. Then, I had them try doing pushups with no air in their lungs. Some were able to do as much as 80 pushups with air in their lungs, while others were able to do 50 pushups with no air in their lungs.

The problem with the pushups is that the exercise doesn't really warm the body. Therefore, I encouraged everyone to move around by jogging in place. In time, everyone had completely adjusted to the cold.

At that point, the cold was no longer a problem. Instead, we were having a fun time doing all these different types of playful movements. I told them that this is the type of feeling I get when I expose myself to extreme colds. If the body is trained, anyone is capable of playing in the cold for an extended period of time!

Remember: Practicing gradual exposure can lengthen the amount of time you are able to stay in the cold.

After the movement session in the windy pasture, we took a break. I took the time to explain this story to them:

"Last week, I was on a television show where blindfolded psychics had to guess who I was. I was located in the Rotterdam container terminal. It was a chilly evening and the wind was strong. It was my job to judge which psychic did the best. When they all finished their presumptions, I would score them and present it to the cameras.

After an hour of them walking around me and trying to figure out who I was, I was asked to go inside of a temperature controlled container of -28°C (-18.4°F). I had to stay in there for ten minutes wearing only shorts. It was the psychics' goal to find me. The tricky part was that there were thousands of containers in the terminal. They needed to use their senses to locate exactly where I was.

I prepared myself mentally before going into that container. I knew that it would be extremely cold, so I prepared my body for that. Soon after entering, my body began to shield the cold away from my core. I had lit the fire within myself.

Next to my container was a heated car. Every ten minutes, they were supposed to open the container and let me go in and warm up; however, I didn't need to leave the container, I was completely comfortable. I stayed in the container for a full hour!

After the hour, I stepped out of the container and felt a warm breeze brush against my skin. You may ask, "Why did the cold wind feel so warm against your skin, Wim?" Well, when I was in the cold, my body adapted to the temperature of the chilled container. It became more alert and wiling to change with the environment. When I got out, the air felt warmer because my skin temperature had adjusted to the temperature on the inside of the container."

The workshop participants nodded with excitement.

Soon after, we all left to travel to the beach of the North Sea where we would go for a cold swim. The wind on the beach was frigid and the water itself was 2°C (35.6°F)!

In their minds, they knew what they had to do, but their body was telling them a different story. Despite the strong avoidance responses that their bodies were giving them, they seemed determined to jump in and get it over with.

We all went into the water together. After the initial shock was over, they all seemed very calm. We began splashing waves at each other and swimming around comfortably. With the right direction and enough energy, anyone is capable of doing this.

After a few minutes, we all left the water and returned to the beach to get dressed in our clothing, but before anyone could begin changing, I shouted, "That exercise was just the beginning!"

Before anyone could figure out what I was talking about, I took off running.

Although they were dazed at first, within seconds they had begun to chase after me. Each was running in their bathing suit, barefooted through the cold sand. With each step, the sand sucked the heat away from their feet.

After five minutes of running, I saw five people become red with an explosion of warm blood flowing through them. This was my goal. I wanted their bodies to readapt to the new cold environment. For those five people, it was a success.

With this type of adaptation, you can last much longer in the cold. It is a natural reaction. We are all capable of it.

My methods may have been unorthodox, but these people were able to see what their bodies were capable of. Each one had experienced the power of the cold.

Thanks Jaap, for the opportunity to teach these wonderful people! I'd also like to thank the participants from the bottom of my heart for their patience and endurance during my instructions. Thank you for looking past your limits!

CHAPTER 29:
ALMOST THERE...

With four weeks left until the workshop, my life became really hectic. I had just spent $940.00 on a plane ticket and my supplies were running low. To save money, I would buy large pizzas and portion them to last me for days.

I had hoped that my course work would lessen as the semester went on, but the complete opposite had occurred. To have enough time to work at The Deli, go to class, and work in my research lab, I had to sacrifice some homework. There were days where I would go through my assignments and calculate which ones were worth the least amount of points. I chose to sacrifice those points in exchange for a little more time. Usually, I'm a very good student, but I had never been so overwhelmed in my entire life. Tactically deciding which assignments were worth completing seemed like my only option.

Sadly, there was no time for my Iceman training either. My last exercise was a run downtown in the snow. Even though I had raised all the money I needed to attend the workshop, I wasn't ready to lift my hands in victory just yet. There was still a lot of schoolwork that needed my focus. The only time I had to "*relax*" was when I was dishwashing. The work had become second nature and gave me an opportunity to free my mind. I guess you could say that it was somewhat therapeutic. It definitely helped maintain my sanity during those busy days.

With three weeks left, I turned in my two weeks notice to The Deli. I planned to use the extra time during the last week to finish studying for my finals, which were all rescheduled for that Tuesday. I also had three research papers and two online assignments to turn in the day before those finals. Time was running out, fast. The amount of work I had to do made Poland seem so far away.

On April 10, 2010, an aircraft of the Polish Air Force went down in Russia. Many Polish political leaders died in the crash, along with the President and his wife. When I first heard of this disaster, I thought it was quite a coincidence. In all my years, I had never heard of Poland ever being mentioned on the news. Yet, a little under three weeks before my trip, the Polish President died in a plane crash. It seemed like a bad sign.

Skeptical, I called my parents and told them the news. They thought I was joking at first, but once they realized my serious tone, they became worried. Immediately, they started telling me about how the streets of Poland would probably be in utter chaos and that my safety was now compromised. I calmed them down by sending Wim an email.

He told me that we would be fine because we would be in a very secluded part of Poland, away from large groups of people. That didn't exactly settle my parents' stomachs, but they let it go. They didn't want to push their worries onto me if I planned to go no matter what.

Then on April 15, 2010, air travel became impossible in northwest Europe due to the eruption of Eyjafjallajökull. I was at my girlfriend's house doing my homework when I first heard the news. It was the second time amidst my studying that I was forced to think about Poland.

No one knew how long the planes were going to be grounded. Tons of people were stuck and unable to fly to their destinations. I hadn't predicted such extreme circumstances. All I could do was hope that the planes would be able to travel again in time for my flight. Six days later, my hopes were answered and air travel was possible again.

The eruption and temporary grounding of flights caused my parents to become more desperate. Even though they didn't have the money, they offered to reimburse me if I decided to stay. They believed that the planes being grounded in Europe was a sign that I shouldn't go. I didn't see it as a sign. I saw it as a test. I wasn't going to be scared away by a couple of unforeseen circumstances.

...

I felt like a giant weight was lifted off of my shoulders when I had finished my last shift at The Deli. It had been a year since my weekend trip to California and I hadn't had a vacation since then. This was my first time not having to worry about incorporating my work schedule into everything else.

Despite the large amount of work I still needed to complete for school, I began to feel a little better. So, I went home and sent Wim an email telling him that I was excited to come, and then asked for detailed information about what to do when I arrived in the Amsterdam airport, which is where he lived and suggested I fly into.

On the Wednesday before my last week in State College I made a decision. There was a time difference of six hours between my home in Pennsylvania and where Wim lived. I wasn't about to waste my first few days in a new country being constantly tired because of the jet lag. No, I was going to be ready.

Luckily, I had purchased a bottle of melatonin pills a few months back. I initially bought them to fix the sleeping problems that my late nights at work created, but now they had a much more important purpose. I would use them to set my biological clock to Wim's time (CET), six hours ahead from where I lived in Pennsylvania (EST). I also thought it would be a great opportunity to escape the noisy college environment and study for my finals in solitude.

The first few nights of my most recent endeavor proved to be rather difficult. My new sleep schedule had me going to bed between 7:00 PM and 8:00 PM and waking up between 3:00 AM and 4:00 AM. I would lie in bed for hours, trying to drown out the sound of my roommates partying in the living room by covering my ears with pillows.

When my alarm went off, I would force myself to wake up and take a shower. I dreaded leaving the comfort of my blankets, but I continued to tell myself that if I didn't get in the shower, I would fail my classes and crash in a plane on the way to Amsterdam. I know what you're thinking, not exactly a reliable consequence, but the satirical extremes were enough to get me on my way.

It wasn't until Monday when the new sleep schedule had finally set in. My roommates still partied, but I had bought earplugs and a facemask to block out the sight and sound. It worked like a charm.

After my morning showers, I'd eat a quick breakfast. I would then proceed to make five peanut butter and jelly sandwiches for the day's meals. When I finished, I would grab my backpack and head on over to the research lab to work on my homework.

Those walks in the early mornings were always interesting. I would typically encounter many intoxicated students that were walking back to their apartments or dorms after a long night of partying. I found it kind of funny. As they were passing out, I was beginning my day.

When I would arrive at the Moore building, I'd take the elevator up to the fourth floor and go to my little cave. The room that

I worked in was extremely dusty, full of storage, and had no windows. Some nights, I felt like I was locked in a prison. I had no concept of time except for the watch I wore on my wrist. The only thing I really remember clearly from those days was the overabundance of peanut butter and jelly sandwiches. I'm surprised that I can still eat them today.

Luckily, my friend Dave was also stressing over finals. He joined me in Moore for a few hours during those late nights. It was nice to have company. It reminded me that there was more to life than working and studying for school, which was my life for those previous few months. Studying those few nights with Dave made my schedule bearable.

It *was* bearable, until I developed a debilitating eye infection. With the long hours in that room and no air circulation, the dust must have irritated my eyes past the point of their tolerable threshold. They were constantly itchy and my eyelids were always heavy. You would think that heavy eyelids would make it easier for me to sleep, but it didn't. Whenever my eyes were shut, it felt like thousands of eyelashes were scratching against my retinas.

Over the next few days, I continued to force myself to work in that room, despite my infection. It was the only place that was available to me that late in the night. My eyes continued to get worse, but I was nearing the end of my workload. By Thursday, seven days after I had initially asked Wim what to do when I arrived, he still had yet to reply.

My parents continued to badger me with questions.

"Do you know where you're going?"

"Have you thought of everything that could go wrong?"

"You have already figured out where you're going to meet him, right?

I was so preoccupied with school that I always answered my parents in the same way, regardless of the true answer: "Yes, I'll be fine, don't worry about me. It'll all work out."

I didn't want them to worry anymore than they had to, even though I was beginning to worry myself. There were two days left until my plane for Amsterdam departed and I still had no clue what to do when I arrived in the Amsterdam airport.

Finally, on Tuesday, minutes before taking my final exams, I received this email from Wim:

Date: Tueday, Apr 27, 2010 -07:42 AM
"Okay Justin
I will be waiting at the gate past the customs.

Right on!
Wim"

...What? That was it? So much for the explicit detail about what I was supposed to do. What if something went wrong and there was no way for me to get a hold of him? I was frantic. I later found out that he was extremely busy traveling and hadn't had time to check his email. Terrible timing, I guess.

Anyway, I received the email as soon as it came in, so I immediately sent one back to him asking for a phone number where I could reach him if something went wrong. Luckily, I got a response a few minutes later. My nerves eased and my worries washed away. Of course, most of the questions my parents asked were left unanswered, but at least I had his phone number.

Seconds after his reply, I packed up my things and left for my exams. There were three tests total that I had to take in a matter of hours, but I wasn't worried anymore. The stress was gone. There was no more time for me to go back to the books and review the information. Knowing that there would be no more studying for the rest of the semester lifted a giant weight off my shoulders.

The finals were difficult, but I expected nothing less. I probably would've been more nervous if I had actually cared about my grades, but my mind was too focused on Poland. In a matter of 48 hours, I would be standing next to the infamous "Wim Hof, The Iceman!"

When I got back to my apartment, I frantically tried to figure out what I would need to take to Poland. I knew that I couldn't have my suitcase weighing over 50 pounds or I would need to fork over extra money that I didn't have. I was clueless.

What should I bring? I thought. *Should I take a lot of t-shirts and shorts because we'll be training in the cold? Should I take a lot of pants and long-sleeve shirts because I'll need to warm myself up afterwards? Is he going to think I'm a wuss if I bring a jacket?*

Despite worrying about what I should bring, I was even more concerned about the fact that I hadn't trained in months. My body wasn't used to any cold whatsoever and I didn't want to freeze to death.

This thought made me decide that I should bring some of everything. The only information I got from Wim about the workshop was that I needed to bring my bathing suit. That's it. I didn't know what to expect because I had been told virtually nothing.

On my three-hour drive home, everything that could possibly go wrong was being played out in my head. *Maybe I'll die of hypother-*

mia. If I get lost or lose my passport, how can I get back home? What if I really haven't been talking to Wim this whole time and I'm going to be murdered or taken advantage of by some stranger?

When I pulled into my driveway, my mind was in shambles, but there was nothing I could do about it. All I knew was that the following day, I would get on the plane and hope Wim Hof would be waiting for me on the other side.

CHAPTER 30:
WELCOME TO POLAND

The following morning I woke up at 3:30 AM. I started my day by printing out my plane tickets and playing a little guitar. By 7:00 AM, my parents were up and I could hear them discussing me in the kitchen. I walked in and hugged them both. I could tell that they were terrified of the possibility of losing their first-born child, but I could see it in their eyes that they were also proud, proud of who I had become. They both hugged me and told me that they would pray for my safety.

My mother made me breakfast while I said farewell to my sleeping siblings. I hugged each of them goodbye as if it was the last time I was going to see them. I didn't know what the next week would bring, but I hoped it eventually brought me back to them.

After eating breakfast, my dad hugged and kissed me goodbye and told me that he loved me. It was a rare occasion for him to show emotion, but his timing meant a lot to me. My mother would be driving me to the airport, so we said goodbye to my father and went on our way.

My mom cried numerous times on the drive there. Between telling me how much she was proud of me and how much she was going to miss me, there were many tears. I appreciated her kindness and openness, but my mind was in another world, particularly Europe. My body was filling with excitement even though it would still be many hours before I reached Amsterdam; I was ready.

When we arrived at the airport, things moved rather quickly. While checking in my bags, the woman who was doing the processing saw the sadness in my mother's eyes and gave her a special pass that would admit her beyond security to see me off at my gate. It seemed unnecessary, but my mother was extremely grateful.

I comforted my mother while I waited at my gate for my plane to arrive. She then began telling me everything she thought I needed to know to remain safe in a foreign country.

"Don't talk to strangers."

"Always watch your belongings."

"Always have your passport on you."

They were things I already knew, but I patiently listened to her advice. Besides, I didn't know if it was the last time I would see her. Something *could* go wrong. There's always that chance, but I didn't want to tell her that. It would just ruin the moment.

When my plane finally arrived at the gate, I hugged my mother goodbye and told her that I loved her. With tears clouding her vision and a forced smile, she told me, "Be careful. I love you more." With that, I handed the flight attendant my ticket and walked through the gates.

My first flight was a short one from Pittsburgh to Washington, only taking one hour and fifteen minutes total. When I arrived in the Dulles International Airport in Washington, I had approximately two hours before my next flight left. I grabbed some dinner and took a seat at the gate where my plane would be departing. I phoned my family, Brooke, Jarrett, and Dave to tell them goodbye and to thank them for their consistent support.

My flight from Dulles left at 5:29 PM (EST). It was scheduled to be a 7 hour and 36 minute flight, arriving in the Amsterdam airport at 7:05 AM (CET). It was my first international flight and I didn't know what to expect. The plane was a lot bigger than my previous flight. My seat was located near a window at the back of the plane. On the back of every seat was a small screen that had the option to play movies, television shows, or an overview of the map. I was amazed by the amount of effort that the airline put into making the flight an enjoyable experience.

An hour after departure, I was served a delicious tray full of chicken, pasta, mashed potatoes, and a little brownie for dessert. After finishing my meal, I began to feel very tired. It was almost 7:00 PM (EST) and according to my newly revised circadian rhythm, it was bedtime. I reclined my chair to a comfortable resting position, plugged my headphones into my iPod, and fell asleep listening to classical music.

Day 1: April 30, 2010

I woke up to the feeling of someone tapping me on the shoulder; it was the person sitting next to me. The flight attendants were bringing around breakfast and he was kind enough to wake me up for the meal. I looked at my watch and the face read 11:37 PM (EST), meaning it was 5:37 AM (CET). I had less than an hour before we touched down in Amsterdam. My eyes were still heavy, but I fought the urge to go back to sleep and awaited the flight attendant.

The cheese omelet that I was served for breakfast was filling. It provided me with the energy that I needed to not fall back asleep. With half an hour left before landing in the Amsterdam airport, my mind ran wild.

What if he forgot and doesn't show up?

What if it was all a joke and no one would be waiting for me in the airport?

What would I do for the next several days?

Where would I sleep?

I calmed myself down by remembering that if something went horribly wrong, I could phone home to my parents and work something out. At that point my mind let go of the "worst case scenarios" and began to think of all the amazing things that would happen if the infamous Iceman was actually waiting for me in the airport.

My plane stopped at the gate at 7:04 AM (CET). By the time I had cleared customs and retrieved my bags, it was 8:05 AM (CET). There were hundreds of people standing around the gate. I looked around for a few minutes, but Wim was nowhere to be found. I considered asking security for help, but when I had finally found someone working for security, I noticed a giant gun strapped around his neck. It wasn't the handgun that you typically see an officer carrying in the line of duty; it was a weapon that looked awfully similar to a machinegun. I decided to take my chances on my own.

After an hour of walking around the place, searching for Wim, I sat down in a Starbucks located on the opposite corner of the building. I pulled out my laptop and tried to check my email to see if he had sent me anything, only to realize that the Internet was not free. *Fail.* So, I decided to go for the next best thing. I pulled up Wim's phone number from my computer and went to find the nearest payphone.

On the way to the payphone, I realized that I had no European currency on me. Luckily, when I came to this realization, I was standing near a currency exchange booth. I converted the $150 that my parents had given me in case of emergencies, and then went to find the nearest phone booth.

At 9:00 AM (CET), I finally found a payphone. It took me another 10 minutes to figure out how to use the thing, but eventually the phone was ringing and a little boy's voice answered the phone.

Boy: "Hallo, wie is dit?"
Me: "Um... Hello. Is Daddy or Mommy there?"
Boy: "Mama!"
A woman's voice answered.
Woman: "Hallo, wie is dit?"
Me: (*Please let this be the right home…*) "Um, hello. My name is Justin. May I please speak to Wim Hof?"
Woman: (In a Dutch accent) "Ohhhh! Justin! Hello, this is Caroline. Wim is there looking for you. He was running late, but he should be there now. Has he found you?"
Me: "Oh, not yet. I tried looking around for a while, but I can't seem to find him."
Caroline: "Well, he's wearing blue jeans, a blue jacket…"

I didn't catch the rest of what she had said because at that moment, I saw a familiar face among a crowd of people.

Me: "I'm sorry Caroline, I think I just found Wim! I need to go chase him down. Thanks!"
Caroline: "All right! Good luck!"

I hung up the phone and started running toward the place where I had spotted him. He was gone. Where was he? I looked around for a while longer and had no luck. I returned to the phone booth and called Caroline once again.

Caroline: "Hallo?"
Me: "Hello Caroline! I'm sorry to bother you again, but it seems that as soon as I got off the phone with you, Wim disappeared. Do you happen to know how I can get a hold of him?"
Caroline: "Yes, actually. There is a place in the airport where most people go to meet. It's in front of the Ticket Information desk, where people can buy their train tickets. Go there and I will call him on his cell and have him meet you there."
Me: "All right! Thank you Caroline! I hope we can meet some day!"
Caroline: "Me too! Have fun in Poland!"

I hung up the phone and went looking around for the Ticket Information desk. To my surprise, I came across three information desks. I made three rounds, checking each information desk over and over again. Forty-five minutes after I had ended the call with Caroline, I finally spotted him. He stood a few inches shorter than I and seemed to be in great physical shape. I couldn't believe it was him. It was the first time I had seen someone famous, let alone talk to them, but I somewhat gathered my composure and walked over.

"Hello," I whispered incase I had mistaken his identity, "Wim?"

"Justin!" he said while opening his arms in an attempt to hug me. "How is everything? I am glad you are here!"

I embraced him and replied with, "I'm glad to be here too. I'm sorry about the confusion. It took a lot longer to find you than I thought it would."

"Everything okay," he replied. "Let's go to the car, yes?"

Hearing Wim talk gave me a better understanding of the content of his emails. In his emails, I sometimes thought he was angry because he would send short responses. I now realized that it was just the way he spoke. I had also forgotten that he wasn't a native English speaker. Later I learned that his first language was Dutch, but altogether he spoke eight different languages. Wim is quite the linguist.

He grabbed my larger suitcase and started walking toward what looked like the exit. We walked through a set of revolving doors and into the fresh air. It was nice to finally be outside of an airport again. The sky was cloudy and the temperature seemed pretty chilly as the wind brushed across my skin. There were frequent gusts of wind blowing through the streets, but it didn't seem to scare people away. Thousands of people filled the streets outside of the airport.

"Wim, are there usually a lot of people around here in Amsterdam?" I asked.

"No," he replied with an elevated tone. "Today is the celebration of Queen's Day. A lot of people come and sell stuff in the streets. Like a giant market with a lot of fun."

"Are we going there?" I questioned.

"No, we need to get going on the road. It's a long drive to Poland. Perhaps we will go for a swim when we arrive. Did you bring your bathing suit?"

"Yes, I did. I'd be down for swimming. Sounds fun!"

Several minutes later we approached a monstrous vehicle. If a hummer and a jeep could produce offspring, this vehicle would be its child. For all intensive purposes, I'll refer to this vehicle as a jeep. Beside the jeep were two men, one of which was smoking. When he saw us coming, he promptly threw the cigarette to the ground and snuffed it out with his shoe.

"Justin," Wim introduced, "This is Henny and Konrad."

"It's a pleasure to meet the both of you," I said as I shook both of their hands.

"Henny is my cameraman, we have been friends for a while. Konrad is one of Henny's friends who will be joining us. Both are very good people."

"My goal for this trip is to quit smoking by the time we get back," Konrad said to me. "It's a bad habit that I need to stop to save money."

I nodded and smiled. Konrad was an interesting fellow who stood a few inches higher than myself. He had dark blond hair and a slender physique. I couldn't see his eye color or tell when he was looking at me because he was wearing a dark pair of sunglasses. I quickly learned that the jeep belonged to Konrad and he would be the one driving us to Poland. Konrad was a friend of Henny's that he had met during a game of squash.

Henny seemed to be a very kind fellow. He reminded me of an estranged GQ model. His glasses were the feature that stuck out to me the most. They seemed to be really expensive and customized. Perhaps it was because they were made in Europe rather than America, but as the first pair of glasses I had seen in a new country, they fascinated me. As far as physical appearance goes, Henny looked to be about the same age as Wim. Although Wim was wearing loose-fitted jean pants and a jean jacket while Henny wore tighter-fitted clothing, as far as I could tell, they had similar body types.

We all got into the jeep and began driving. Henny and Konrad mentioned that we needed to stop at a friend's shop to pick up some parts for Konrad's bike. On the way there, we stopped at a gas station to fill up with diesel. Wim asked Henny to pay for the gasoline and said that he would reimburse him at the end of the week. I was glad to have paid all of my dues to Wim prior to arriving. The stress and worry of money was finally over for me. I could relax and enjoy the company of the people around me.

After filling up at the gas station and picking up a spare part for Konrad's bike, we were finally on our way to Poland. The landscape of Amsterdam was much different compared to my home in Pennsylvania, where there are many hills and valleys. Amsterdam was extremely flat. Another noticeable feature was the overabundance of windmills. I had seen several windmills on farms in the U.S., but they looked like toddlers compared to the giants of Amsterdam.

Those were the two features that stuck out to me the most about the landscapes of Amsterdam. I probably would've seen a lot more, but my attention was more focused on Wim. Ever since we first got into the car at the airport, we had been constantly talking.

For every question I had about Iceman training, he was able to answer it completely. Although for a few questions, Wim told me to wait and see until we arrived in Poland. He said that there were some teachings that could not be explained through words, only experience, which is what the workshop in Poland was for.

After exhausting all my questions about certain Iceman techniques, I began to ask Wim about his achievements that I saw on television or read in the news. Actually, all of the stories that Wim told in this book, I heard in the long car ride to Poland.

Wim then moved on to telling me about the new scientific breakthroughs in relationship to his autonomic nervous system. I was extremely impressed to hear that there was scientific data supporting The Iceman's lifestyle. With the worry of doing damage to my body while pushing to the brink of hypothermia, it was encouraging to hear that I may eventually receive the same benefits from the cold.

When we finally arrived at the Poland border, I noticed a dramatic change of scenery. The roads were extremely narrow and they were filled with unavoidable potholes. Being that I had inherited extreme motion-sickness susceptibility from my father, the drive through Poland was quite the unpleasant experience. During this time, Konrad was telling us stories about his life from when he had lived in Poland. I was unaware that he was Polish up until that point.

He told us that there is a stereotype out there that men in Poland love to bulk up at the gym so that they can pick on people. He didn't confirm or deny whether or not it was true, but nevertheless, it frightened me a bit. It somewhat confirmed my mother's worrying in that I may get into trouble and have no way to get out of it because they don't speak English.

I relaxed a bit when I found out that Konrad was fluent in the Polish language and Wim was more than proficient. At this point, Wim told me that their goal for the week was to "make a wonderful video for YouTube." He wanted to show people that the workshops could be fun and hopefully spark more interest via the Internet. Wim also told me that in-between the few hours of meeting Konrad and picking me up at the airport, they had come up with an idea to try to organize a 5-kilometer barefooted snow run in Karpacz, Poland.

Wim thought it was a marvelous idea and a great opportunity for the community to join in on a great experience. Konrad was in a great position to organize this because his cousin had a lot of political power in Karpacz. Wim told me that I could help organize the event and also run in it when the time came; I was ecstatic. After only being in Europe for half a day, I was already invited to come back to participate in a unique event with the one and only Iceman!

It was early in the evening when we arrived at a medium-sized home in the small town of Przezdziedza. The outside appearance of the "house" reminded me of a barn. Running around the area, inside of the fence, were four or five chickens. Wim opened the gate to the property so Konrad could drive the jeep inside. The property, named "Time-Out" is allegedly run by the mother of Wim's youngest son, Caroline.

"Missshu, Miiiiishu!" Wim's voice reverberated off the walls of the building.

I was clueless as to what he was doing. After a couple more yells, my answer came in the form of a large dog with the build of a bear. Mishu galloped to Wim and stopped by his side, letting him pet the gigantic beast with both hands. Although large, Mishu's soft grey coat and gentle face made him look like an overgrown puppy. He didn't bark, just walked around, letting all of us pet him.

We grabbed our belongings from the car and moved them into the house. When I first walked in, I was greeted by a warm, comfy feeling, despite the cold air that filled the stone walls. I was impressed by how much it already felt like home. Perhaps it had to do with Wim's personality. It's hard not to like the guy. His personality is warm and he speaks to you as if you've been friends since birth. Nevertheless, his home immediately felt like my home, even though it was thousands of miles away from what I normally call "home".

Wim gave us a quick tour of the house. When you first walk in, to your right there's a small wooden piano that's extremely out of tune. To the left of the piano is the room that holds the common area. Inside there is a fireplace, a couch, a computer using dial-up Internet, and a table to eat on. Continuing past the piano and to the left, there's a pantry. Directly across from the pantry is the kitchen. In-between those two rooms is a stairway that leads to the second floor. If you're standing at the top of the stairway, behind you and to the right is the room where Wim slept. Across from his room is his personal bathroom. If you're still standing in the stairway, to your left is a room with seven beds with a door inside that leads to another bathroom. My bed was the first on the right as soon as you walk in.

To reach the attic, there's another stairwell from the hallway on the second floor. Tons of beds were stored there. Wim told us that Caroline uses the place to give people a place to sleep. He said it is similar to hostiles in Europe, a place that can be slept in for cheap to help people who needed it. I could tell that there was still some work to be done in the attic. There were several floorboards missing. We were careful to watch our step.

We each placed our belongings next to the bed where we would be sleeping that night. Henny, Konrad and myself would be sharing a room while, Wim would be sleeping in the bedroom across the hall. After settling in, we all met in the common room by the fireplace.

"We go for a swim?" Wim asked enthusiastically.

"I'd like to try," Konrad said, "but I think I will wait until later on in the week. It was a lot of driving and I think it will be better if I wait."

"No, thank you," Henny replied while shaking his head. "Not for me."

"Sure! I'll go get my bathing suit!" I chimed in. I didn't go to Poland to sit in a house all day; I came to train!

"Okay," Wim continued, "we go for a swim and Henny, you bring your camera and make a beautiful picture for YouTube."

Henny nodded.

I ran upstairs to prepare myself for my first swim. I opened my suitcase and pulled out both of my thermometers, my bathing suit, and a towel. The air temperature was somewhat warm so I assumed that I would be a lot warmer as soon as I got out of the cold water.

It had been ages since I last performed my cold water immersions in my bathtub at college, but I felt comfortable enough wearing only my swimming trunks, a sleeveless t-shirt, and my running sandals.

A few minutes later I met everyone downstairs in front of the house.

"The place where we will be swimming is a ten minute walk from here." Wim announced. "It is where I go in the winter to do my cold exercises."

We left Mishu at home and closed the gate behind us. We walked along the side of the dirt road, passing houses on both sides of us. At one point, Wim raised his hand toward a property, similar to the size of Time-Out.

"A woman lives there that takes care of Mishu and the chickens when I am gone," he declared. "She collects the eggs and leaves them in a basket near the fireplace for when we return. Nice woman."

We continued walking along the road until Wim told us we had gone far enough. We cut across the grass through some shrubbery, until we found ourselves at the opening of a river. On our right was a few logs lying next to a pile of ashes.

"People come here sometimes and make a bonfire. It's relaxing," he said. "We'll dive in here and do a quick swim, 600 meters or something."

Now, being that I'm from America, I'm not familiar with the metric system. I hadn't done any conversions in years. I used this to my advantage. Not knowing how long 600 meters were in feet or miles was less intimidating to me. I ignored the distance he gave me and listened to the word: "quick." I'm not a swimmer; I'm a runner. But, I do know *how* to swim. Well, let me rephrase that. I know how to stay afloat and slowly propel my body forward.

"Yeah!" I replied. "Sure, I'll try it!"

While Henny prepared his video camera, I took out one of my thermometers and measured the temperature of the water. The thermometer read 48°F (8.7°C). Even though the temperature of the water was several degrees warmer than the water had been in my bathtub, I wasn't sure what to expect. I tried to remain hopeful, but I didn't want to look weak in front of The Iceman.

When Henny had the camera ready, Wim had me stand by him. Henny began recording and Wim started talking to the camera. He explained how far we would be swimming and how cold the water was.

At the end of his speech, Wim took of his shirt and threw it to me. To get a running start, he took a few steps away from the river. After yelling loudly, "Yeah! Go!" he took off with full speed and dove into the water.

I thought he was going to wait for me to jump in before starting our challenge, but I was wrong. He started swimming in the direction that he previously pointed out to me.

I guess that means we won't be swimming side by side, I thought.

I took off my shirt, backed up, and jumped into the water. The cool water instantly chilled my body. It had been a while since I had been completely exposed to the cold. I had forgotten how *cold* the cold could really be.

After surfacing from my dive, I shook my head, to get the water out of my eyes, and began swimming.

"He did it!" I heard Konrad yell. "Hey, you my heroes!"

I smiled at Konrad's remark as I pedaled my arms in a forward motion. Wim was so far away; I wished he would slow down.

After a minute or so, my body was adjusted to the water and I no longer felt the cold sting. I remembered the familiar sensation and welcomed it. To my right, I saw Konrad and Henny walking along the riverside, taking pictures and recording videos.

Wim continued at a fast pace and put more distance between us.

"How do you feel?" he yelled back to me.

"I am good!" I replied.

At about seven minutes into the swim, the cold began to creep back into my body. My fingertips and toes were affected first. It became extremely hard to spread my fingers apart. I also noticed that my pace was slowing down significantly. It was hard to stay afloat, but I used all of my energy to keep myself moving forward. A few times, I noticed the river become shallower. When available, I walked across the bottom of the river to give my arms a rest.

After twelve minutes, it became extremely hard for me to move my limbs. My body wasn't numb anymore; it just felt cold, really cold. Up ahead, I noticed Wim exiting the water. *Finally*, I thought, *I'm almost there. Just a little bit more.*

Luckily, there was another stretch of shallow water and I was able to use my legs to walk. For the last four minutes, I walked through the water, making my way to the edge where Wim had just exited. Henny, Wim, and Konrad were cheering me on, but I ignored them. I was focused on trying to figure out how much damage I had done to my body.

I was moving very slowly; my hands and feet felt like rocks. I had no feeling in them whatsoever. When I had finally reached the edge of the river, I tried pulling myself out, but my arms were incapable of supporting my bodyweight. I was forced to find a ledge underwater to push myself up.

After getting out, Wim looked at me and asked me how I felt. When I responded with "fine," my teeth chattered and my body shook from a cold chill. Wim looked at me and I could tell he knew I was not actually "fine." So, I admitted to him that I couldn't feel my fingers or toes.

"Let's do an exercise to fix that," he said.

He stood upright with his legs together and began swinging his arms back and forth. His arms crossed over each other and slapped his back, as if repeatedly making a hugging motion.

"Do this and it will bring the blood back to your fingertips," he explained.

I copied his demonstration. Henny and Konrad joined in for the heck of it. After a minute or so of slapping my hands against my back, Wim began squatting close to the ground, and then standing up again. It reminded me of doings squats in the gym, except his legs were side by side. The three of us repeated this motion together.

"Are you feeling better?" he asked after several more sets of squats.

"Not yet," I replied, "I feel like I'm getting colder."

"That's the afterdrop. Henny, Konrad, please take our belongings. Justin and I will jog back to the house and meet you there."

Wim and I started jogging up the path along the road. My body felt tight and the motor skills in my leg were still slow. I felt uncoordinated. After a minute or so of jogging, my stomach began turning. A feeling of possibly throwing up washed over me. My motion sickness was kicking in, but why? I was so confused.

"Wim, I feel like I may throw up." I admitted.

"Oh," he said, "that's not good. Let us walk."

My nerves settled, but my body remained cold. Once Wim and I got back to Time-Out, he made coffee to warm me back up. I also grabbed one of the sweatshirts from my suitcase and put it on. By this point, my body was suffering from uncontrollable shivers. When Konrad and Henny arrived back at the house, Konrad suggested that I sit inside his jeep, which had been sitting in the sun for the past few hours. *It couldn't hurt*, I thought. I was willing to try anything.

I brought the coffee into Konrad's jeep and sat there for the next hour. While the warm air slowly reheated my body, I regretted how little I had done to prepare myself.

There I was, in the presence of the master of the cold, and yet I couldn't last a fifteen-minute swim in cold water. Disappointment washed over me, but as my body slowly began to stop shivering and I regained control, I saw potential. I saw my first swim as a good reference point to look back on at the end of the week, to see how much progress I had made.

When I felt like I had regained my composure, I exited the car and found Wim. Everyone was sitting next to the fireplace discussing dinner plans.

"Why don't we drive to town and get groceries. Then, afterward we can go to a local place and buy dinner," Wim suggested.

Everyone thought it was a good idea. We got into Konrad's jeep and drove 15 minutes to reach the town of Lwowek Slaski. When we got there, Wim suggested that I grab the guitar and my Frisbee from the trunk, so we could play around in the local park after getting the groceries. While on our way to the store, we ran into two young Polish girls. Konrad stopped and asked, in Polish, if they'd like to join us in the park in twenty minutes to hear us playing guitar. They agreed and we continued on our way to the grocery store.

When we arrived at the store, I left the guitar and Frisbee outside with Konrad while he smoked his cigarette. Wim and I looked around for ingredients that would fit all of our needs. Henny and Konrad were both vegetarians, so we would be having meatless meals as long as they were around. After purchasing the food, we made our way to the local park, which was right across the street from the grocery store. The park wasn't that large, it only took up about an acre of land, which was more than enough for our purposes.

Wim sat on the ground in the middle of the park and took out the cookies and beer from the grocery bags. The beers were in warm cans. I'm not really a fan of beer, warm beer at that. But when he offered one to me I didn't want him to think that I was rude, so I faked a smile and cracked it open.

Wim grabbed the guitar and began playing Spanish love songs. I was unaware of how well he could play guitar up until this moment. The girl's from earlier must have heard his singing because they walked around the corner a few moments after he had started. They sat down on the bench and tapped their feet to the rhythm of the music. Henny, Konrad, and myself threw around the Frisbee while Wim continued playing the guitar.

Hearing Wim's music inspired me to want to do a backflip. It had been a while since I had attempted one, but I wanted to do something that could impress Wim. Stupid, I know, but it was the thought that came to my mind at the time.

Anyway, I asked Henny to assist me by being my base. Wim thought it would be a good idea to put it in the YouTube video, so Konrad took Henny's camera and began recording. Within a couple of minutes, Henny understood the role that I wanted him to play.

On the count of three, I stepped into Henny's interlocked hands. He lifted me with all of his force and threw me into the air. Milliseconds later, I was back on the ground and Wim was clapping. I high-fived Henny and thanked him for his willingness to help me. Wim then told us that he used to do backflips as well. His training in Yoga made his body more flexible and more able to perform difficult stunts. I was impressed and hoped to gain the honor of seeing him do one some day.

Soon after the two girls stood up to leave, our stomachs began to rumble. Wim suggested we drive to a local Pizzeria and grab something to eat. We returned to our vehicle to put the groceries and guitar away, and then decided it would be faster to drive to the Pizzeria. Our stomachs required sustenance.

The Pizzeria was one of the nicer establishments I saw in Lwowek Slaski. The walls were painted light orange and were covered in large murals of birds and trees. It had a nice, subtle "jungle" feel to it. I couldn't read the menu, so I asked Konrad to order me a pepperoni and chicken pizza with hot sauce; it smelled delicious.

While we were eating our pizza, Wim mentioned that one more person would be joining our workshop the following day; his name was Marco. He said that Marco would be traveling by bus and we would need to pick him up.

We quickly finished our dinners and decided it was time to head back; we had a long day. Wim paid for the pizza and we drove back to Przezdziedza. The sun had set and the air was even cooler. We wished each other good night and went to our respective beds. I laid there for a few minutes, reflecting on the day's experience. I pulled out my laptop and tried to write down and document as much as I could. Eventually, the weight of my eyelids grew too heavy for me and I fell into a deep sleep.

Day 2: May 1, 2010

The next morning when I woke up, I heard voices coming from downstairs. I didn't want to miss out on any fun so I quickly got dressed and walked down the steps. Henny, Konrad, and Wim were sitting at the table by the fireplace, talking.

"Good morning Justin!" said Wim in a joyous tone. "Would you like some coffee with milk and sugar?"

"Sure," I replied. "Thanks."

Wim ran out of the room into the kitchen to fetch me some coffee. I took a seat across from Henny at the table.

"Good morning guys. How'd you sleep?" I asked.

Henny and Konrad replied in unison, "Good."

Wim came back into the room a moment later with coffee.

"Here ya go. Here's some sugar and a spoon if you'd like to add more." He placed both the sugar and my coffee in front of me. "It is hot, so be careful."

"Thanks Wim! So what's the plan for today?" I blew on my coffee to try to cool it off.

"We were talking when you were asleep. We were thinking about driving to the other side of town. There are rocks there that we can use ropes to climb down. It should be fun, yes?"

"Sure, I haven't done something like that in a long time."

"First, I want you to try some breathing exercises. Perhaps after breakfast you can go back upstairs and try them while we clean up down here."

"Okay," I replied.

"Start off," he continued, "by taking 30 breaths to saturate your body. Then, after your last breath, take one big breath in and blow it out completely. Hold it for as long as you can with no breath in your lungs. When you need to breathe again, take one big breath in and hold it for 10 seconds. Close your eyes and maybe you'll see some lights going on. If it doesn't happen right away, it will hopefully happen in the future. After you did that three times, I want you to try to do 30 breaths and then hold your breath for as long as you can. Time yourself for all of these. As you do it more and more, your time will increase. It is a cleansing exercise."

"Sure, I'll try it. I have a quick question though. What's the most important part of the cold exercises? Is it the breathing or the cold exposure?"

"It is both. The breathing gives you control, while the cold gives you experience and conditions the body."

"All right, thanks! I'll do the exercises."

I made myself a bowl of cereal to go with my coffee. When I finished my breakfast, I went upstairs to attempt the breathing exercises.

My first three trials of holding my breath without air in my lungs resulted in the following times:
1st Trial: 1 minute 33 seconds
2nd Trial: 1 minute 45 seconds
3rd Trial: 1 minute 22 seconds

I didn't see the lights that Wim had mentioned, but I had little hopes for it happening the first time I tried it. I then proceeded to try holding my breath after inhaling.

I only tried it once, but my time was:
3 minutes 36 seconds

I usually don't hold my breath, but I thought 3 minutes and 36 seconds was good for my first attempt.

By the time I got back downstairs, Wim was already done packing the ropes, carabineers and harnesses into the jeep; everything was ready. We all jumped in and drove 30 minutes to the rocks. When we pulled in, Wim explained where we would be rappelling.

"The rocks that we will rappel down are hidden behind these trees," Wim said. "We must climb the path a bit. Then we will see them."

We grabbed the gear and started hiking. Twenty minutes later, our group was looking down a 90-foot drop (27.4 meters).

"Here we are," Wim declared. "This is where we will rappel. It's about conquering fear. If you are going to be in the cold, you have to be willing to look past the danger and focus on the moment. You must stay attentive or you could hurt yourself. Be like a cat with precise and acute reflexes. Prepare yourself."

As encouraging as Wim's speech was, I was terrified. I've rappelled down fake rock walls at camp before, but not real ones. The camp rock wall was made out of plastic. Also, with the rock walls at camp, we were belayed down and controlled by someone else. In this scenario, we would all be in control of our own fate. I noticed that we also didn't bring any helmets. With one wrong move, I could easily slam my head against the rock and fall to my death.

I told myself that I had to go down. I didn't want to look like a coward. What would Wim think of me if I were too afraid to rappel down a few rocks? I kept my fears to myself and bit my tongue. I had no choice but to do as he said and live in the moment. If I succumbed to any other emotions, I would jeopardize my safety and it would be no one's fault but my own.

Wim went down first to test out the rope to make sure he had tied it correctly.

"It's always scary being the first one to go down, even I feel it," he said while dangling over the edge, "but we must accept it if we wish to gain the riches of success."

With that, he bent his knees and pushed off the wall with all his strength. He flew down at an incredible speed. He landed at the bottom in under 30 seconds, with no injuries whatsoever. This guy made it look easy.

Henny and Konrad went next. Both of them went down smoothly. Konrad and I had discussed before he descended that he too was afraid. Yet he told me that he was excited to try something new. To Konrad, this week was about changing his lifestyle and experiencing life for all that it had to offer. His words motivated me. Hearing that someone else was intimidated by the heights made me feel more comfortable.

Watching Konrad descend before me made me feel more capable. When he reached the bottom, I approached the top where Wim was sitting. There were no safety ropes to prevent me from slipping, so I sat on the ground next to him. I slid the harness on and prepared myself.

"Everything will be okay," Wim assured me. "You will be fine. You have a strong mind and a strong soul. I believe in you."

With those words, he tied the carabineer to my harness and wished me good luck. I slowly slid my body toward the edge. Wim held the rope so it wouldn't get snagged on a rock.

"When you're ready, turn around and put your feet flat against the wall, then lean back."

I did as I was told. He let go of the rope and my life suddenly came back into my hands. I pushed myself off the ledge of the rock and leaned backwards. I positioned my legs so that they were flat against the wall. I released the grip on the tight rope with my right hand; my body suddenly jerked downward. I reflexively gripped the rope again. *Too fast*, I thought. I slowly let the rope slide through my fist and then performed a small horizontal jump off the face of the wall.

"Good job Justin!" Wim called from the top. "Well done!"

I smiled at Wim's encouragement, but remained focused on the wall. I tried lowering myself down more smoothly by keeping a steady, but constant release of the rope. After a few more kicks, I got the hang of it.

"Hey Justin!" I heard someone yell from behind me. I turned my head and saw that it was Konrad. "Keep looking over here. I want to take a picture."

It was hard to stabilize my body against the rocks; gravity wanted me to continue going downward, but I held the rope tightly and did my best to look back and smile at the camera. A few clicks echoed off of the surrounding walls. I took that as a sign that I could continue down.

"Thanks!" Konrad yelled in appreciation.

Descending the rest of the way was a piece of cake. The only extremely scary part about rappelling down the rock was stepping over the edge. Everything else was simple. I knew that if something went wrong, I would have no control over it. I guess you could say I was comforted in knowing that I could only control what was in my power, everything else was left up to God -- in my opinion.

Once my feet touched the ground, a surge of adrenaline rushed through me. I was itching to do it again. I disconnected myself from the rope and yelled up to Wim, "Clear!" to let him know that the rope was free. I then jogged up the path, back to the top of the cliff. By the time I had reached the top, Konrad was already on his way down again. I noticed Henny packing up the gear, but when Wim saw me, he asked if I wanted to go once more.

"Sure!" I yelled in excitement. "That was awesome!"

When Konrad reached the bottom and had disconnected himself from the rope, Wim connected my harness once more.

"Have fun," he said while patting me on the back. He held the rope, which allowed me to get into position once more. When he let go, I felt the weight of my life in my hands again. It was a powerful feeling. This time, I wanted to try to go down faster.

Simultaneously, I loosened my grip on the rope, tucked my knees and pushed off with an exaggerated force. My body soared toward the ground, picking up speed on the way down. Right before I was in the position to make my final kick, I tightened my grip to slow my body down. Soon after, I was safely on the ground once again. What an exhilarating experience!

A few minutes later, we had taken all the equipment down and packed it back into the jeep. We then drove back to Lwowek Slaski to wait for Marco's arrival. It took us an hour or so before we found the bus station where he would be arriving. We thought we had missed him until we checked the bus schedule. It said we still had another two hours before his bus arrived. In the meantime, we began playing guitar and throwing the Frisbee around in the streets.

While Konrad and I were throwing the Frisbee, Konrad told me that he used to play Ultimate Frisbee with an organized group. I could tell that he wasn't lying because his throws were fast and accurate. I mentioned my time playing on Penn State's club team during my freshman year. It was nice to have something to relate to with Konrad. He seemed like a good guy and I hoped I would get to know him better. I could tell he meant well.

Buses came and went. Around 5:00 PM, Marco finally showed up, but not by bus. I was the first to see him, emerging from the bushes behind us. He told us that he had been walking around town for a while, looking for us. He had apparently arrived earlier that day and went to check out the town hall in his spare time.

Marco had a strong build and an evident tan. Born and raised in Ecuador, Marco was known for traveling around Europe to learn about Yoga. He was searching to find enlightenment. Marco was a good fellow with a kind soul. He stood a little shorter than I, but we had the same haircut. We both had buzzed, black hair. We could be passed off as brothers, being that we both have Spanish backgrounds, therefore Spanish features. His skin complexion showed he was young and healthy individual.

"So, what now?" I asked after we all had been acquainted. "What should we do?"

It was Konrad who spoke up, "Well, why don't we drive to Karpacz, where my cousin lives, and we can find a place to have dinner there?"

"Sounds good to me," said Marco.

"Sure," said Henny.

"Yes, let us go," Wim chimed in at last.

We walked back to the jeep with our new friend, Marco, and began driving to Karpacz. Karpacz was about a 25-minute drive from Lwowek Slaski. Karpacz was also the town where Wim and Konrad were hoping to organize the 5k run in the snow that upcoming winter.

On the ride over, Wim and Konrad filled Marco in on their plan and invited him to participate in the run as well. Marco also had a slew of questions for Wim about Iceman training. Marco's questions carried on all the way until we arrived at a restaurant called Kolorowa in Karpacz. It was a beautiful place with a very interesting menu. For the first time ever, I tried beat stew. I typically don't like beats, but the flavor was amazing.

During dinner, the conversation switched back to the barefoot snow run. Wim and Konrad were trying to figure out marketing plans and specific information. I told them, "Perhaps I could be of help and try to spread the word in America. I have a few friends that may be interested in participating in something like this."

They seemed excited and continued to discuss the potential. Wim's goal was to show the world that anyone could train to do what he had done. He figured that the barefooted snow run was an opportunity to get people interested in pushing past their body's perceived limits. It was exciting to be involved in this type of talk, to be apart of something bigger than myself. I felt very honored to be included.

After dinner, Wim said that we should all climb Mount Blanc with him. Apparently, in the first week of August, he was scheduled to ascend Mount Blanc. He told Marco and I that we were welcome to join to help encourage our training. I didn't want to get my hopes up, but I told Wim that I was interested, if he thought it was possible.

"Of course it is possible," he countered when I questioned him. "If I can do it, you can do it. We all are capable. The spirit has no age."

These few words lit up my face. "The spirit has no age." It is something that Jarrett and I had believed in wholeheartedly. To hear someone whom I had never expressed those views with before, say it on the opposite side of the world, came as a huge shock to me. It was comforting to know that someone else had come to that same conclusion on their own. At this moment, I knew Wim was something spectacular. Him and I were the same in a way, we both wanted to see what life had to offer and not let any obstacles keep get in our way.

Wim was no longer some celebrity to me. I saw him for what he really was... Selfless. He wanted to make a difference in the world and offer his services to anyone who needed it. He recognized the potential in his ability and wanted to share it with the world, not keep it to himself. He was the type of guy that competitively challenged people to push themselves to be better. Everything I saw in Wim was everything I hoped I would become.

After dinner, we went on a short walk. Wim and Konrad were trying to locate a hidden path to a waterfall, but because it was dark and neither of them had been there in a few years, they failed. We ended up walking by an old monastery. Marco took many pictures of the place. It seemed to fascinate him. Henny kept quiet and followed along as Konrad and Wim continued to talk about their 5k event.

Eventually, we all grew tired and deemed it time to go home. On the drive back, Konrad got a little lost. We drove in one direction for a while, and then tried to correct it by taking Wim's directions.

Instead of a 25-minute ride home, it ended up taking us 2.5 hours.

By the time we arrived back at the house, we were all exhausted. We had barely enough energy to drag our bodies to our beds before passing out. I used my last few minutes of consciousness to write a journal entry in my laptop to document the day's events. When I finished, I hit the power button on my laptop and closed the lid. I fell asleep as soon as my head hit the pillow.

Day 3: May 2, 2010

The following morning, I woke up to Wim's face peeking into the room through the door.

"Good morning Justin," he said.

"Good morning Wim," I replied. "What are you doing?"

"I just wanted to see if you guys were up yet."

I looked over to where Marco was sleeping. He was now sitting up in his bed with his attention on the door. I also noticed that Konrad and Henny were missing from the room, yet I couldn't hear any sounds indicating that they were downstairs.

"I just did some breathing exercises in the barn with the chickens around me," he continued. "I feel great now. I want you guys to try the breathing exercises again. Do them before you have breakfast. They have a better effect when you are on an empty stomach."

I nodded and smiled while giving him an exaggerated thumbs up. He then proceeded to explain the breathing exercises to Marco, while I started on my own. My ability to hold my breath was much better than the day before.

The best time for each were:
Holding Breath (without air in the lungs): 2 minutes 20 seconds
Holding Breath (with air in the lungs): 4 minutes 5 seconds

My ability to hold my breath was noticeably increasing. I didn't want to announce it to Wim until I had seen the results of the third day. So, I kept my time to myself and went downstairs to meet Wim while Marco continued his sets of breathing.

When I arrived at the bottom of the staircase, I noticed Wim was the only one sitting at the table.

"Where's Henny and Konrad?" I asked.

"They went for a bike ride with Konrad's brother," he answered. "They will be back later. For now, we eat breakfast and then go for a swim."

"All right," I said. I was feeling less energetic than I had the day before. The previous late night had really worn me out.

"Would you like some coffee?" Wim asked.

"Why not? Hopefully it will help wake me up. Thank you Wim," I answered.

He jogged into the other room and came back with a cup of coffee and placed it in front of me. I thanked him and proceeded to make myself a bowl of cereal. A few moments later, Marco came down.

As I was eating my cereal, Marco asked a lot of in-depth questions about how the breathing was related to yoga. I knew nothing about yoga so I ignored the conversation and tried to imagine what it would be like to climb Mount Blanc, wearing only shorts and sandals.

"You ready to go for a swim?" Wim asked.

"Huh?" I replied, snapping out of my daze and back to reality. "Yeah, sure. Sorry I must have zoned out."

"No problem whatsoever," he replied. "Let's go!"

I washed out my cereal bowl and ran upstairs to put on my bathing suit. Wim and Marco were already outside by the time I had finished changing. Wim was juggling a soccer ball in the air with his feet. Marco was using his camera to record Wim juggling. When Wim saw me come out, he kicked the ball away and began whistling.

"Mishu," he said, "time to go!"

We walked out the front gate and closed the door after Mishu.

"We have to be careful with Mishu," Wim explained. "There is a law that if a dog bites someone outside of our property, people can come and kill the dog."

"Well that doesn't sound too pleasant," I replied.

"Yes, but it is okay. We will be fine. Mishu is a good dog"

A few minutes into our walk, we came into a large opening. To our left was a small mountain.

Wim pointed and exclaimed, "Sometime this week, we will climb there. We can climb to the top and meditate. I know a good spot. I have done it before."

Marco seemed pleased with the idea. He smiled and used his camera to take a picture of the mountain where Wim had just pointed.

The four of us, including Mishu, continued walking until we arrived at the spot where Wim and I had been a few days earlier. We took off our shirts and placed them on the ground. Mishu jumped in first, making a gigantic splash. Marco recoiled as a few droplets of the cold water from Mishu's dive, came in contact with his skin.

"What should I do to try to stay warm?" Marco asked.

"Focus on your breathing," Wim answered. "Relax and try to let your body adapt. It will readjust on it's own."

I checked the water with my thermometer to compare it to the last time we had jumped in. The thermometer read 48.5°F (9.2°C). It wasn't as cold as it had been the first time, but it was still chilly enough to train in.

Wim jumped into the water, splashing Marco and I. I then followed Wim into the water. It stung, just like the last time. It didn't shock me as much as it had before. Even though I suffered from a few gasps for breath, I was able to quickly take control of my breathing, focusing the airflow through my nose.

"Should I jump in completely?" Marco called out to us.

"Yes," Wim answered. "Let the whole body adapt."

With that, Marco took a few steps back and picked up a running start. Jumping into the water feet first, he made a small splash. He came up out of the water gasping for air. He looked extremely uncomfortable. Immediately, he began swimming back toward the water's edge. He seemed to be in a lot of pain.

"Nice and easy," Wim said. "Try to relax. Easy does it."

Marco slowly pulled himself out of the water and stood on the shore. He bent over in pain grabbing his knees.

"My knees, they hurt," he said. "I've had problems with them for years. As soon as I jumped in, it felt like needles were being shoved into my knees."

"Oh, okay. I understand," Wim replied. "Move around a bit and try to get warm. Jog where you stand. Is it okay if Justin and I keep swimming in here to train for a bit?"

"Yes," Marco replied, now running in place. "That is fine, I will be okay. I'll be warm again soon. Living in Ecuador, we are not used to cold temperatures. My body is used to the heat, not the cold."

"I think you are correct," Wim replied. "We will try again later. Perhaps next time we will only go up to your knees. We will find a spot in the water where you can stand and not have your whole body exposed. The cold has the ability to help your knees and circulate your blood flow. They will improve by the end of the week. You will see."

While Marco tried to warm his body up on the land, Wim and I treaded in the water. We swam in circles for the next 18 minutes. By the end, my limbs were numb again and felt slower than normal. I told Wim about my condition and he suggested we get out. I swam to the edge and he helped pull me out of the water. Him and I changed out of our wet swimming trunks into the extra dry clothes that we had brought with us. We then began slapping our hands against our backs like we had the day before.

After five minutes of doing "warm up" exercises, I felt my afterdrop begin to kick in. This time, I was mentally prepared for it. I saw it as a challenge. I tried to control my shivering by taking careful breaths; it proved to be extremely difficult. Wim became aware of my afterdrop when he noticed my shivering.

"Let's get back to the house and try to warm up," Wim directed.

On the way back, Marco asked about my shivering.

"Why is he shivering like that?"

"It is the afterdrop," Wim answered. "It is when the warm blood in the body mixes with the cold blood. It makes you feel cold, even if you are standing in a warm environment."

"Will that ever go away?" Marco continued.

"Yes, with training. In time, the amount of time it takes to recover will decrease until it disappears completely. Right now, I am experiencing no afterdrop even though I was in the water just as long as Justin. Even though I am a lot older than him, my body is still strong. Remember, the spirit has no age!"

When we got back to the house, Wim asked me to stay outside in the heat while he made me some tea. I juggled around the soccer ball while waiting for him. The shivering was still pretty violent. Focusing on the soccer ball helped take my mind off the uncontrollable shakes.

Wim came back outside and gave me my tea. I passed the soccer ball off to him while I consumed the warm liquid. Marco began recording Wim while he juggled the soccer ball.

We were both amazed with Wim's handling skills. He was performing tricks that I had learned during my soccer years. I watched him as he flicked the ball into the air and stalled it flat on his back, a trick that I loved performing myself. Watching him play inspired me to join. I downed my tea and placed the cup on the bench. Marco told us he wasn't much of a soccer player, so he watched from the bench and recorded our playing.

After kicking the ball back and forth for a bit, Wim and I transitioned to juggling the ball in the air by and passing it off to the other person without the ball touching the ground. I was so engaged in the juggling that I didn't even notice that my shivering had stopped.

"Let's take turns juggling the ball in the air," Wim suggested. "Try to get one hundred touches without the ball hitting the ground. Don't use your hands or arms. You can go first."

Flicking the ball up with my right foot, I bounced it off my knees, feet, head, and shoulders. Eventually, I had hit the ball 100 times without it touching the ground once.

"Marvelous!" Wim yelled. "My turn!"

I kicked the ball in his direction and he began. I sat next to Marco on the bench, watching Wim with locked eyes.

...55...56...57

Every touch that Wim made looked intentional and graceful. I had an appreciation for the man. He wasn't just "The Iceman." He was a guy that loved to have fun doing whatever he could. I felt a strong connection when playing soccer with him. We both shared the love of knowledge and experience, even if it was for something as simple as playing soccer.

...98...99...100

I stood out of my chair and clapped. "Nice one, Wim! Well done!"

He took an exaggerated bow, obviously joking, and rose with a huge grin on his face.

"How are you feeling now?" he asked. "Is your afterdrop gone?"

"Yeah," I replied. "I think moving around helped a lot. I didn't even notice it disappear. It's weird though. During the first ten minutes of the afterdrop, I felt a strange sensation in my stomach. It made me feel like I was going to throw up. Maybe it's because I get motion sickness sometimes. I inherited it from my father."

"Oh, well why don't we try an exercise to fix that? Let us both spin in circles 100 times. We need to condition the body. When we are done, we will try to stay on our feet and readjust."

It reminded me of an exercise I had tried once earlier that year. I had been tired of getting motion sickness on roller coasters and long car rides, so I set up an exercise where I would sit in my desk chair and spin in circles for minutes at a time. The first time I tried it, I nearly threw up. It took me five minutes to find my equilibrium.

The next day, I tried it again. That time, it only took me two minutes to readjust, but I still felt sick. The following day, I tried it once more. After spinning in circles at a rapid pace for 60 seconds, I was able to readjust in only 30 seconds. Not only that, but I also didn't feel like throwing up anymore. It goes to show that conditioning the body can go a long way with determination.

Anyway, I was excited to try Wim's exercise. It had been a few months since I had last tried my desk-chair exercises, but I hoped for the best. Wim and I started spinning in circles, counting out loud. By the time I got to 50, I was having a lot of trouble with staying on my feet. To prevent myself from falling over, I slowed down the rate at which I was turning.

When I got to 70, I heard Wim yell, "100!" By the time I reached 99, he had declared that he was already readjusted. When I stopped spinning at 100, I grabbed onto the wall to stop myself from falling over. My world was spinning and there was nothing I could do to control it. I fought to keep the strength in my knees to support my weight. I regretted not continuing my desk-chair training.

Wim and Marco made their way over to me and looked into my eyes.

"Your eyes are pointing in different directions," Marco stated, amused.

"Wow, incredible. What do you see Justin?" Wim asked.

"Um... everything is blurred together and spinning very fast," I replied.

"Okay, well relax and try to let your body readjust," he directed.

Two minutes after I had stopped spinning, my vision stabilized. I took a seat and tried to settle my churning stomach with deep, controlled breathing. I felt beads of sweat drip down my face and fall off my chin.

"If you continue to practice this exercise in the future," Wim advised, "I think your motion sickness will slowly go away."

Yes, in the future, I thought. *For now, I need to focus on the cold training.*

"Thanks Wim," I said aloud.

Wim stood up and grabbed his rucksack and bathing suit. "Okay, let's go back to the water and go for another swim. This time, we will take it easy and find shallower water."

I was surprised that Wim wanted to go back to the water again so soon, but I didn't want to question his methods. So, I grabbed my backpack, with my wet bathing suit inside, and walked toward the gate. Marco was right behind me. We left Mishu behind this time.

On the way back to the river, it started to rain, but only a light sprinkle. When we arrived at the new, allegedly shallower part of the river, we changed back into our wet bathing suits and prepared to swim.

"Marco," Wim said, "I want you to go in slowly. If you can, walk in the water until it's up to your knees. Try to relax through the pain and let your body adjust. Everything will be okay."

Marco nodded in agreement. The three of us slowly walked down back into the water. Marco and Wim went in first; I got in last. The water was still shocking, but being that it only came up to my knees, it didn't take long to readjust. Marco, on the other hand, was bent over again, clutching his knees in agony. Wim was by his side, encouraging him.

"You can do it. Let the cold numb your knees. Everything will be okay. Readjust."

After a couple minutes, Marco's face finally relaxed in relief. He remained bent over with his hands resting on his quads, but he seemed much more at ease.

"Nice job man!" I said earnestly. "Well done!"

Marco smiled. I could tell from his face that he was happy with his success.

"Okay," Wim said, "That's good for now. We'll come back later and do some more. Let's get back to the house."

We collected our bags and began walking back to the house through the rain. Marco walked with head held high, happy with his accomplishment.

When we arrived back at the house, Marco and I went upstairs to change. Wim had gone outside to grab some firewood. By the time I got downstairs, he had already started the fire. He placed our bathing suits on the brick walls that encased the fireplace. Marco was still upstairs changing.

"Listen Justin," Wim said while gazing into the fireplace. "I am very impressed with you. I can see that you are persistent and have the heart and motivation to do great things. I tell you this now because I think you will be breaking records soon. I can tell."

"Wow Wim," I replied, probably blushing, "That really means a lot to me. Do you really think Mount Blanc would be a good goal to shoot for?"

"We shall see. I am being sponsored by television, so I don't know if they will allow you to go, but we shall see."

Mount Blanc sounds like a great opportunity if it works out, I thought, *but if it doesn't, I will still have my chance at the snow run in Karpacz.*

We heard footsteps and Marco appeared in the doorway.

"So what's next?" he asked.

"Konrad left his keys," Wim answered, "So, I think it would be good to take his jeep and go to Lwowek Slaski to grab more groceries. Then, if the rain stops, we can go and rappel down the rocks again. We did it yesterday, but I want you to experience it too, Marco."

"Okay, sounds great!" Marco replied excitedly.

By the time we got to Lwowek Slaski, the rain had stopped. We stopped at two grocery stores and picked up enough food to last us for the rest of the week. We also bought a large portion of assorted chocolates to snack on between meals. Once we had finished shopping, Wim drove us back to the rocks that him and I descended down the day before. We grabbed our gear and made our way to the top. The ground was somewhat muddy from the earlier rainfall, but the rocks looked dry enough to rappel down without slipping.

When we got to the top, Wim reconnected the ropes, as he had done the day before, and tested their safety by rappelling first. After he had returned to the top of the rocks, it was Marco's turn.

As Marco slowly descended down the face of the rock wall, his face lit up with joy. He seemed to be really enjoying himself. Eventually, his body disappeared as the surrounding trees blocked him from view.

I decided to take advantage of the alone time with Wim.

"So, what are you goals now, Wim?" I asked. "Now that you've completed all of these world records, what will you do? What will make you happy?"

"Well," he started, "I no longer have any desire to break records. I have done all of that; there is nothing there for me anymore. Now, I just want to teach. Like how I am teaching you now. I want to teach you so that you can become fruitful and teach others."

"Well, I appreciate the opportunity."

"No thanks necessary. I used to charge people 1400 euros for 3-hour seminars, but I only asked for a few hundred from you and Marco because I understand both of your financial situations. It is an opportunity I do not want you to miss, so I lowered the price because I see that you are great people."

"That means a lot Wim, thank you."

"Just take the training I give you and do your best. Continue on. Next year, when we do the run in Karpacz, I am going to be running too. I want you to train so you can beat me. I will not hold back, but I want you to give me your best and try to beat me. I believe in you."

"I'm clear!" Marco called up from below.

"Your turn," Wim said looking at me with compassion. "Have fun!"

I locked myself into the ropes and he held onto them as he had done before. I stepped over the cliff and rappelled smoothly to the bottom.

Several minutes later, the three of us were sitting on top of the rocks, watching the sunset. We cracked open the box of chocolates and enjoyed our delectable treats. Not much was said. We just sat there and enjoyed each other's company and the silence that surrounded us.

After about ten minutes, Wim broke the silence.

"How about we swim once more. Marco, you can go up to your knees, then Justin and I will swim 600 meters as we had done before."

Marco agreed. We all agreed that it was a great idea. We packed our stuff and returned to the jeep. I felt like the three of us had a stronger bond. Engaging in these training activities connected me to these strangers. Even though I had only known them for a couple days, I felt like I could trust them with my life. I could tell that they were genuine and unique individuals. Both of them had a strong love for knowledge, wisdom and understanding.

When we got back to the house, Konrad and Henny still hadn't returned, but that wouldn't change our plans. We quickly grabbed our bathing suits and left before the darkness set in. Soon, we were walking down the familiar dirt road to the river. When we got to the shallow portion of the water, Marco pulled out his camera and handed it to me, asking if I could record his immersion. I happily agreed.

When he first stepped in, he gasped for air, but after a few careful breaths, he was able to regain control. His face contorted in pain as his joints and knees locked up, but he stood strong. After five minutes, he came out of the water and did a few squats to restore the warmth in his legs.

"They tingle," Marco admitted, "but it's a good kind of tingle. They feel more loose."

"Fantastic!" Wim yelled, "You are getting better! Nice one!" He gathered his things and threw his backpack over his shoulder. "If you are ready, let's go. Justin and I need to finish swimming before it gets dark."

Marco switched out of his wet bathing suit and into his dry clothes. He followed behind us as Wim and I led the way to our spot.

"Do you mind carrying our things while we swim?" Wim asked. "It is not very much, just two rucksacks."

"No problem at all," Marco replied.

As soon as we were ready, Wim and I dove into the water and began swimming; we didn't want to waste any time. The cold shocked my body once again, but it took even less time for me to adjust. My breaths were normal when my head emerged from the water; there was no gasping whatsoever. Wim pulled ahead of me again with an astonishing speed. He looked like a swan, propelling himself gracefully through the water. There was no way I could keep up with him. I remained focused and stuck with my steady pace.

This time, I noticed that I was able to keep the warmth in my body for much longer. There was no stinging in my fingertips and I had perfect control over my limbs. The cold did not set into my body as it had the previous time; I was comfortable and warm. When Wim and I reached the end of the 600 meters -- him first, me second -- I emerged with triumph. My body had stayed warm the entire time and I had no pain in my extremities. I was improving!

I remained excited until the afterdrop kicked in a few minutes later. I told Wim and he suggested that we all jog home, not just for my afterdrop, but also for extra exercise.

My new goal was to decrease the amount of time it took for my afterdrop to dissipate. After my first time swimming the 600 meters with Wim, it had taken me one hour to completely feel comfortable again. After my second experience, treading water earlier that day, my afterdrop had taken 30 minutes to dissipate. I hoped to see even less time knocked off this recovery period.

By the time we returned to the house, we were all physically exhausted. The sun had completely set and darkness engulfed Time-Out, save for the few lights that were switched on inside the house. I sat myself down next to the fire and waited for my afterdrop to fade away. After 23 minutes from the time I had left the water, my body readjusted. I had dropped 7 minutes off of my recovery time. I was ecstatic!

We all had a few bowls of a cereal for dinner and discussed our progress so far. It was an encouraging conversation. We reflected on all that had happened and looked forward to more amazing experiences.

Before we went to bed, Wim phoned Konrad to figure out his and Henny's whereabouts. Konrad mentioned that Henny had returned home because he had business to attend to. He also mentioned that he was still hanging out with his brother and wouldn't be returning for a couple of days.

When Wim get off the phone, we spoke a bit longer and then headed to bed. As tired as I was, I managed to document the day's events in my laptop before drifting off to sleep.

Day 4: May 3, 2010

I woke up in the morning feeling well and rested. After lying in bed for a couple of minutes, I decided to go downstairs and find Wim to let him know I was up. He was downstairs checking his email.

"Good morning Wim," I said, announcing my presence.

"Good morning, would you like some tea?" Wim offered.

"Sure."

He handed me a cup of tea and we chatted for a few minutes about the previous day's events. When I finished my tea, I returned upstairs to my bed to begin my breathing exercises.

My best times for each set were:

Holding Breath (without air in the lungs): 1 minute 9 seconds

Holding Breath (with air in the lungs): 3 minutes 25 seconds

My breath-holding endurance seemed to have dropped significantly. I was disappointed in myself. I began questioning my abilities.

Can I really become like Wim? I thought. *Maybe yesterday's breathing exercises were a fluke. This sucks.*

I hid my shame and returned downstairs. Marco and Wim were sitting at the table. Marco and I ate a bowl of cereal while Wim talked to us about a new endotoxin experiment that doctors wanted to try out on Wim. The talk of research and experiments gave me an idea.

"Hey Wim, do you think you can consciously heat up a specific part of your body without being exposed to the cold?" I asked with hopes.

"I think so," he replied. "I have never tried it. What do you mean?"

"Well, if I ask you to heat up your hand while just sitting here, could you do it?"

"I think so. I can try." He stuck out his hand and placed it on the table in front of me.

"Wait a second. I want to measure your skin temperature before and after with my infrared thermometer. I can also record it with my laptop so we can put it on YouTube."

"That's a good idea!" he exclaimed. "More footage for YouTube!"

I pulled out my infrared thermometer from my backpack and turned on my laptop. When the red light turned on to indicate that it was recording, I aimed it at Wim's arm and took the temperature in the palm of his hand. My infrared thermometer read 30.1°C

(86.18°F). I then told him to do his thing and heat up his hand. Five minutes later I took the temperature again in the same spot, it read 32°C (89°F), which was an increase of 1.9°C (2.82°F)!

The simple feat fascinated me. It showed me that his ability was real and not some cheap, parlor trick. He had left his hand on the table in front of me and warmed it up right there in front of my eyes. It would be quite the interesting clip for YouTube.

Wim then encouraged Marco and I to try too. Yet after five minutes, neither of us could raise the temperatures in our hands.

"Don't be discouraged," Wim said. "Now you know the potential exists. Let's grab our things and go climb the small mountain we walked by the other day."

Marco and I ran upstairs to change.

A few minutes later, we were walking along the dirt road again with Mishu by our side.

"He enjoys long hikes," Wim told us.

When we came close to the river, we diverged from the path and started walking toward the mountain. As we approached it, I noticed that it rose several hundred feet into the air. Large, rocky overhangs cast shadows at our feet.

I wish I had a small mountain to climb near my house, I thought.

It took us about a half hour to reach the top. Although the climb was steep, the sweat dripping off our faces indicated a great workout. Wim led us to a spot at the edge of a cliff overlooking the entire river. The terrain was steep and covered with loose rocks.

We each searched and found a spot where we could sit comfortably without sliding down over the edge. We sat quietly, gazing out over the valley. After several minutes, Wim spoke.

"Now we sit and meditate. Try to think about your goals and your life. Visualize who you want to be and what you want to become. Try to understand yourself. Open your mind and let it run free."

Mishu plopped himself down next to me. His heavy breathing made it difficult to concentrate, but after a few minutes, I was able to think clearly. Here were my thoughts:

I can't believe I'm in Poland. I can't believe that all my hard work has finally paid off. After all those weeks of scraping dishes and completing homework assignments, it was all worth it. I have found someone who is very much like myself. His hunger for knowledge and understanding is magnificent. This is what it must be like to have someone that inspires you.

After meeting Wim, there's no way I could settle for anything less than extraordinary. I have seen the results of the devotion and dedication he put forth throughout his life and I want the same for myself. I can't settle for keeping my head down and accepting mediocrity. I now believe that it is possible for one person to make a difference in the world.

Wim's intentions are pure and selfless. I have never seen a man so vulnerable to ridicule, yet choose to bare the weight and use it as motivation. He must have fought through years of teasing before people treated him with respect.

I'm eternally grateful for the opportunity he has given me. I will not squander my potential. I owe it to Wim to do everything I can to help him make his dreams come true. I now see him as a brother, not a celebrity. I want to be like him -- someone who is willing to sacrifice everything to improve the quality of life for other people in the world. Even though his message may appear insane, he will no longer stand-alone.

I will help him spread his message that the cold is not our enemy, but a key to understanding our body's full potential. Don't forget this experience Justin. Nothing will compare to what you are doing this week. Never forget the gift that Wim has given you. Use it.

We sat there for an hour before I heard Wim moving. I opened my eyes and he was looking back at me, smiling.

"You guys ready to go?" he asked. "We can go for a swim in the river on the way back."

"Sure," Marco and I replied simultaneously.

We carefully rose from our respective seats and began making our way back down the mountain. Mishu ran ahead of us and led the way. There was a spring in all of our steps as we jogged down the mountain.

When we reached the bottom, Mishu ran ahead of us, back to the house.

"Don't worry," Wim said, "Mishu will be okay. My neighbor will let him back into the gate."

It only took us a couple of minutes to reach our swimming spot. We changed into the bathing suits that we had previously stuffed into Wim's backpack. Marco expressed his interest in submerging his body deeper into the water this time. He seemed excited to push further. The meditating on the mountain must have boosted his confidence.

"We won't do anything strenuous right now," Wim declared. "We just hiked a mountain and I want us to stay rested for tomorrow. Tomorrow we will go to Karpacz and climb their tallest mountain. It will take a long time and a lot of energy, but for now… we swim. Easy does it. Justin, I want you to come into the water with me first. I want you to try holding your breath underwater."

"All right," I replied taking off my shirt. "Let's do this."

Wim dove into the water and I followed after him.

"Good," he said. "Now, I want you to put your face under the water and try holding your breath. I'll hold on to you to make sure the current doesn't take you downstream."

"Sounds good, I'm ready!" I announced.

"One..." he counted. "Two... Three!"

I took a deep breath and dunked my head under the frigid water. It was really hard to stay in one place because of the strong currents, but after grabbing my knees and curling up into a ball, Wim placed his hand on my back and stabilized my body. I figured I wouldn't be able to hold my breath as long as I normally could because my focus was on staying warm, rather than holding my breath.

When my lungs grew tight and my head began to throb, I pulled my face out of the water and sucked down air.

"1 minute and 45 seconds," Wim said. "Not bad for your first time. I am impressed!"

I smiled back at him and began swimming to the edge of the water.

"All right Marco, your turn," Wim called to him.

As I pulled myself out, Marco lowered himself into the water. At first he only let his knees in so that his body could adjust slowly. After about 30 seconds, he lowered himself in to the point where the water reached his navel. Wim stood by him, encouraging him as his body readjusted. After several minutes had passed, Marco raised himself out of the water.

"Nice one!" Wim said as he pulled his body out of the water. "Easy does it. That's the way to do it. Slowly put more and more of your body in until all of your body can handle it. Good work! Let's go back home and eat some dinner!"

Not much happened once we arrived back at Time-Out. Wim prepared us a delicious vegetable and pasta dinner.

"You both did a great job today," he said while smiling. "Tomorrow we will take on a big challenge and climb the mountain in Karpacz. It will be cold up there and hopefully we can find some snow!"

After dinner, we listened to some music and looked over the pictures and videos that we had recorded thus far. Surprisingly, there was a lot of good footage.

"When I look at our YouTube video in the future, I will cry," Wim admitted. "I will cry because I will remember the bond we shared and the good people that you both are. I love you guys!"

Wim built a fire and we sat there, enjoying each other's company for the next few hours. We laughed and reflected on the memories that would last us a lifetime.

Eventually, my eyes grew tired and I required sleep. So I bid Wim and Marco good night and went upstairs to my room. After documenting the day's events in my laptop, I fell asleep, the happiest I had been in years.

Day 5: May 4, 2010

The next morning I woke at 9:00 AM and immediately ran downstairs to greet Wim.

"We are going to go to Karpacz, are you ready?" he asked.

"Yeah," I replied, "but is it okay if I quickly run upstairs, do my breathing, and get a shower?"

"Yes. Easy does it."

What a peculiar phrase. I took it to mean, "Take your time." I ran back upstairs and performed my routine breathing exercises.

My best times were the following:
Holding Breath (without air in the lungs): 2 minutes 32 seconds
Holding Breath (with air in the lungs): 4 minutes 32 seconds

Awesome! My breath-holding endurance was increasing again! I jumped into the shower and began cleaning myself. It was my first shower since I had arrived in Poland; I was filthy. After drying myself off, I packed my things into my backpack and rushed downstairs to make myself breakfast. Marco and Wim spoke next to the fireplace while I ate my cereal. Shoving spoonfuls of food into my mouth, I finished in seconds.

"All right!" I announced. "I'm ready! Thanks for being patient while I prepared. Let's go climb that mountain!"

The drive from Przezdziedza to Karpacz only took about 30 minutes with traffic. Along the way, we listened to music from my laptop. I had learned from the previous night that one of Wim's favorite bands was Coldplay, so the sound of Chris Martin's voice filled the jeep as we drove to Karpacz.

When we arrived in the town of Karpacz, we found a place to park and made our way to the base of the mountain. Wim bought 3 tickets and handed one to each of us.

"Let's climb!" he said.

We made our way toward what looked like the entrance. The first part of the incline looked to be about a 40° angle.

"There are several different areas that we could potentially climb to," he explained, "but we will be summiting on Mount Śnieżka. The top is at 1,620 meters, or about 5,315 feet for you, Justin. We are starting to climb here at 640 meters [2,100 feet], but we still have a long way to go. Normally, it takes people 3 hours to reach the top. Let's try to beat that!"

Wim led the way at an incredible pace. He suited his philosophy well, "the spirit has no age." He was climbing as if there was no incline at all. Marco and I trailed behind him. I could tell he had noticed our slow pace, but he kept his cool and didn't try to rush us.

On the way up, we only stopped once to take a picture. For the first hour, the temperature was really warm. It was about 77°F (25°C) that day. The amount of heat we generated resulted in a heap of sweat. Marco and I were having a lot of trouble, but Wim continued to seem perfectly fine.

Eventually, the temperature began to drop. The sweat that had accumulated on our bodies began to freeze and chill our skin. It was hard to focus on climbing while our bodies were fighting to stay warm. So, Marco and I pulled out our jackets and continued on.

Soon after, a wall of fog greeted us. A few minutes into the fog and we finally saw our first snow! It was to the side of the stone path, mixed in with some dirt. I was amazed to be seeing snow near the end of spring.

The fog became thicker, lowering visibility. Patches of snow filled the ground around us. We formed a single-file line to conform to the narrowing of the path. At one point, we were in danger of slipping off the mountain by walking over a slick stone edge covered in snow. We took intentional, careful steps to make sure that we would make it safely across, but Marco and I were still intimidated by the imminent danger. Luckily, none of us fell to our deaths.

As the path opened up, we passed a restaurant on our left.

"Perhaps we can come back here on the way down and grab a bite to eat," Wim suggested. "For now, let's keep on!"

Several hundred feet higher, and we were finally standing atop Mount Śnieżka. I wasn't sure if it was completely accurate, but my infrared thermometer told me that the air was 32.5°F (.3°C). Visibility was low due to the vast amount of fog. I felt like I was in a dream or some sort of limbo. The terrain resembled that of a frozen wasteland, consisting of rocks and frozen dirt. Sadly, snow was nowhere to be found. The wind must have blown it off the side of the mountain.

After walking around for a little, we noticed a sign that read "Czech Republic."

"Oh, I think this is the border between Poland and the Czech Republic," Wim announced. "Watch this!" He began jumping back and forth between Poland and the Czech Republic. After doing this several times, he stopped abruptly and pointed, "Look, now we see some air. There's a good panorama."

I looked to where he was pointing and noticed the fog breaking. There was an area, the size of a football field, covered in loose rocks.

"Let's take off our shirts and change into shorts so we can do some training, yeah?" he advised.

We placed our stuff down and undressed. We did a few poses and recorded the shots with my laptop and Marco's camera. Wim also performed his infamous peacock on a rock. The peacock, as Wim explains, is when you use one of your arms to hold your entire body off of the ground horizontally. It is called the peacock because it's supposed to look beautiful and majestic. It also takes a lot of strength and balance. Marco and I both attempted the peacock, but we could only slightly succeeded by holding the pose with two arms.

We hung out on top of Mount Śnieżka, shirtless, for about 20 minutes before Wim decided to head back. Our growling stomachs must have given away that we were hungry. We put all of our layers of clothing back on and made our way down to the restaurant.

Along the way, we passed a large patch of ground that was covered in snow. Wim came up with an interesting idea.

"Why don't we get back into our shorts, then sit and meditate in the snow for the camera. It can be in the YouTube video! Also, it will be great training!"

Marco and I loved the idea, so we happily agreed.

I set my laptop on top of a flat rock and pushed record. Wim had already been sitting in the snow for a few minutes by the time Marco and I undressed. It had been almost half a year since I had last walked through the snow barefooted.

Climbing up the slope to sit in the snow was a daunting task. The place where Wim advised us to sit was on a slope of about 45°. I slipped numerous times while attempting to get into position, cutting my bare feet and knees with little chucks of ice. After building a leveled area for myself to sit on, I was finally able to relax -- well, as much as you could relax when sitting half naked in the snow.

I looked down and noticed that Marco had just gotten into position below me. His body was shaking violently. My body began to shiver as well. With each gust of wind, my body tensed. It was extremely uncomfortable. Yet somehow, Wim was sitting perfectly still.

"Let's sit here for five minutes," he announced. "Try not to move."

For the next five minutes, I tried to slow my breathing and focus on staying warm. I lost concentration occasionally when strong gusts of chilled air blew against my back.

Eventually, the five minutes were up. I couldn't feel my butt cheeks anymore, so I used them as my way of sliding down the slope.

"I can't feel my feet," Marco said.

"Me neither, they're numb!" I replied.

"Everything will be okay," Wim said comfortingly. "We'll go to the heated restaurant and warm up our feet and bodies. I'll also buy us hot chocolate."

After putting the layers of clothes back on to our bodies, we continued back down the mountain toward the restaurant. Being that I couldn't feel my feet, I paid careful attention to each step that I took. I didn't want to make one wrong move and slide down the slide of the mountain.

Finally, the restaurant came into our sights.

"Awesome!" I yelled.

We made our way to the wooden building and walked inside. The establishment was beautifully furnished with fine wooden tables and a large selection of food items. Marco and I placed our feet next to the heater to warm up our shoes while Wim ordered us food.

Over dinner, Marco and I discussed how our feet felt when we were climbing through the snow. Wim chimed in with a story.

"I used to train people to walk through the snow. The first time they would put their feet in, they would only last for a few seconds. I then made them go inside and warm up. Ten minutes later, after their feet were back to normal, I made them come back outside and walk through the snow again. This time, they were able to walk for ten times as long. It is a mixture between a certain mindset and conditioning. Your ability to walk barefoot through the snow will come with practice. Trust me."

After dinner, we gathered our belongings and threw on our jackets. We walked back into the cold air and made our way back down the sloped path. Our stomachs were full and our thirst for adventure was quenched.

We reached the bottom 90 minutes later. Instead of returning home, Wim suggested that we go to the waterfall that him and Konrad had previously tried to find the other night. Marco and I didn't mind, so we got back into the jeep and went waterfall hunting. Wim asked the people around town if they knew where it was located. No one could give us the correct directions. Eventually, Wim settled on resorting to his memory and retracing the steps that he made the last time he had been to the waterfall.

Finally, after about an hour of searching, we were in the presence of the "wooooshing" sound of the waterfall. It was hidden at the end of a winding path, inaccessible to vehicles. Trees on all sides surrounded the waterfall. The only exposed part to sunshine was the waterfall itself. The rays of light reflected off the water's surface and lit up the scenery. The beautiful view looked like it belonged in the Garden of Eden.

"The water that flows down from Karpacz is usually very cold," Wim stated in a matter-of-fact tone. "Much colder than the water in the river. This will be good training for the both of you."

I grabbed my thermometer out of my backpack and approached the water. The thermometer read 5.1°C (40°F).

"Okay," Wim began. "Marco, Justin and I will go into the waterfall first and stand beneath it for a while. Our bodies will be completely submerged in the high-pressured water. When we come out, I want you to meet us on the giant flat rock and meditate with us for a bit."

Marco nodded in understanding.

I looked over at the waterfall. The water seemed to be coming down pretty fast, smashing into the rocks below. I'll admit I was slightly afraid of my body being ripped to shreds by the pressure of the waterfall. I checked out Wim's face; it was completely calm. He seemed extremely sure of himself, as if he knew everything was going to be okay. So, I trusted his judgment and let go of my worries.

Marco pulled out his camera and turned it on. He set it on a rock facing the spot where the action would take place and clicked "Record." He gave a thumbs up to Wim and I, signaling that it was time for us to go out into the waterfall.

Wim and I decided to go out barefooted, which probably wasn't the best idea, but it was our only option. He led the way, stepping down into the cold, rushing water. I waited for him to make his way to the first rock platform before I stepped out. When I saw that he had made it safely, I stepped down into the water. The current was much stronger than I had anticipated. I struggled to maintain my balance on the slippery surface below my feet. Several times, I lost my footing, but I always caught myself before going down.

Right as I was taking my final step to stand on the giant rock platform that Wim was standing on, I slipped. The water took away all of the friction between my feet and the rock. There was nothing I could do but wait to fall. My feet continued to slide. After spinning 180° degrees, my right foot found itself against a dry part of a rock that was sticking out of the water. I had found friction again! I took one more careful step to bring myself to Wim's side.

Together, we walked through the rushing water and positioned our bodies directly below the waterfall. My knees caved several times as I tried to maintain my balance against the brute force of the water. I felt as if thousands of needles were repeatedly piercing my skin, but I stood my ground. I opened my eyes wide enough to see Wim standing by my side, firm as a rock. This man was a beast, stronger than anyone I had ever seen. Seeing Wim like that gave me renewed strength. I tightened my muscles and stood solid. Then, all of a sudden, the pain stopped and my body adjusted. I was warm again.

A moment later, I felt someone tugging on my arm. I opened my eyes to see that it was Wim pulling me from the waterfall. It was time to move on to meditating on the rocks with Marco. I pulled myself free of the waterfall's grasp and followed Wim to the rock. I slipped several more times, but luckily Wim was there to catch me. He held my hand, preventing me from being carried away by the strong current.

Once we arrived at the flat rock where Marco was now seated, he let go of me and took a seat beside him. I sat on the edge of the rock and tried to scoot over to sit closer to Wim and Marco, but the water picked up my light body and slid me farther than I wanted to move. Once again, Wim was there to catch me and seat me beside him.

Exhausted, yet feeling accomplished, I closed my eyes and began to meditate. The sound of the running water made it easy for my mind to float free. I imagined myself back in the waterfall. When I was standing there, it felt like the whole world was pressing down on me. At first, I had tried to fight it, stand up against it, but it wasn't until I had accepted the situation did I come to understand it. I realized that accepting the cold was the only way to survive in it. Resistance caused suffering and pain, while acceptance provided wisdom. It was my most important realization yet.

After five minutes of meditating on the rock, Wim announced it was time to go. We all carefully removed ourselves from the slippery surface and returned to our dry clothing.

"Woo hoo!" I yelled.

"That felt great!" Marco admitted.

Wim looked at us and patted us both on the back saying, "I'm proud of you guys! Nice one!"

As we drove back to Time-Out, we all felt a sense of accomplishment. We had summited on Mount Śnieżka and had a great experience at the waterfall. We listened to Coldplay's "Yellow" on my laptop as we drove into the sunset. It was the perfect way to end a perfect day.

Day 6: May 5, 2010

The next morning, I performed my breathing exercises before going downstairs. I felt energized and wanted to get a head start.

My best times were:
Holding Breath (without air in the lungs): 2 minutes 40 seconds
Holding Breath (with air in the lungs)): 5 minutes 6 seconds

Those were my best times yet! I ran downstairs and told Wim the good news. He was excited to hear that I had been able to hold my breath over five minutes (with air in my lungs) after only a few days of practice.

"So, what do you do when you hold your breath?" he asked. "What do you feel?

"Well," I started, "at first I do the 30 breaths like you asked me to. Then, when I hold my breath, I feel nothing for a long time, no pressure, no signs telling me that I should stop, nothing. After a while, at about four minutes, tightness appears in my chest. From that point on, I know that I can last another minute or so by fighting that tightness."

"Well then," he replied looking somewhat disappointed, "I am glad you are seeing results, but I think you are going about it the wrong way. You do not want to force it. Forcing can hurt you and take you back a few steps. Focus on relaxing; don't force it."

Hearing that I was doing it wrong was a shock to my ego, but I felt comforted knowing that I didn't have to force it anymore. I figured that the tightness was natural and I just had to push through it, but I was wrong. I encoded his advice in my memory and went into the kitchen to fetch myself a bowl of cereal and some coffee.

When I walked into the kitchen to grab myself a bowl, I ran into Marco holding a frying pan.

"Good morning Justin," he said. "I was thinking about making some french toast. Would you like some?"

"Sure! Is there anything I can do to help?"

"I should be okay. Thank you for offering."

During breakfast, Wim made an announcement.

"Today, we are going to take it easy. We had a long day yesterday, so I figure that we deserve to relax. I'll light a fire and we can just hang out around the house."

That sounded good to me. My body was very sore from standing beneath the waterfall the day before. Resting would do me some good. It would also give me the opportunity to work on the You-

Tube video with the accumulated footage.

After breakfast, Wim told me that he and Marco were going to go to the mountain and do some more meditating. I told them I would be okay staying at the house to work on the YouTube video, so they went on without me. I had never worked with video-editing software before, so it took me a while to get the hang of it.

After a few hours had passed, Wim and Marco returned. When they got back, Wim exclaimed that Marco did his first full-body immersion for a full minute! I was sad to have missed it and also missed out on an opportunity to go in the water, but I had an important job. I needed to finish the YouTube video to help promote Wim's workshops.

Time flew by that day. I spent several hours working on the video while Wim and Marco just talked. For dinner, Wim cooked again and made a marvelous meal. Konrad had stopped by earlier on in the day and told us that he was on his way to go speak with his cousin about the barefoot run. He had also dropped off a couple bottles of wine as gifts. Therefore, wine was served at the dinner table.

After dinner, I went back to work on the video. Marco went to sleep early and Wim stayed out to continue sipping on wine. We talked for a good while about the potential of cold changing the world. Eventually, the topic of Mount Blanc was brought up.

"You should do it, Justin," he said. "Join me on the climb to Mount Blanc."

"But you said it may be difficult with the television crew organizing it," I replied, confused.

"Ahh, don't worry about them. If you can raise the money to get yourself to Europe and pay for your gear to climb, I will make it happen. I am The Iceman; they will have to listen to me. You are my friend and I want you there. We are like brothers."

"Brothers?" I asked.

"Yes, spiritual brothers. We both have similar visions. We want to change the world. People want to leave it the way it is and live ignorantly, yet we have wisdom and can show them a better way of living. We have the power to change the world. All my life, I have been ridiculed. I was called crazy, and insane! But now, with this new research developing about me being able to control my autonomic nervous system, they won't laugh anymore. It's a deep and powerful technique. My way of living is redefining science!"

"Well Wim, if you really want me to be there, and you are serious about this, I will do everything in my power to make sure that I can come back to Europe the first week in August. I will climb Mount

Blanc with you."

"Yes!" Wim exclaimed. "Spiritual brothers!"

We embraced one another, as if we were family.

"I love you man!" he said with tears in his eyes. "Thank you for believing me. Thank you."

"I love you too, Wim," I said with a smile, holding back tears of my own. "Thank you for showing me that there are things in this life that are worth pursuing. I will do everything in my power to help you spread your message."

We hugged once more and he wished me good night.

"Tomorrow we will do more training," he said. "Marco will swim 50 meters in the cold water. You and I will swim 1 kilometer together! As brothers!"

I continued to watch the doorway as his footsteps faded up the stairs. *That man is going to make history*, I thought. *He is going to change the way we live our lives. And from this day on, we will call each other spiritual brothers.*

I decided to stay downstairs and work on the video a bit longer before going to bed. Half an hour after Wim went to bed, the power went out. The eeriness of the pitch-black house freaked me out. I used my laptop's screen as a flashlight to find my way to my bedroom. After typing up my journal for the night, I closed my eyes and fell asleep.

Day 7: May 6, 2010

The next morning I awoke and immediately did my breathing exercises, however, I didn't bother to record the time because I didn't want to have any reason to force myself. Instead, I took my time and relaxed. I still hadn't seen the lights that Wim had talked about, nor did I break any time records, but I did feel much better when I was finished. I felt relaxed and peaceful. I didn't know if that's what was supposed to happen, but I accepted it for what it was.

When I went downstairs, Marco and Wim were already up and talking to each other. I prepared myself a bowl of cereal and joined in on the conversation.

"So what's the plan, Wim?" I asked.

"Well, we're going to do things a bit differently than I had explained last night," he said. "Instead of doing the kilometer swim, we are just doing to do 800 meters, nice and easy. We'll take baby steps. If you can do 800 meters with no problem, then we will move on to one kilometer. As for Marco, we decided that he's going to swim against the current with his whole body exposed. It will be good training for the both of you."

"All right," I said. "Sounds like a good idea. When are we going?"

"When you finish your cereal," he replied.

While I finished my breakfast, Marco and Wim left the room to change into their bathing suits. When I was finished, I placed my bowl in the kitchen and ran upstairs to change too.

Fifteen minutes later, we were standing in front of our familiar swimming spot. Wim and Marco had gone into the water to swim against the current. I was watching from above, holding Marco's camera. Marco seemed to be doing really well in the 9.8°C (49.64°F) water.

After five minutes of swimming against the current, Marco's face contorted into an interesting expression; it looked like determination. Wim also noticed the expression and began to say things I didn't understand -- later I found out that he was reciting Sanskrit mantras from memory as a form of encouragement. It seemed to give Marco strength. He was able to last for another five minutes in the cold water!

After Marco had swum to the edge and dried off, it was my turn. I dove into the water and treaded with Wim. When Marco told us that he was ready to walk along the river, Wim announced that it was time to swim our 800 meters.

"Let's go!" he yelled. We began swimming.

Once again, Wim pulled ahead of me and maintained a steady

pace. I remembered his advice about not forcing, and continued on at my own pace. Throughout the entire swim, my body remained warm and my breathing was relaxed.

When I had reached the end of the 800 meters, my body was exhausted. In total, it took me 16 minutes to swim 800 meters. There was nothing wrong with my body, heat-wise. I was just physically exhausted. Other than that, I felt great. My fingers felt fine with no numbness at all. The same was true for my toes.

As I emerged from the water, I remembered that my afterdrop would come on quickly. Therefore, I asked Wim if we could jog back to the house in an attempt to suppress my afterdrop. Sadly, it didn't work. My afterdrop kicked in completely by the time we were halfway home. My shivering was uncontrollable.

The afterdrop lasted a total of 32 minutes. That's significantly more time than my last afterdrop episode, but you must also consider that we added another 200 meters to the original swim.

When all was said and done and I was warm again, I reflected on my achievement. I had seen substantial progress. I felt more comfortable while I was in the water. There had been no pain or discomfort. I realized accepting the cold worked was working to my advantage. It gave me the ability to generate more heat to stay warm longer.

When we got back to the house, Wim lit a fire. After talking for a bit, we realized that we were pretty hungry. Wim suggested that we catch a taxi into town and eat at the Pizzeria again. We would have taken the jeep, but Konrad took it with him to go visit his cousin in Karpacz.

Thirty minutes later, we were being dropped off at the Pizzeria in Lwowek Slaski. Apparently, the taxi driver was a friend of Caroline's, and told Wim that he would be willing to pick us up in a couple of hours to take us back. He said that we didn't even have to pay him until he had returned us home. We took him up on his offer and asked him to pick us up in two hours.

We made our to the restaurant and discussed other possible ways to promote the barefoot-snow run in the winter. While we ate our pizzas, Wim told us about how happy he was to have us as friends.

"I really think of you guys as my family. Thank you for being here."

After dinner, we made our way back to the taxi and rode back to Time-Out. It was about 9:00 PM by the time we arrived back at the house. I was still exhausted from the earlier swim. We spoke around the fire for a bit, but soon my eyelids were too heavy to keep them open. I said goodnight to Marco and Wim and went upstairs to my

Day 8: May 7, 2010

The next morning, I fixed my bed and went downstairs to meet Wim and Marco. I always seemed to wake up later than they did. Perhaps I still wasn't used to the time change. Either way, I never woke up later than 9:00 AM, which wasn't too bad.

Wim and Marco were eating breakfast and drinking tea when I entered the room. Wim suggested I do my breathing exercises outside in the nice, warm sun. I took him up on his advice. I walked outside and sat on a nearby bench.

Performing the breathing exercises felt much more relaxing than they had the first day. After each set of breath holding, I felt more alert and energetic, but also centered and controlled. Since I had implemented the "don't force" rule, it didn't feel like a chore anymore. It was quick and easy to do, with no effort required whatsoever.

Walking back inside after finishing my exercises, I noticed that Wim and Marco's teacup was empty.

"Would you like more tea?" I asked, already reaching for their cups.

"Yes, thank you," they both replied.

I took their glasses and made more tea while I also made myself cereal. While fixing up breakfast, I came up with an idea. When I got back to the breakfast table with the tea and cereal, I told them my idea.

"Hey, so why don't we go back to the river and swim one more time before we go. Along the way, we can stop somewhere, if there is a field close by, and throw a Frisbee around. Then, perhaps we can go to the river and have some fun by throwing the Frisbee at each other and catching it while jumping into the water."

"Great! Nice one!" Wim exclaimed enthusiastically.

"Okay, let's do it," Marco replied while smiling.

While I finished up breakfast, Marco and Wim went upstairs to change.

"We'll meet you outside," they said, grabbing the Frisbee that was sitting on top of the piano.

I finished my bowl of cereal and took it to the kitchen. Running upstairs to change, I saw Wim through my bedroom window, throwing the Frisbee with Marco.

In just a matter of days, I thought, *I have been to come into a new country and build friendships that will last a lifetime. I now have ties with amazing, intellectual pioneers. I can't believe that it all started from simply watching a television show featuring "The Iceman." Wow.*

I finished changing, gathered my things, and ran outside to meet my friends. We walked along the dirt road toward the lake, one final time. Later that day, Marco would be getting on a bus and moving on to his next adventure.

I'm going to miss this, I thought.

Eventually, we arrived at a giant field with two soccer nets on each end.

"Here is a good place," Wim declared.

We spread out across the field, throwing the Frisbee back and forth. The field was filled with thousands of dandelions. What kind of insect loves dandelions? That's right… Bees. Along with the thousands of dandelions, there were hundreds of bees everywhere we stepped. Simply throwing around in the field turned into a game of "Don't stay in one place too long or you'll get stung… quick throw the Frisbee!" We had a lot of laughs. Luckily, no one was stung.

After an hour of throwing, we decided to move on to the river and swim one last time. When we got to our normal swimming spot, I took out my laptop and placed it in a position where the camera would be facing us. When everything was ready, I took the Frisbee and stood next to my laptop, perpendicular to the spot where we usually jumped in.

"On the count of three, Wim, I want you to run and jump. I'll throw the Frisbee to you. Ready?" I asked.

"Yeah! Go!" he yelled back to me.

"Haha, okay. One… Two… Three!"

Wim sprinted toward the edge at full speed and leapt forward. I threw the Frisbee and it just missed his outstretched arms.

"So close!" he said as his head emerged from the water. He threw the Frisbee back to me. "I want to try again!"

As Wim swam back to the edge, Marco dove in. I threw the Frisbee to him, but he also narrowly missed it. We couldn't seem to get the timing right.

We each took turns throwing the Frisbee at each other. After fifteen minutes of throwing and catching, I was the only one to catch it. We probably would have tried for longer if it weren't for the water being so cold. It's not that the cold was affecting us in the way that we were losing heat, but whenever we would dive in, the impact from hitting the water would sting our sides and backs; it was extremely painful.

After catching the Frisbee, I decided to stay in for a bit and swim around. Before leaving Poland, I wanted to feel the afterdrop one last time. I enjoyed having the ability to just walk down the street and jump in a freezing cold river. I was going to miss it.

I stayed in the water for about fifteen minutes. Marco jumped in once more and swam around for a little too. It was relaxing, not having to think about the cold and just enjoy swimming. We had come a long way from our first day of training. It was comforting to know that progress had been made.

Five minutes after getting out of the water, during our walk home, my afterdrop kicked in. I welcomed it. Even though it was uncomfortable, I now looked at the afterdrop with gratitude. Like the burn in the muscles that you receive after a long day of working out, the afterdrop let me know that I had pushed my body to its limits and was in the process of recovering.

As we approached Time-Out, we heard a loud horn from behind us. We turned to see it was Konrad in his jeep. He met us back at the house and told us that his trip to Karpacz was a success. His cousin was going to let us hold the barefoot race in Karpacz! This was great news!

I went inside to bathe myself and clean off. In the tub, I reflected on everything that had happened over the last few days. I thought about the cold swims, climbing up to Mount Śnieżka, and sitting in the snow. I had gained a lot of experience and had significantly improved as far as my Iceman training goes.

I also recognized that I had a long way to go if I wanted to catch up to Wim, but I was willing to keep trying. I didn't want to leave my training in Poland. I hoped that this Mount Blanc challenge would force me to continue practicing daily. The first week of August was only a short three months away. I finished up my bath and went downstairs to work on the YouTube video some more.

Konrad noticed me working on it and asked me to show him my unfinished video. He was amazed.

"You guys sat in the snow?" he asked with excitement in his voice. "That's incredible! Wow, you are my heroes."

After watching the video, Konrad began taking pictures of the house. He explained that he wanted to take pictures of Time-Out back to Holland to show his friends. During this time, Marco was upstairs packing his stuff. It was almost time to take him to the bus stop in Lwowek Slaski.

When Marco was finished packing, we all met outside in the front yard. Konrad was holding a bottle of alcohol and a lit candle.

"I want us to try something," he said. "I am going to put hot wax on the cap of this bottle to seal it. I want us all to use our fingertips to seal the wax. Then, when we have completed the barefoot run in Karpacz, we can come back here and drink this bottle together."

We all thought it was a good idea. He poured the hot wax around the lid and we all took turns pressing our fingers against the wax. It was a nice, sentimental gesture by Konrad.

We arrived in Lwowek Slaski 45 minutes before Marco's bus showed up. In the meantime, we threw around the Frisbee in the streets. Konrad took more pictures of us to keep as memories. Wim and I also tried a few breakdancing moves in the street. He did the peacock while spinning in circles, while I did my two-handed peacock and walked forward. It was a nice, relaxing way to end our time together.

When Marco's bus arrived, we were sad to say goodbye. We had planned to see him again in the future, so it wasn't really goodbye, just a temporary "see you later!" We each took turns hugging Marco and wishing him the best of luck on his upcoming adventures. As the doors closed and the bus pulled away, we waved goodbye to our new friend.

Wim, Konrad and myself walked back to the jeep and drove home. When we arrived, we began packing up the jeep for our return to Amsterdam. Wim and I took a break from packing to record his voice for the YouTube video. With the voice track completed, I only needed another half hour to complete the video. I was ecstatic.

When we had finished putting our things into the jeep, Konrad placed the wax-sealed bottle on top of the cabinet, next to the fireplace. As we got in the car, we said our goodbyes to Mishu and Time-Out one final time.

It was a long drive back to Amsterdam. We left the house just as the sun was setting. We stopped at several gas stations and rest stops along the way. Wim and Konrad took turns driving. I would've driving too, but I didn't know how to drive stick in a manual vehicle. I didn't mind though, it gave me the opportunity to finish working on the video in the backseat. When it was polished and set up the way I liked it, I closed my laptop and took a nap.

Day 9: May 8, 2010

I awoke to the sound of a car's horn. I looked outside the window; we were back in Amsterdam. My watch read 6:55 AM. In about 13 hours and 10 minutes, I would be on a flight departing from Amsterdam Schiphol to Frankfurt, Germany. It was almost time to go home. At 7:15 AM, we stopped on the side of the road and Wim got out.

"What are we doing?" I asked.

"I am dropping Wim off," Konrad replied. "He has something to attend to so he won't be hanging out with us for the rest of the day."

My heart sunk.

"I am sorry," Wim said. "Konrad will take care of you until your flight leaves. He'll make sure that you get to the airport on time too. I wish I could stay, but I need to go see my family."

"It's okay Wim," I said, looking him in the eyes and forcing a smile. "I understand."

Konrad and I got out of the car and helped unpack Wim's belongings. Wim and I embraced each other one last time. As he turned to leave, he looked back at me and said, "Goodbye my spiritual brother. I will see you again on Mount Blanc!"

With that, he turned away and walked behind a building.

"Goodbye brother," I muttered under my breath.

"All right," Konrad said. "Let's go!"

We got back into the car and began driving. Before going back to Konrad's house, he mentioned that we would need to stop by his friend's to pick up a key. I didn't know what the key was for, but he said it was important.

We drove 25 minutes to a town called Harlem, where his friend lived. We stopped at his house and tried knocking at the door, but no one answered. He tried calling his cell phone -- still nothing.

"Come on, let's go find a coffee shop and I will buy you some coffee," he said, seeming frustrated that his friend was unavailable.

We found a coffee shop on a nearby corner and took a seat. Konrad struck up a conversation with the owner while I reviewed the video of Poland on my laptop. When we had finished our coffee, Konrad tried calling his friend once more. This time, he answered. Apparently he was very sick and couldn't get out of bed. To avoid catching the sickness, Konrad told his friend that he would come back for the key at another time.

"I have an idea," Konrad said. His eyes lit up. "Do you want to go for a cold swim?"

"Um...sure," I said hesitantly, "but where?"

"You will see."

We jumped into his jeep and drove thirty minutes back to Amsterdam. We made a turn and then drove another ten minutes toward an area that I was unfamiliar with. The landscape opened up and the ground flattened out. In the distance, I could see water.

"It's the North Sea!" Konrad said, revealing the surprise. "Let's go!"

We grabbed our bathing suits, towels, and Konrad's camera from the back of the jeep and made our way toward the water.

"I think it would be nice to make a video for Wim," he thought out loud. "We can record us going into the water to show him that even though he is not around, we will still continue training."

"Okay Konrad," I thought it was a silly idea, but I figured Wim would probably love it.

After changing into our swimming trunks, Konrad took his camera out of its bag and turned it on. He laid his shirt on the ground and placed the camera on top of it.

"Okay," he said, obviously excited. "Let's go!"

We ran out into the ocean and swam around for a good ten minutes. The water was freezing, but it was nothing compared to the frigid waterfall at the base of Karpacz. Although I hadn't expected to do anymore Iceman training before leaving Europe, it was a nice surprise.

We changed back into our dry clothes and walked to a nearby restaurant located on the shore.

"How about I buy you cup of hot chocolate and then we go, okay?" Konrad asked.

"Why not?" I replied.

We entered the restaurant barefooted. I felt bad bringing sand into the establishment, but when I noticed that the floor was already covered in sand, I stopped worrying. There was a fireplace sitting near the giant windows facing the North Sea.

After Konrad had bought two hot chocolates, we made our way to the fireplace and sat beside it. We lifted our sandy, wet feet up and placed them on a footrest near the open flames. As Konrad and I sipped on our hot chocolate, we looked out the window, taking in the beautiful landscape. At that moment, life seemed perfect.

I couldn't believe that for the past week, I had been training with the original Iceman, whom I now called, my *spiritual brother*.

CHAPTER 31:
GOING HOME

*L*ater that evening, Konrad dropped me off at the airport. I checked in my bags, went through security, and made my way to the gate. It had been a great experience, but I was ready to get back to good ol' America. I missed my family and my friends. The only thing standing in the way of that was my final trip home.

My flight schedule had me arriving in Frankfurt, Germany at 9:10 PM (CET) and leaving at 8:25 AM (CET). From there, I would fly from Frankfurt to Chicago, IL. From Chicago I would have to go through customs and board one final flight leaving at 2:20 PM (EST) and arriving at 4:54 PM (EST). In case that was a little hard to follow, I still had over 24 hours before I would be picked up by my family in Pittsburgh, Pennsylvania.

My first flight from Amsterdam to Frankfurt was quick and painless. The flight attendants were really nice and the flight itself only lasted an hour. When I arrived in the Frankfurt airport, I was intimidated. I was in a fairly large airport in a country I had never been to before. I tried speaking to a few of the people working there, but none of them spoke English.

When I arrived, my first goal was to find the gate where my plane would be leaving in the morning. Along the way, I noticed that there were a lot of convenient stores and restaurants. I decided to grab some food after I had found my gate and then, hopefully, find a place to nap.

Well, I found my gate, but by the time I had walked back to the miniature restaurants and convenient stores, they were all closed! I looked at my watch and it read: 10:02 PM. Everything must have closed at 10:00 PM. Ugh! I was extremely frustrated. It was the *perfect* way to start the evening.

Great, I thought, *now what am I going to do?*

I walked down the hallways of the airport for a bit longer, hoping to find one convenient store that was open late. There was absolutely nothing. So, I sat down and turned on my laptop. Well, it turns out that the Frankfurt airport doesn't have free wireless Internet. Disgruntled, I repacked my laptop into my backpack and continued to walk around the airport.

Eventually, I came across a computer that offered Internet access, but I needed euros to operate the machine. Luckily, I had a few coins in my pocket. What wasn't so lucky was that it took me until my last coin before I understood how to operate the machine. Finally, with that last coin, I was able to send a quick email to my family and Brooke, letting them know that I was safe in Frankfurt.

Finishing my battle with the computer, I decided to return to my gate and find a place to plug in my computer, so I could turn on my alarm and fall asleep. When I returned to my gate, which was about a fifteen-minute walk from where I was, I found a seat in the corner. I sat down and pulled out my laptop and power cord, only to find out that the power outlet I was going to connect to had metal rods inside of it, preventing me from using the power source.

You have got to be kidding me.

I would like to take a second and make a side note really quick… In no way am I blaming my unfortunate sequence of events on the Frankfurt airport. It was all because I was unprepared. I should have researched the airport before I purchased my tickets. This part of the story is just emphasizing my "coming to terms" with my interesting predicament.

Anyway, back to the story. So, with no way to set an alarm -- mind you, the alarm function on my watch was broken -- I was uncomfortable falling asleep. I was desperately afraid that if I fell asleep, I would miss my flight. I didn't know how rescheduling flights worked, but I wasn't interested in finding out.

I sat there for a few hours, staring out the window. I was waiting until I grew extremely tired before I used the rest of my laptop's battery life to watch a movie. Hopefully, the movie would be enough to stimulate my mind to prevent me from falling asleep.

Around 3:00 AM, it became extremely difficult to keep my eyes open. I forced myself to get out of my seat and get a change of scenery. I walked a few gates down and settled in a comfortable chair by the bathroom. If I was going to watch a movie, I figured that it would be better if I used the restroom first, that way I wouldn't have to shut everything down, use the restroom, and then turn everything back on. So, I forced myself to get back out of the chair and use the restroom.

After quickly using the restroom, I found my way back to the chair and turned on my laptop and played the movie. During the movie, several times I saw the janitorial staff riding giant vacuums and floor cleaners. Actually, during one of the more action-packed scenes of the movie, I had a strange feeling that someone was watching me. I looked up and saw one of the staff staring me in the face, standing no more than two feet away.

"Um... hello," I said timidly.

He was holding two giant-sized pretzels. When I spoke to him, he extended the pretzel in his left hand and put it in my face. I grabbed it.

"Thank you." I said.

He smiled.

I smiled back.

Despite the creepiness of the situation, I was more than happy to accept food from a stranger; I was famished. I watched the man walk away and around the corner. I hurriedly shoved the pretzel in my mouth and tried biting down. It was incredibly stale.

Whatever, I told myself. *This is the only food I'll be getting until the shops open in the morning. Are you really going to reject free food, Justin?*

My answer was no. I carefully nibbled on the rock-hard pretzel until there was nothing left. Soon after, my stomach began to relax and my desire to eat diminished. I returned to my movie.

An hour later, the movie was over. According to my laptop, I only had half an hour left of battery. I promptly shut it down in an attempt to save the rest for an emergency. The clock on my watch read: 5:00 AM. I felt more awake than I had before turning on my movie. Luckily, the movie had been very entertaining and was able to hold my interest the entire time, which most likely aided in giving me more energy.

With a few hours left, I went into the restroom and decided to clean myself up. I shaved, brushed my teeth, washed my face, and took off my shirt to wash my back, chest and arms. My mini-shower in the bathroom woke me up even more. I packed away my electric razor and toothbrush, and left the bathroom. I walked around for the next couple hours to keep myself active. I was willing to sacrifice my sleep in order to insure boarding my flight.

Around 7:00 AM, I noticed the lights in the convenient stores turning back on. I walked back to my gate and looked for the closest place that sold food, which happened to be a yogurt shop.

"May I have a yogurt please?" I asked. My stomach was begging for food again.

She stared at me blankly.

I resorted to pointing at a yogurt cup.

She held up two fingers. I assumed that she meant two euros. I pulled out my wallet and handed her the proper amount of currency. She grabbed the yogurt cup and handed it to me smiling.

"Thanks," I said, grabbing the cup and smiling back. I walked back to my gate and dug into the delicious treat. My stomach was pleased.

After eating, time flew. Before I knew it, I was onboard my flight to Chicago. I praised myself for staying up all night and not missing my flight. Exhausted, I fell asleep soon after taking off into the air. I awoke when the pilot's voice came over the loudspeaker and announced that we were descending. I wiped the drool off of my complementary pillow and sat straight up in my seat. Even though the sleep had returned most of my energy, I was still tired from traveling. I just wanted to get back home and see my family.

Going through customs took forever. I thought it would be like going through airport security, but I was wrong. Nevertheless, when I got out, I still had an hour left to catch my flight. I made my way to the gate and sat down, placing my belongings under my seat. I turned on my phone and texted my parents and girlfriend, to let them know I that was safe.

I then decided to pull out my laptop and use the remaining battery power. Now that I was in the U.S, I was free to use my debit card again. So, I purchased access to the airport's Wi-Fi and was finally able to upload the YouTube video of our workshop. If you would like to see it, please go to this URL:

http://www.youtube.com/watch?v=3WmmPrWL9mo

After uploading the video, I sent a quick email to Wim with the link inside, once again thanking him for the opportunity. Soon after, my flight began seating people. I packed up my things and boarded my final ride home.

A couple hours later, I was riding down an escalator to baggage claim.

"I see him!" I heard a voice say. I looked to my left and saw my little sister Natélie, waving at me. On her sides were my girlfriend, Brooke, and my mother.

"Hi guys!" I said while walking over to them.

Brooke looked at me. I could tell she was holding back tears. She walked over and dug her head into my chest. I hugged her. She made a gasping sound as she tried to catch her breath. She was crying.

"I missed you so much," she said into my chest, muffling her voice.

"I missed you too, baby," I looked over Brooke's shoulder; my mom and Natélie were smiling. I could see that they were anxious to hug me as well.

"I got you this," Brooke said. She held up a stuffed monkey. "Except when I bought it, I didn't know it was a puppet." She turned it over and showed me the hole where his backside should be.

"It's beautiful, thanks for thinking of me. I love it." I let go of Brooke and walked over to my mom to hug her. While I wrapped my arms around her, Natélie ran over and hugged me from behind.

"I want you to know," my mother whispered into my ear, "that I wanted to hug you first, but I waited because I knew Brooke was really sad and wanted to see you. So I told Natélie that we should wait to hug you until you came to us."

"I love you," I hugged her harder.

"Your dad is bringing around the car. Let's go see him."

We grabbed my checked bag from the conveyor belt and made our way outside. My father got out of the car and hugged me. He told me that he was glad I was home safe. We packed my things into the car and began driving home.

During the hour and a half drive, I laid my head in my girlfriend's lap and told my family the stories from my adventures in Poland. It was good to be home. Time to prepare for Mount Blanc.

CHAPTER 32:
THE ENDOTOXIN EXPERIMENT – A GREAT FIGHT

*F*our years after the beginning of The Iceman research, I finally stumbled upon an opportunity to prove my point that we can influence the immune system and fight diseases by the power of our mind.

While I was immersed in the ice bath at Radboud, Professor Netea was one of the people watching me with excitement. Professor Netea is well known for his research as an immunologist. He's a celebrated scientist and a well-known member of academia.

I have met many world-record holders in sports and other numerous disciplines; the ones with strong spirits do not boast. The same goes for Professor Netea. He remains humble despite his numerous achievements.

His most recent research on the immune system using the Endotoxin Experiment is astounding. It focuses on what happens when the inflammatory marks in the body, which are the cause of numerous diseases, flare up too much and cause damage to human tissue.

Being that I am a trained person who shows unusual results when exposed to extreme temperatures, he thought it would be an interesting opportunity to see how my body differs from everyone else that he had tested.

I accepted his invitation over the phone and agreed to take part in his research. He had gained approval to perform the endotoxin experiment, despite my age! I was convinced that we could consciously influence the immune system and Professor Netea would be my way to show the world that it was possible.

Even though the experiment would get universal coverage and would probably be all over the newspapers and televisions, I was only focused on proving that anyone was capable of directly influencing the autonomic nervous system.

We set an appointment to do the first check up and collect basic data. The data showed that I was a perfectly healthy, older man, in great physical condition. My heart rate at the time of the test was 39 beats per minute.

Normally, an overactive immune system causes damage to human tissue. The experiment would see if I could suppress that overactive response. If possible, we could potentially develop a method that would enable millions of people to improve their own immune systems.

Inflammatory marked bodies can create inflammation, which is the cause of almost any disease. Therefore, being able to influence the immune system, by meditation and specific breathing, could be a natural weapon that mankind uses against disease.

The morning of the Endotoxin Experiment, I woke up at 4:00 AM and performed my routine breathing exercises. I was in full spirits and ready to give my all at the hospital in Nijmegen. I was excited to show my stuff to the doctors, professors, medical team, and TV crew who would be there to watch me.

I was anxious and nervous; yet I was fully aware of the challenge I had to overcome. Suppressing a disease by sheer will without any external means would be nothing short of a gigantic breakthrough.

A few hours later, I was lying in a hospital bed surrounded by scientists, the medical crew, and a television crew in a 7x5 meter (23x16 feet) room. The doctors wired me to numerous machines to record data.

There, I would have to fight against an injected toxin. Not only would I have to fight against the disease, but also against the pressure of the people around me. Their expectations were high and I wanted to fulfill them.

Even though I didn't know what impact the injected poison would have on me, I had prepared my body the best I could. I began my breathing technique to give myself a head start. With each breath, I imagined that I was charging my immune system with more power.

Right before I was injected, the doctors explained that I would feel the effects of the endotoxin soon after the injection. So I prepared my body and received the poison as it was released it into my blood.

During the first few minutes, I felt nothing. There was no change. I told the doctors this and they explained that most of the inflammatory marks would be present in my body 90 minutes after injection.

60 minutes past and I was fine. 75 minutes past and I was still okay. I was waiting for any noticeable change in my body so that I could counter it. About 90 minutes after injection, I felt a little headache begin to come on. I had finally found my opponent, but it was

far less than what I was expecting.

Soon after focusing on the hostile force, the headache was gone and the pressure was relieved. What had happened? I was expecting a war and all I got was a little headache.

Regardless, my immune system was ready and alert. When I felt the headache, I had simply stimulated the immune system to work more efficiently. In this case, it meant suppressing the inflammatory bodies with sheer willpower. In a matter of minutes... It had gone.

After about forty withdrawals of blood and 10 hours of being wired into a hospital bed, it all came to an end. The professor and doctors were delighted with the results. They were amazed that I hadn't experienced anything more than a headache.

My feeling was that of victory and I cried several times that day. A long time of waiting to see if my beliefs were true had finally come to a victorious end. I felt relieved, as if a giant weight had been lifted off my shoulders.

It was my greatest adventure in bed, ever.

After the experiment, an enormous appetite had developed and my desire for food was intense. After eating, I went to a nearby hotel and slept. The following day, I returned to Radboud for another check up.

Everything was fine and my body was in great condition! I drove home with my friend, Ben, who was there for me on this adventure. We sang songs with our hearts full of joy.

Yes, it is possible to influence the immune system and fight disease. We will show everyone!

CHAPTER 33:
THE WIND TUNNEL EXPERIMENT

*O*ne day, Maximum TV called me and asked if I was still interested in doing television performances. Since it's the way I make my money, I told them "yes." They were happy to hear my response. That's when they started talking about what they wanted to do, "The Wind Tunnel Experiment."

They had two ideas that they wanted to pursue in the experiment. One of them was to strap me to the outside of a truck driving 80 kilometers per hour (49.7 mph) in temperatures near freezing. The other idea was to travel to Vienna where there is a wind tunnel capable of creating winds that are 120 kilometers per hour (74.5 mph) with a temperature of 0°C (32°F). I had never done anything like that before so I was interested in both of the ideas. I was ready to test my body and mind once again.

A couple of weeks later I flew to Frankfurt, then Munich. There, I met the 27-year-old Dennis. Typically a journalist and a soccer player, Dennis was now going to host the show and join me in the experiment. He was eager to do a good job and give his best.

The following morning, ten of us began our 160 kilometers (99.4 miles) drive from Munich to Memmingen, Germany. Once we arrived, we stopped at a truck company that specialized in airline transport vehicles. One of their vehicles and an ambulance accompanied us to the nearby airport.

When we arrived at the airport, the television crew began to set up. The medics checked on us to make sure we were in good condition. They checked our core temperature, blood pressure and heart rate. They declared us healthy individuals.

The producer's goal was to strap Dennis and I into the back of a truck and then drive 80 kilometers per hour (49.7 mph) in the rain at 4°C (39.2°F). After the final preparations were made, the truck began to move. At 80 kilometers per hour (49.7 mph), the rain feels like hail as it hit our skin.

I was barely clothed while Dennis had the advantage of wearing a raincoat. The combination of rain, cold temperature and high winds took the heat from the body at a rapid pace; however, it made for a wonderful endurance test.

Despite the hail-like rain, we quickly discovered that the extreme stunt was possible to do while remaining somewhat comfortable. Even for an untrained person like Dennis, he was able to maintain his composure and stay energetic. He suggested that maybe it was my presence and advice that gave him the ability to endure the cold. Either way, during those hours we "chilled out" and had a great time.

After many hours of driving, the television crew was finally satisfied. We packed up our stuff and started driving to Vienna. We stopped 150 kilometers (93.2 miles) short of Vienna. It was late, so we found a quaint hotel to stay in where we quickly fell to sleep. The next morning we rose at 5:00 AM and quickly got back on the road.

Soon after, we arrived at the thermo-test facility. It was a huge compound that had the capacity to simulate a wind tunnel. When we first entered the building, we noticed an enormous refrigerator. There were pipes 10 meters in diameter, covered in insulation, feeding into the wind tunnel. Using a propeller that is seven meters high to generate wind, this facility holds the largest wind tunnel in the world.

When the emergency team arrived, which included a doctor and his assistant, we were ready to record. People were running all over the place to try to make all of the necessary preparations. I prepared myself mentally for the test.

Eventually, we made our way to the front of the wind tunnel. Normally, they test trains' resistance against temperatures from -40°C (-40°F) to 60°C (140°F). They are also able to simulate rain and snow during these tests to mock the outside environment. They told us that we would be doing the shot with the wind tunnel running at 100 kilometers per hour (62 mph) at 0°C (32°F).

Dennis and I got our final check ups from the medics. My heart rate was at 68 BPM while Dennis' was at 122 BPM. Being that I am more experienced when it comes to these situations, my heart rate stays relatively low while I am preparing for the event. Soon enough, the cameras were ready and it was time for the shot.

A few moments later, Dennis and I were standing in front of the tunnel and the massive propeller began to spin. The tunnel was 12 meters high, 120 meters long, and controlled by a computer to create any possible weather condition; it was a beautiful sight. Dennis was wearing a jacket, but not me. He was standing a meter behind me. Of course, we were both a little anxious about what was to come because neither of us had experienced anything like it before. We didn't know what to expect.

The sound from the propeller became louder. *Fou, fou, fou, fou, fou, fooo, fooooooo.* The wind strengthened and we had to position our feet in a way to prevent us from being knocked over. At 0°C (32°F) and 100 kph (62 mph) winds, it felt like a storm. It wasn't comfortable, but we were able to hold our ground, despite the wind stinging our face and sucking the heat from our hands.

After 10 minutes into the storm, Dennis had endured all that he could handle. He raised his hand to signal to the crew that he was done. I was running in place and I had felt extremely comfortable prior to them turning off the propeller, but the first attempt was over and it was time to relax.

We went back into a heated room to drink some tea and warm up. After an hour had passed, we were ready to go again. This time, they would turn up the wind speed to 120 kph (74 mph), lower the temperature even more and add rain into the equation. In the meantime, more shots were taken of our preparations. The television crew worked constantly to acquire as much footage as possible. Time was money and they had little time to get the right shots.

Back at the tunnel, Dennis was now wearing two raincoats and waterproof pants, and I was wearing clothes that could easily soak the rain and keep it pressed against my body. We were ready. The cameras began to roll and we positioned ourselves in the middle of the tunnel. The powerful roar of the propeller came on and drowned out all other sounds.

The rainfall came on pretty quick. By the time the wind speed reached 120 kph (74 mph), I was soaked. I also quickly became aware that it is incredibly difficult to remain balanced in 120-kph winds, but I managed to do so anyway.

However, now that the wind speed was much faster, the rain felt like hail stones. I was constantly being hit in the faces with these rock-like water droplets. Dennis was having a lot of difficulty with the pain as well; he couldn't stand it. After four minutes, Dennis gestured that he was done. When they turned the propeller turned off, he explained to the crew why he had stopped. Then he returned to the heated room to warm himself back up.

My turn.

They turned the propeller back on and the rain began to fall once again. I was able to easily hold my ground from the practice that I had in the last attempt. I was in the zone. I began to tap my heel and sing while the winds approached 120 kph (74 mph). Harder and harder, the wind picked up speed. I continued to go deeper into my song, and myself, to try to bring out my spirit.

After going deeper, I began to sense a presence. I felt like I was not myself. It felt like there was an Indian spirit inside of me. I was singing chants and I felt connected to the wind; I could identify with it. The cold of the winds didn't bother me anymore. I was in a trance and in total control. I felt like I was facing a great force, but felt no fear or danger. I was facing it with total tranquility.

I had never experienced something like this feeling before; it was incredibly intense. I felt like I was on top of the world. Even my experience on Mount Everest couldn't compare. The camera team was mesmerized, but the their cameras continued to roll. The doctor was telling the crew to break off the experiment, but they were all too intrigued by the peace I was showing. I felt so much in balance that I raised one foot of the ground and was now fighting against 120 kph (74 mph) winds while only standing on one foot, like a flamingo.

Soon after, someone heard the cry of the doctor and signaled to turn off the experiment. They didn't understand that I was perfectly fine, but they broke it off anyway. I felt nothing but greatness. I had seen the identity of the wind and the spectators told me that watching the experience had emotionally touched them.

Deep down, we all have a part of us that has the ability to connect with the elements of nature. We have the potential to connect with it fully and have our bodies adapt. Indians, who were close to nature, understood this very well and had the wisdom of the land. In civilization, we have lost that ability. Nature has the ability to make us whole -- to fulfill us.

Therefore, we must strive to become "*wholy*."

CHAPTER 34:
PREPARING FOR MOUNT BLANC

I didn't get to spend much time with my family after returning home. I needed to get back to work to pay for my rent at college. Not only that, but I needed to begin saving up for my trip to Mount Blanc. My parents were sad to hear that I would be returning to Europe again in just a few short months. They felt that climbing a mountain in only shorts and sandals was pushing my luck, but I was determined to go.

Brooke and I drove back to State College only two days after I flew in to Pittsburgh. The first thing I did when I returned to Penn State was visit my ex-manager at The Deli. I went in the morning, before the restaurant opened, to speak with him. I found him sitting at the bar reading a newspaper.

"Good morning Joe! How's it going?" I asked.

"Fine," he replied. Joe wasn't much of a talker.

"Well, I wanted to stop in and see how you were doing. I also thought I'd see if you still had any full-time positions open as a dishwasher."

"Dishwashers… No. Only part time. It's dead in the summer after all of the students leave. I only need part-time people right now."

"Oh," I replied, slightly disappointed. "Well, okay. Do you think you could let me know if any full-time positions open up?"

"Full-time? Yes. I will." He took a sip from his coffee and went back to reading his newspaper. I took that as my cue to leave.

"Well, it was good seeing you Joe!" I began walking toward the entrance.

"You too. Goodbye. Wait, how was Poland?" he asked. I was surprised he had remembered.

"Oh, it was good. Had a nice time. Thanks for asking."

"Glad to hear it. Take care, Justin." He gave me a quick smile and returned to his newspaper.

I was overcome with disappointment as I left The Deli. I had hoped to get my old job back as a dishwasher and begin making money. Working at The Deli was my only plan. I had no clue as to how I was going to raise however-many thousands of dollars to get to Mount Blanc.

On my way home, I tried coming up with other ideas. I considered working at other restaurants, but I knew that it could take weeks before I would actually get my first paycheck. I needed to begin making money, immediately. That's when it hit me -- I could apply for Penn State's Summer Work Study program and work in the research lab for money instead of credits! The question was: would it be enough?

When I got home, I phoned my friends in the research lab and asked about the Work Study program. Anthony, the graduate student that I worked under, said it would be okay to work in the lab for money. I just needed to apply to the program via the university's website. After I got off the phone, I went online and signed up. I didn't know how much I would be able to make, but I hoped that it would be enough.

While I waited for a response from the Student Aid office, I realized that I would also need to take two summer courses, 4 credits each. As I went through the course list to pick out my classes, I found only two that really appealed to me: Russian 001 and Russian 002. What I didn't realize at the time was that they were intensive courses. This means that each class stuffs a semester's worth of information into two weeks. I signed up for the courses and told myself that, if everything worked out with the Work Study program, I could hopefully find a way to juggle the workload. I knew that if I survived, it would all be worth it.

A few days after applying, I heard back from the Student Aid office. I had been approved for the Work Study program for the amount of $2,500 dollars while working full-time. This meant that I could work up to 40 hours a week, every week, until I had accumulated all 2,500 dollars. Hopefully, it would be enough money to pay for my living expenses, food, and cover my costs for Mount Blanc. If I were going to make all of that money in time, I would need to put in 40 hours, every week, until I left. It was overwhelming to think about.

Regardless, I knew what I wanted to do. If I wanted to climb Mount Blanc, I would need to raise the money. It wasn't just for me; it was to support Wim. We were spiritual brothers and I wanted to make sure that he could always count on me. I didn't spend a week in Poland just to move on when I came home. The experience had changed my life; there was no reverting back to the old me.

After I got things organized with my research lab and the financial office, I called Brooke to tell her the good news. She was happy for me, but seemed a bit sad. Apparently, her lease was ending soon and would need to move back home. I told her that she was welcome to stay at my house for the summer, as long as she didn't mind me being gone most of the day. She was delighted and more than happy to take me up on my offer. She moved in over the next few days.

Soon after Brooke moved in, my work in the research lab began. For the first few weeks, it was easy work. Most of my time was spent organizing the lab drives. After a while though, the work began to pick up. The Principal Investigator of my lab, Dr. Reginald Adams, was leaving for a month and wanted me to help take over a project of his. When he left, there was a lot of miscommunication on my behalf. The matter sorted itself out eventually, but it created a problem that spiraled downward. Regardless, I made a point to come to the lab daily, usually working for 7 to 8 hours in a row. I always made sure to stop when I had reached my total of 40 hours.

As the middle of June approached, so did my Russian classes. I had never taken Russian before, but I was always interested in learning. The language intrigued me.

Starting the middle of June, my class hours were Monday through Friday, 9:05 AM to 3:30 PM with a 30-minute break for lunch at noon. This schedule threw me for a loop. I hadn't anticipated class to be that long. Regardless, I sucked it up and rearranged my lab hours to fit my schedule.

My weekday schedule now looked like this:
  6:30 - 7:30 AM: Eat breakfast and go for a run with Brooke
  7:30 - 8:00 AM: Take a shower
  8:00 - 8:35 AM: Study Russian
  8:35 AM: Begin my 30-minute walk to class
  9:05 - 12:00 PM: Russian Class
  12:00 - 12:30 PM: Brooke makes me food and we meet me for lunch
  12:30 - 3:30 PM: Russian Class
  3:30 - 4:00 PM: Eat a quick snack/Walk to the research lab
  4:00 - 12:00 AM: Work in the research lab
Sometimes, if I had to miss an hour or two from the research lab, I'd make it up on the weekends to fill my 40 hours. It was a hectic schedule. I was lucky to have Brooke staying with me for the sum-

mer; otherwise I wouldn't have had anyone to talk to. She made for great company.

During the weekends, I would spend my time either studying Russian or making up missed hours in the research lab. Sadly, there was no time for Iceman training. My goal was to make it to Mount Blanc. I figured I could begin training again once my Russian classes were over.

...

The days dragged on and I quickly grew tired of the routine. I felt like I was a prisoner. Numerous times, I reminded myself that I was working for a good cause, that soon I would be back in Europe climbing Mount Blanc with "The Iceman." Sometimes, it was enough to calm me down. Other times, I would lay awake at night, asking myself if it was really worth it. I was always able to talk myself into sticking with the routine, even though there were a few close calls when I had come close to quitting. The day after my last Russian class had ended, I received this email from Wim.

"Hi Justin,

The total amount that you will have to pay in Europe will be 700 euros. This includes climbing Mount Blanc and transportation from Amsterdam Schiphol airport.

You will need to arrive in Europe no later than August 4. We will arrive back in Amsterdam on August 11.

You will need to bring a rucksack, sleeping bag, clothes etc. Climbing equipment will be available at the location, provided by the group (Chamonix).

We will prepare our own food and buy groceries before we go.

We'll stay at the campsite first, and then take a trolley up to 2,400 meters (7,874 feet) to acclimatize. As soon as everyone acclimatizes, we'll make our final climb to the top. It is best to leave early, something like 3:00 AM. It will then take us four or five hours to reach the summit.

It is a beautiful challenge, which I'm sure you already know.

Greetings,
Wim"

700 euros is the equivalent of about $1,014; that's pretty expensive for a college student. I was cutting it close. At the time, I was two weeks away from receiving the rest of my $2,500 from the Work

Study program. After receiving this email, I did something that was either very brave or very stupid; I went online and purchased my plane ticket.

The total cost was $1,190.90, a giant dent in my wallet. My reasoning for doing so was to put myself in a situation where I would feel like my only option was to succeed. Sadly, that is **not** how I felt at first. After purchasing the ticket, I severely regretted it.

Take a moment and consider my cost of my rent each month. Including utilities, it's about $400. If you multiply that by the three months I lived in my apartment, that's $1,200. Luckily, some of my college loans paid for some of my housing, knocking off $600. This left me with only paying $600 for housing and about $150 for food. This also made me very conservative about what I ate. To save money, for weeks I would only eat pasta, peanut butter and jelly sandwiches, and items from McDonald's dollar menu. It may not have been healthy, but at least I didn't starve.

After subtracting living expenses and the total cost of my plane ticket, I only had about $559 after I had received my final paycheck. That's a little over half of what I needed to pay Wim for Mount Blanc. With no other forms of income, I resorted to other means. I began giving plasma again, which my parents didn't like, and started selling some of my older possessions. In total, that gave me $900. I was so close, but my flow of income had stopped.

One hour before I left State College, after I had packed all of my things that I was taking to Europe, I came up with one last idea. I had been saving all of my Psychology books that I had bought over the years, to use for future reading. I decided it was time to sell them back to the bookstore and use the money for my trip. I searched through my house and found twelve old Psychology books. Throwing them into a bag, I made my way downtown to the bookstore. They gave me $250 for the lot of them, bringing my total to $1,150! I was ecstatic. I was the happiest I had been in a long time. All my worries were washed away and everything was *finally* set up. All the effort I had put forth felt worth it.

My family warmly greeted us when Brooke and I had arrived at my house. Once again, I could tell from their faces that they were worried. After giving everyone hugs and bringing my stuff into the house, my father approached me.

"Listen Justin, I know you really want to go climb this mountain, but I want to give you another option. I will reimburse all of the money you paid for your plane ticket and fly you to Hawaii instead, if you change your mind about climb Mt. Blanc."

"Thanks Dad," I said, "I really appreciate it, but this is something

I really want to do. I want to support Wim and do something with my life. I don't want to be like everyone else that he trained and leave it in the past. I want to become like him. I want to become The Iceman too."

"So, nothing I can say will change your mind?" he asked, putting his hand on my shoulder.

"Sorry Dad, but I have to do this. I have committed to it."

"Okay Son, I love you. Just do your mother and I a favor and come back to us safe, please."

We embraced each other and I thanked him once more for caring.

CHAPTER 35:
HELLO... SPAIN?

August 2, 2010

The day of my departure, I received this email from Wim.

"Hi Justin,

> I know that you are on your way to Amsterdam now.
> Great adventures are awaiting us; there is no doubt.
> I am excited, however, the weather is dangerously bad on Mt. Blanc.
> I might reconsider the location.
> Whatever happens, we will go deep and straight like an arrow.

Live life,
Wim"

What? What was he talking about? Even though I hadn't trained for the past couple months because I had been so busy, I was still expecting to climb Mount Blanc when we got there. I was suddenly glad that I purchased a plane ticket that took me there a day early and was flying me back two days after we were supposed to return from Mount Blanc. At least I would have some flexibility.

That's when I realized that there was absolutely nothing I could do. I certainly wasn't going to tell my parents about Wim's surprise email. They took what comfort they could in knowing where I would be at all times. If I told them that I was going to Europe for a week with no idea where I'd end up, they would freak out and probably rip up my plane ticket. So, I kept up the facade and pretended like I had never received that email.

Around 11:00 AM (EST), my mother and Brooke drove me to the

airport. They both shed tears during the car ride. When we arrived at the airport, we unpacked my luggage from the car and walked in. While I checked in my bags, Brooke and my mother disappeared. They came back a moment later with a brown paper bag.

"What's this?" I asked.

"We wanted to buy you a gift," my mother replied, "so you would remember us."

I took the contents out of the bag. It was a solar-powered keychain with my name on it. "Pittsburgh" was inscribed on the back.

"Every time it's in the sun," Brooke said, "your name will blink. We hope you like it." Brooke's eyes filled with tears again.

"I love it, thanks guys." I hugged them both and they began crying in unison.

"We'll miss you," they said together.

With one last squeeze, I told them that I loved them and walked toward security.

"Thanks again guys!" I called back.

After clearing security, I located my gate and immediately boarded my flight.

Welp, I thought, *this should be interesting.*

...

When I arrived at Amsterdam's airport, Konrad was there to pick me up. I found him looking at a giant screen that showed the flight arrivals.

"Hello Konrad," I muttered. He turned around, surprised to see me. His face was shaved and he looked much skinner than the last time I had seen him.

"Oh! Hello Justin," he replied. "Wim sent me to come pick you up. He will meet us at my house later. Is that okay?"

I laughed, "Of course that's okay. What am I going to say, no?"

He bought me a ticket for the train and we rode back to his house. It had been a long time since we had seen each other. It was refreshing to see a familiar face. It reminded me of our times in Poland. Through previous emails, I had heard from Wim that Konrad would be joining us on our trip to Mount Blanc.

When we arrived at his house, he told me that he wouldn't be going with us on the trip. He had run into an unfortunate set of circumstances that had left him with no money. I was disappointed that he wouldn't be going.

A few hours later, Konrad received a call from Wim.

"Wim says he will be here soon. He is riding his bicycle over,"

Konrad told me.

"Great!" I said enthusiastically.

Wim walked through the front door of Konrad's apartment half an hour later.

"Hello Justin!" He embraced me. Wim was wearing a crimson sweatshirt and long brown pants.

"It is good to see you again, my friend," he said.

"Yeah, it's good to see you too," I replied. "So, what's the plan?"

"We are not going to Mount Blanc. The weather is too dangerous there -- avalanches and such. Instead, we will go canyoning in Spain. We will meet my son, Enahm, there."

"Uh, wait… Canyoning in Spain? Isn't it hot there?" I started to regret packing all of my winter clothes. I only had one pair of shorts!

"Yes, very hot, but do not worry. Everything will be okay."

"Well, how much is it going to cost? I only have the 700 euros you told me to bring." I began to worry.

"The same price. It will be enough to cover your expenses. I am not charging you to be with me, but we will all split the expenses."

"Oh, okay. Wait a second. I thought Konrad wasn't going. Who "all" do you mean?"

"It will be you, me, Enahm, and Dennis, but Enahm will meet us there. We have to pick up Dennis later today."

"Who's Dennis?" I was starting to realize how much I didn't know.

"He is a good guy. I met him a few days ago."

"Okay Wim. Well, I guess I'm up for whatever."

He looked at me and smiled, "Great! Now, I have to go meet Caroline in the park. You guys should come. Meet me there in an hour, okay?"

He left as quickly as he had come.

"I guess we're going to the park," I said while smiling.

…

About an hour later, Konrad and I had found Wim in the park. He was talking to a blond-haired woman and a little blond-haired boy. We approached them.

"Hello," Konrad and I said in unison.

"Hey guys!" Wim said back. "This lovely woman is Caroline," he placed his right hand on her left shoulder and smiled, "and this is my boy, Noah."

Konrad and I shook hands with Caroline and waved to Noah. Noah seemed shy; he clung to his father when we tried speaking to him.

"He doesn't speak English, yet," Caroline informed me.

"That's okay. Does he like to play?" I asked.

"Yes!" Wim said. He told something to Noah in Dutch, and then looked back at me. "He wants to be like his father. He likes doing yoga positions and gymnastics, yet he's only 7 years old! He'll show you."

Noah ran over to a nearby log and climbed on top of it. He looked at me and smiled. All of a sudden, he bent down and threw his body into a cartwheel.

"Wow!" I said, giving Noah a thumbs up. "Well done!"

He continued to show off for the next ten minutes. Eventually, I joined in and did a few somersaults as well. When we grew tired of that, we grabbed a pair of sticks and pretended they were swords. I had a lot of fun with Noah; he had a lot of energy, like his father.

While Noah and I played around, I could hear Wim and Konrad talking about the barefoot-snow run in Karpacz.

"Listen," Konrad said. "If we are going to do the run in Karpacz, I need more details. I need to start organizing things. Otherwise, my cousin will cancel the event altogether."

"Yeah, yeah," Wim replied, "it will all work out. These things always work out. Just give it time. We will figure it out later."

"But Wim," Konrad insisted, "we can't wait anymore. I think it would be best to try to organize the run somewhere else. Maybe we can hold the run in Karpacz after it's held somewhere else first."

"Okay," Wim replied, "let's do that then."

Soon after, Wim came over to Noah and hugged him goodbye. "I have to go," he told me. "I will pick you up from Konrad's house first thing in the morning. I will be there early, so be ready."

"All right," I said, "Goodbye Wim."

He jumped on his bike and rode away. Konrad and I stayed for another ten minutes, talking to Caroline. When Konrad remembered that he was running out of time on the parking meter, we ran back to the car and returned to his house. Konrad re-told me what him and Wim were discussing in the park; he wasn't aware that I had overheard them talking. I expressed my concern and proposed that we could try doing the run in the U.S.

"That's a good idea," he said. "It could be a lot of work. It will be up to you to organize it."

"I'll figure it out," I told him. I was excited to have the opportunity to organize the event in the U.S. I put it in the back of my mind to think about later. My main focus was Spain. I didn't know what to expect. It was something that I had come to understand from being friends with Wim: he always had surprises up his sleeves.

I awoke the next morning at 5:00 AM to get a shower. I didn't know how long of a car ride it was to Spain, but I assumed that it was farther than Poland, meaning that we would be on the road for a *long* time. While I was in the shower, I tried to imagine myself canyoning in Spain. The images that popped into my head were of me falling off cliffs into a hole the size of the Grand Canyon. I shook my head, trying to rid my mind of the pessimistic thoughts. I knew that I would be with Wim and he was usually very safe to be around. I knew I could trust him.

When I got out of the shower, I went on my computer and emailed my parents and Brooke, letting them know I would now be going to Spain instead of Mount Blanc. I figured that they wouldn't take it very well, but their response wasn't going to stop me. I was in Europe under the care of Wim. I had no choice where I was going to go. My last words in the emails were "I'll try to be safe." It was the only comfort I could offer them, and the only promise I could keep.

Around 6:30 AM, Wim pulled up in a small green car that I had never seen before.

"Hey Wim!" I called as he opened the driver's side door. "Whose car is this?"

"I borrowed it from a friend of mine," he replied. "His name is Manely. He is doing a documentary on me. Since Konrad can't come and he needs his jeep, I needed to find another way to transport us to Spain. Come on, we have to go pick up Dennis."

We packed the car with my stuff and bid farewell to Konrad. We drove thirty minutes into the town of Amsterdam until we had arrived in a vacant parking lot.

"He's meeting us here," Wim said.

"Where are we?" I asked.

"The place he told us to meet him."

Wim and I sat in the car for a few minutes, waiting for Dennis, until we noticed a coffee shop nearby. We got out of the car and walked over to grab a couple coffees while we waited. We took a seat near the window so that we could watch when Dennis pulled in. Soon enough, an unfamiliar car drove in and parked next to our small green car.

Wim paid for our coffees and we made our way outside to meet Dennis. When the car door opened, a tall blond man with braces emerged. He had bright blue eyes and was wearing a tight black shirt. He seemed to be slightly older than I.

"Hello Dennis!" Wim yelled, extending his arms to hug him.

"Hello Wim!" Dennis accepted his hug and turned to me.

"And you must be, Justin?" he asked.

"That is correct," I replied, extending my hand to shake his. "Pleasure to meet you, Dennis."

Several people got out of the car and hugged Dennis goodbye. I assumed it was his family.

"This is my wife," he said.

"Be careful," the woman told me. She appeared to be the same age as Dennis. I grabbed her hand and shook it.

"All right," Wim announced, "Time to go! We have a lot of driving to do."

We said goodbye to Dennis' family, jumped into the car, and began our journey to Spain.

During the first few hours, Wim, Dennis and myself spent some time getting to know each other. I learned that Wim had met Dennis a few days before at one of his world record attempts. Dennis had asked about joining one of Wim's adventures sometime soon, so Wim invited him along. I also learned that Dennis was a motivational speaker and loved the power of the mind. He was selling his interior design company to become a life coach. It all seemed very interesting.

Eventually, the barefoot-snow run was brought up.

"Dennis," Wim said, "Justin and I are organizing a barefoot-snow run in Poland!"

"Wait a second," I interjected, "aren't we not doing it in Poland anymore?"

"Oh yes," he said, "I forgot."

"Well," I continued, "I was thinking... What if we did the barefoot-snow run in the U.S.? There is a park near my house where we could try to organize it."

"That is a great idea!" Wim said. "Oh! I can even break a world record, while sitting in the ice, to draw more people in to the event. We can do a workshop too!"

"Yeah, that doesn't sound like a bad idea. My family owns a small business back home and they rent out a building. You can break the world record and do the workshop in there."

"Perfect!" he said, visibly excited. "Let's make it happen. I'll let you organize it, Justin."

"Speaking of running barefooted," Dennis said, "have you ever seen these shoes before?"

He lifted up his feet and presented his strange footwear. "They are called, Vibram FiveFingers. This particular model is the KSO. They are amazing. They simulate barefoot running and are supposed to be better for your knees, joints, and feet."

"That's awesome!" I said. "I'll have to look into those." I really liked the design of the shoe. It gave me a great idea. If I were going to participate in the barefoot-snow run, I would need to start running around barefooted. On the sidewalks and streets at Penn State, you can sometimes find broken shards of glass. You could understand why it's not an ideal environment to run on barefooted. I also noticed that the material on the shoe looked relatively thin, assuming that there would be less protection from the cold. Dennis' Vibram FiveFingers shoes quickly became a viable option to allow me to run barefooted through the snow at Penn State, without cutting up my feet.

Soon after the conversation about the barefoot-snow run ended, I fell asleep. The jet lag had finally caught up to me.

CHAPTER 36:
THE SPANISH PYRENEES

Our drive took us from the Netherlands took us through Belgium, France, and finally Spain. Justin slept a lot because he was still jet-lagged from the traveling. In that time, Dennis and I conversed in Dutch and got to know each other on a deeper level. He expressed that he came on the trip because he wanted to learn about The Iceman from the intellectual side.

When we passed through the South of France, the atmosphere changed. The architecture of the buildings looked older and much more unique. Eventually, we crossed the France border and entered the Beisla tunnel, leading us into Spain.

As we drove through the Sierra de Guara, which is a desert-like area just south of the Spanish Pyrenees, I had a strange feeling. It had been 10 years since I was last in the Spanish Pyrenees. I felt like I was finally coming home.

We arrived at 2:00 AM and found Enahm sleeping in a hammock at the campsite. He had arrived a day early and set up the tents so that we could crash as soon as we got there. It was a long day of driving, so we left the introductions for the following day.

Sunshine greeted us in the morning. It was a typical day in the Spanish Pyrenees. When I opened my eyes, I noticed a Baccata Big-nonioides tree to my side. They are well known for providing a lot of shade as well as large beans.

We met for coffee at the restaurant, located on site, and discussed our plans for the day. Eventually, we all decided to start with canyon-ing and end with puenting.

Canyoning is a great way to become one with nature. It a very play-ful and an exciting experience. Water channels that eroded away at the space between the mountains produced the canyons in the Pyr-enees. We now use ropes and other safety equipment to rappel down it. We left our car at the site and we all drove together in Enahm's van.

Enahm is a 28 year old who loves spending his time canyoning. He's a tall guy with a very contagious smile. He loves the outdoors and is a very enthusiastic gentleman. His most recent goal has been to set up a canyoning business. He wants me to join him because I have a lot of experience. I worked for 9 years as a guide through the Spanish Pyrenees. Spain is like my second home.

Enahm drives like a racer; we had to hold our bodies against the force of every turn he made. We drove through the desert-like region until we had reached our first canyon, the Barranco del Rio.

The Barranco del Rio is what we call a "water canyon." This means that inside the canyon, there are many holes and paths filled with water. Sometimes, the holes in the canyon are as deep as 50 meters (164.04 feet).

To get to the bottom, we must crawl, jump, and balance on top of rocks and push ourselves to descend further and further down the canyon. On the way down, the beauty of our surroundings are revealed.

Descending can feel like you're trying to find your way through a labyrinth. Mysterious places are all around and it can sometimes be cathartic. Especially if there is cold water flowing along the path, which there usually is.

The shadows danced across the rocky walls as the sun changed its position. The sound of our voices echoed against the rocks. The mouth at the bottom of the canyon opened into a large emerald lake; warm water greeted us as we exited.

Dennis and I coated our bodies with mud from the bottom of the shallow lake. We let the sun dry the mud on our skin to give us a make over. The mud cleans the surface of the body and gives a nice, smooth feeling.

We had a lot of fun enjoying our stay in Sierra de Guara. After a quick picnic and a good bath, we threw our rucksacks back on, wrapped our ropes, and began hiking our way back up the mountain to where we had parked the van.

The heat of the Spanish summer sun soon had us sweating, but the panorama was beautiful and the lake was enthralling. After hiking through the densely covered mountain with many trees and bushes, we finally found our way back to the parked van where we had started hours before.

We placed our equipment in the back of the van and continued to our next activity, puenting. The drive was bumpy again as Enahm kept his foot on the pedal. After several minutes, we had arrived at our puenting bridge. The bridge was raised about 60 meters (200 feet) over the water.

I knew what to expect because I had puented hundreds of times before, with many other people, but the last time I did that was just over ten years ago. I fell silent with excitement. Puenting is an activity where one person has one end of two ropes tied to their harness, while the other end is tied to the bridge. Before putting the ropes on the individual, they are pulled underneath the bridge and tied to the opposite side of the railing. Then, the person fastens the ropes to their harness, using carabineers, and jumps off. The ropes that are tied to the other end of the bridge cause the person to fall straight down until the ropes catch them. At that point, the person swings back and forth from side to side until they lose momentum. You could think of it as a gigantic swing.

During those first few seconds of free fall, it is very common to feel like there is an imminent danger of falling to your death. The tension of the abyss is enormous and sometimes will prevent people from taking the plunge. However, with a little encouragement, most are willing to try.

I decided to go first to make sure the ropes were connected properly. Not knowing is always a scary feeling, but I had experience and was ready to complete my first jump in ten years. I took a few careful breaths and began concentrating.

One of the most important things to remember when puenting is that you must jump straight off the bridge. Any other angle can prove dangerous because you will enter the possibility of swinging into the bridge.

I jumped. The first few seconds of free fall are the best part of puenting. I continually picked up speed until the ropes caught me and swung me to the other side.

Knowing that you are capable of overcoming hesitation can be a powerful tool. It's an amazing feeling that gives you boosts of adrenaline and a rush of endorphins.

After my ride ended, I connected myself to another wire that they had thrown down. I then lowered myself into the water below. After 20 minutes of preparation, it was Dennis' turn.

Dennis is a powerful, analytic thinker. He knows the mind well. All he needed to jump off the bridge was a decision that he was going to be stronger than the fear, which he was. After saying, "mental power," Dennis jumped backwards into the abyss.

After another 20 minutes, it was Justin's turn to jump. Regardless of seeming nervous and tense, he jumped backward off the bridge without any hesitation whatsoever. Although, after a few minutes of swinging back and forth, Justin's motion sickness had kicked in and he began to throw up. He was successful, but a slave to his genetic disposition.

After Justin had detached himself and swam to shore, it was Enahm's turn. No one knew that he was going. He jumped off the side of the bridge while no one was looking. The experience of adventure is what Enahm lives for.

After Enahm disconnected himself and returned to the top of the bridge, we disconnected the ropes and returned to our van. We all felt different, accomplished. On the way home, we stopped by a river where there was a bridge 9 meters (29.5 feet) high. Justin still felt a little sick, so he stayed in the car while the rest of us went to leap off the bridge. From the bridge, Enahm backflipped, I dove, and Dennis jumped.

When we returned to the campsite, we made pasta with a nice mixture of vegetables and wine. Enahm and I played guitar together and sang a beautiful tune.

The next day, we traveled to a canyon 50 kilometers (31 miles) away called La Panilla. The canyon was known for its large rappelling walls made of limestone. Wild horses and other fauna surrounded us as we made our way to the top of the canyon.

When we had reached the top, we put on our harnesses, prepared our ropes, and got our cameras ready. It would be a few hours before we reached the bottom of the canyon, so we also had to mentally prepare ourselves.

We groped, jumped, and balanced our way to the bottom of the first rappelling wall. Rappelling is a calming movement down the rocky walls in nature. You have to surrender yourself to the materials protecting you. It can be scary at times, but you have to overcome that fear. Once you begin, there is no turning back. The only option is down.

When rappelling, people tend to hold on to the rocks and stay as close as possible to the wall. This is the complete opposite of what is necessary. It is important to make sure that there is never any slack in the rope. To do this, you must lean back at all times and stay focused on having your feet flat on the surface. Yes, it may be scary because it's an unnatural position to be in, but it is a necessity to rappel safely. Once accustomed to the material and the way of using it, it's easy to go down very quickly.

At the point when the inhibitions vanish, you are able to enjoy the scenery and view the great panoramas. It's a hands-on way to enjoy nature.

Sometimes, people expect happiness to just enter their lives and change them from the outside, but it doesn't work like that. Those people need to work things out inside themselves. Happiness must spread from the inside out. I know this because I did a lot of problem solving to answer my own riddles. It took me a lot of time and confidence before I could view the world in color, rather than only black and white.

For a while, I was emotionally disturbed. I looked for all kinds of challenges to take my mind off of worrying. Eventually, I found that "nature" was the answer I was looking for all along. The answer varies from person to person, but that is because each person has his or her own path.

We need to contemplate and look inside ourselves. Contemplation is the last stage before clarity. Try to open your mind and experience the world for what it is, not what for you want it to be.

When we finally got to the bottom of La Panilla, we went swimming in a beautiful, sapphire-blue river. Enahm left to go pick up the van while Justin, Dennis and myself got to swim around. It was very relaxing after a long day of rappelling.

When Enahm had returned, we went back to the campsite and made dinner. Guitar music and laughter filled the air until we grew tired and fell asleep.

The next morning we awoke at 5:00 AM. We had planned to go climb and rappel a gigantic canyon, El Mascun. Enahm was not able to come on the trip because he made plans elsewhere, but Justin and Dennis were ready for anything.

We drove through the early morning and crossed Sierra de Guara. After three hours of curvy roads, we had finally reached the little village of Rodellar, which is at the boarder of the natural reserve for Sierra de Guara."

El Mascun is the Arabic name of the place that represents where spirits reside. For that reason, people in ancient times would avoid the canyon because of the sinister atmosphere.

In reality, El Mascun is a living museum with gigantic monoliths everywhere. There are fossilized rocks at the top of the canyon at 1100 meters (3,608 feet). The mountain is the result of tectonic plates moving throughout thousands of years.

We got out of the car and took our backpacks up the winding path of the mountain. Soon, we began to see the mountain for the beautiful place that it was. Cars are not allowed near the mountain, so anyone who wants to rappel it needs to hike a trail for many hours before they can begin to descend.

When we reached the top, iron nails attached to ropes greeted us. The view was magnificent; pine trees surrounded the mountain on all sides. After gearing up, we tied into the ropes and began abseiling. Again, the feeling of overcoming inhibitions washed over me. Where most would feel imminent danger, I felt peace. We all did. Each cliff was a new challenge, one that we were always anxious to overcome.

El Mascun didn't "let us down." It was full of exhilarating twists and turns and we were never bored. We had arrived early in the morning and didn't return until the late evening. It had been a beautiful day and we slept with the weight of success on our shoulders.

Then, came Monte Perdido. Located in Ordessa National Park, Monte Perdido reigns at 3355 meters (11,007 feet). It was the largest mountain we had set our sights on. Enahm was still gone and wouldn't be able to join us for our ascent.

What the Monte Perdido lacks in abseiling, it makes up for in terrain. The night before our final expedition, we rested our bodies on a campground a few miles away from Ordessa. After a hearty dinner, we talked about what we had accomplished thus far and what we hoped to gain on Monte Perdido. When the sun slept, so did we.

The next morning we packed up our sleeping bags and drove to a bus station. On the bus ride to Ordessa, we weaved through many narrow turns. For most of the ride we teetered on the edge of a large crater, similar to America's Grand Canyon.

The bus took us to Ordessa at 1,300 meters (4,265 feet). We grabbed a cup of coffee from the local shop and started the hour hike to the beginning of the Monte Perdido path.

Forests full of pine and fagus sylvatica trees surrounded us. The luscious combination provided beautiful scenery for the hike. Once we arrived at the Monte Perdido trail, the incline became steeper. After an hour and a half of climbing, we made had our way past the point at which trees stop growing and the alpine vegetation begins.

After a couple more hours, we finally arrived at the Clavijas de Cotatuero. This is the point on the mountain where this is no trail. The only way to continue on the path is to climb up metal nails that are cemented into the wall.

Justin, Dennis and myself had our backpacks and sleeping bags weighing us down. We had brought no climbing equipment with us, but we didn't need it. Our mission was about overcoming inhibitions.

If anyone is unfamiliar with this type of climbing, vertigo may be one of the problems that he or she may have to overcome. This was the case for Justin. Despite his fear of heights, he forced himself to continue on with steady hands and careful steps. Even though he may have had a bit of hesitation, he was still able to climb Clavijas de Cotatuero with ease.

In these moments, time seems to stand still. Nothing else matters except for that next step. If your focus is on anything else, you will fall. These moments can teach us to remain in the present.

Dennis was the last to cross the Clavijas de Cotatuero. He made it swiftly and safely across. A great feeling of accomplishment was present in all of us. We took several minutes to rest and meditate on a rock, hundreds of meters above the ground.

After our little break, we continued on our path. When we reached the upper part of the walls facing Ordessa, we pulled ourselves over the cliff. Our eyes were blessed with beauty. Thousands of beautiful blue and purple flowers, known as Iris Xiphioides, were laid out across the land. There was also a miniature waterfall that opened into a stream, feeding water down the center and over the cliff. It was a surreal atmosphere.

To me, this view alone is more beautiful than Mount Everest. It is always the same thing on Everest -- rocks, snow and ice. Nothing grows at that altitude; all life is gone. On Monte Perdido, the climate changes the higher you climb. Therefore, you pass all kinds of vegetation during the ascent, providing the eyes with new surprises every step of the way.

At 2:00 PM we reached a refuge at 2,160 meters (7,086 feet). We rested for half an hour, raised our expectations, and then set sail for the summit. Normally, a climb to the summit of Monte Perdido should be done on a separate day, after resting at the refuge, but we were determined to continue on.

As the path became steeper and more difficult, the air became colder. Justin and I were wearing only shorts and sandals. Dennis was wearing a black t-shirt, pants, and his hiking boots. We had left behind our sleeping bags and backpacks at the refuge. The people that we passed were astounded when they saw us attempting to summit the snow-covered slopes of Monte Perdido, while only wearing limited clothing.

At 3,000 meters (9,842 feet) we were still going strong. The air was thinning out and the path was becoming even steeper. Our minds were being tested to overcome fear and fatigue.

We made our way over the snow-covered rocks, climbing along at a slow pace to preserve our energy. After a while, Dennis stopped and decided to turn around. He had done exceptionally well, but in his mind he had already decided to turn back. We told our friend goodbye and continued onward toward the summit.

Adorned with great views, we felt like eagles -- free from the worries of the world. Our majestic panorama was the result of much physical and mental endurance. It was the fruit of hard labor and constant meditation.

Near the final stretch, Justin and I decided to take a break and sat down on two large rocks.

"Wim," Justin said, "I was waiting for the right time to tell you about something that has been on my mind for a while. I think now is the perfect time."

My ears listened attentively to Justin's every word. Curiosity consumed me.

"I was thinking about writing a book entitled *Becoming the Iceman*. I have been keeping track of all of the stuff that we have done over the past year and I think it would make for an incredible book. Ideally, it wouldn't include only the things that I have learned, but your experiences as well."

"In it," he continued, "I think it would be great to have stories leading up to what made you *The Iceman*. If we combine both of our experiences and include the challenges we had to overcome to become Icemen, it may have the potential to inspire others. We could give people the opportunity to become Icemen and Icewomen, especially if the book contained the method and technique."

My mind was eager and my body language began to show it. Yes, this is what I wanted as a book! I didn't just want a book comprised of methods and techniques. I wanted a book full of experiences that would inspire people to become better and give them the knowledge they needed to succeed.

This book needs to happen, I thought.

"One more thing," Justin said. "I think it would be important to show that it is possible for anyone to do what you have done. To show that we all have the potential inside of us. A skill that just needs to be trained. I think a way we could show that is by you and I breaking a world record together. It could make our words more credible. What do you think?"

"Yes!" I told him. "We need to break a world record together! It will be like I am passing the torch on to you. It would be a lovely way to end the book. This time, I'll come to you. Let's do it in America!"

It was a marvelous idea and a great concept. Out of excitement and appreciation, we embraced each other.

We never finished the climb to the summit, but we came back down in higher spirits than the summit could have ever given us. The idea was reward enough; there was no need to continue on.

With a great feeling of success, Justin and I continued our way back down to the refugee. Our stomachs were tightly clenched, telling us to eat immediately. We ate very little that day and climbed more than 3000 meters (9,842 feet) in height.

There were climbers from many different backgrounds at the refuge. At dinner, many languages were spoken around the table: French, Dutch, English, Spanish, German and even Basque. It's really great to know multiple languages; it helps me communicate and empathize with the random people I meet on a daily basis.

Finishing with wine and food was the perfect way to end our day. There was a lovely sunset outside. Instead of purchasing a room to sleep in that night, we decided to save the little money that we had to purchase breakfast in the morning.

That night, we slept in our sleeping bags on a grassy hill outside of the refugee. I counted many stars in the vast night sky as I lay there trying to fall asleep. My mind was too excited to rest. Eventually, my thoughts died down and the quiet, clear sky helped me dose off into a deep slumber.

The next day, we continued down the mountain. Justin was a little timid because his legs were sore and we had dangerous slopes to climb down without gear, but because he trusted me, we made it down safely. He got rid of his inhibitions and descended successfully.

During our long drive back, Justin and I discussed the possible world records we could attempt together.

"Well, instead of the barefoot-snow run that we were trying to organize in the US," he said, "Why don't we try to breaking a record together, first. Perhaps, we could try sitting with our bodies fully exposed in the ice, like you have done in the past?"

I shook my head, "No. That takes a lot of training and is extremely dangerous, even for myself. No, I know what we should do. We should try to set the fastest time for a 5 and 10-kilometer run, barefoot through the snow! What do you think?"

"I think that's a great idea, however, I will admit that I have had very little training running barefooted through the snow." I could tell from his voice that he was worried.

"Do no worry," I assured him. "It is very easy to learn. Very few people try. If you are determined to do it, you will adapt very quickly. I believe in you. We have to do it for the book!"

"All right, Wim," Justin replied. "I trust you. Barefoot running in the snow will be our record attempts.

The experiences that Dennis, Justin, Enahm, and myself had will never be forgotten. They are deeply rooted in our minds and brought us closer, like a family. Even though our memories of the Spanish Pyrenees will last forever, we now had bigger plans in the making.

CHAPTER 37:
RETURNING HOPEFUL TO AMERICA

I came back to America filled with new energy. Even though I had not climbed Mount Blanc, we had plans for a far greater goal. I was going to try and break a world record with my mentor and spiritual brother, The Iceman.

Classes began shortly after I had returned from Spain, but I didn't care. My mind was more focused on Becoming the Iceman. I had begun to take my training to a new level. I woke up every morning before class and went for a run in a nearby park. As I felt more comfortable, I tried running barefooted on the sidewalks; I watched my steps carefully to avoid stepping on broken glass. For the first few runs, it was extremely painful. I could never run more than a few blocks at a time before my feet blistered up. Each day after my, I would immediately shower to clean my cuts. When I got out, I would put on socks to provide some comfort for my wounds.

When I wasn't wearing socks to heal from running, I tried to remain in bare feet as much as possible. I did away with wearing shoes and resorted to only wearing my running sandals. The problem with running sandals is that they accumulate a lot of sweat over time, making them pretty smelly. Brooke wasn't a fan. So, I decided to go give plasma, save up a bit of money, and invest in the Vibram FiveFingers shoes that I had seen Dennis wearing in Europe.

Within a couple weeks, my KSO models arrived at my doorstep. By then, I had developed a few callouses on the bottom of my feet. Therefore, with and without the KSOs, I was able to run comfortably through the streets without feeling any pain. Although, I did like the KSO's a bit more compared to running barefooted. Running in the Vibrams gave me the chance to focus on my running and breathing, rather than constantly looking at the ground to avoid sharp objects.

As the warmer days of summer faded away and fall set in, I redirected my focus toward organizing the world record attempts. I received an email from Wim asking me to submit a few applications into Guinness World Records to see if we could legitimize our world record attempts. After class one day, I spent a couple hours going through the application process. The two applications I submitted were for fastest 5 and 10k barefoot through the snow.

With the applications submitted, I went back to focusing on my training. I started implementing cold exercises back into my daily routine, specifically, exercises that trained my feet. These included: **Foot Immersions** and **Ice Buckets** [*Refer to **Justin's Method** section for more information]. I performed these exercises several times a day.

As the fall semester continued on, my workload increased. It began eating away at my time for training. Therefore, I decided to make a change. I began cutting back on the amount of hours I slept each night. I learned from the cold water exercises that my body could handle anything I threw at it, so I figured it would be okay with a little bit of sleep deprivation. Now, I don't suggest that anyone else try this. It was just my way of coping with my situation at the time. I was persistent about pursuing further training, while still making time to do my homework.

For months, I survived off of only two hours of sleep. With all my extra time, I was able to finish all of my classroom assignments with a few weeks to spare before the semester ended, which is exactly what I needed. Soon after I had finished my assignments, I received an email from Guinness World Records stating that we would be able to attempt both records as long as we provided adequate proof and adhered to their requirements.   Assuming that I would be running the 5k and Wim would be running the 10k, my time to beat was 30 minutes, while Wim's time to beat was 60 minutes. I was unsure of whether or not I could beat that time, but I knew I had to try.

I began searching around for places that would be interested in holding our world record attempts. I called local parks, colleges, and even my friends to see if they had property that I could use. Everyone turned me down. No one would take our attempts seriously. The only people that supported us were a few friends of mine who were willing to do anything to see the event happen. They donated hundreds of dollars to try to help us organize the event, but when every place we spoke to turned us down, I returned all the money to the donors and wrote each of them an appreciation message. Our options became extremely limited. It looked like our hopes of attempting the world record in the U.S. were dying fast.

CHAPTER 38:
LECTURES FROM THE ICEMAN

*I*n November of 2010, an international conference was held in Florida where Professor Hopman presented her results from my autonomic nervous system test. She presented the results of my experiment from when I stood in a Perspex box full of ice cubes for 1.5 hours.

I had a presentation of my own that I had prepared for 300 doctors, assistances, and physicians in Europe. I have included that lecture for you in this chapter, to give you an idea of what it's like to attend one of my lectures.

"Good evening. Let me begin by saying that I am honored to be here and that I have respect for everything you do.

I usually don't have a lesson plan for my lectures, so I would like to start off by showing you a couple video clips of me swimming under the ice, climbing snowy mountains in shorts, running a marathon beyond the Polar Circle, and finally the research explaining how my body works. Hopefully those video clips will give you an idea of what my body and mind have been exposed to.

*I then proceeded to show them some of my videos that have been displayed on YouTube. After the video clips finish, I continue on with the presentation.

So, what can we learn from this?
Well, I believe that if we can go deep enough into our minds to influence the autonomic nervous system, as well as the immune system, we can prevent diseases from harming our body.

How is this possible?

The cardiovascular system is made up of muscles that we can train. By exposing them to natural stimuli, such as the cold, we can make the muscles stronger. This is easy as taking a 5-minute cold shower after a warm one.

With cold exposure, the muscles in the arteries are trained. The opening and closing of the muscular walls are like lifting weights at the gym. With training, it builds up strength.

With each cold shower, the body improves immensely. The onset of natural adaptation happens rather quickly. Once the muscles in the arteries are strong enough, you will be ready to go on to the next phase.

In the next phase a psychological aspect comes in. Here, you don't want to take a warm shower before turning on the cold. Try stepping directly into a cold shower. This takes a lot more determination. The aim of this exercise is to be able to close your veins by sheer will.

A big part of being able to do this is by focusing on your breathing. Try not to gasp when you are first exposed to the cold water. When you can do this and feel in control, the veins around the vital parts of the body contract, as well as in the skin.

This is all possible after gradual adaptation of phase one. It is an essential step to develop naturally, without force. This phase helps your body consciously control the cardiovascular system.

Through concentrated exercises, you will adapt fast. Your will is also tested through all of these exercises. You may think that it would be much easier to simply turn off the shower and put on warm clothes. This is, in fact, true, but you aren't helping your body. In fact, you are doing the complete opposite.

Listening to your intuition becomes a big part of this exercise. If you are willingly in the cold and accepting the exercise, your body will begin to give you signs that you are ready to move on to phase three: ice-water immersions.

With the exercises in phase one and two, you will have learned how to deal directly with the cold. You will then understand that it takes will power and determination to get through the experience, as well as hopefully knowing your body better.

The psychological development in phase two opens up a new range of possibilities. At this point, you will know how to influence the cardiovascular system and you will have tapped into consciously communicating with the hypothalamus, our mental thermostat.

Once you can control that, why not tap into another part of the brain. When you can consciously steer the hypothalamus, you can bring in visualization. We all day dream at times, but it's mostly done by our subconscious. I implore you to practice visualization by imagining how powerful you will be when submerging yourself in ice water. Imagine yourself going in and feeling completely at ease. Know that there won't be a problem because your body will adapt.

Now, visualize heat in your lower stomach. Imagine that with each breath, you are breathing in fire and it fills your body. It isn't hocus-pocus; this actually works. Thinking that your body is getting warmer will actually make your body warmer. Just try it.

I never had a teacher. I learned from experiences. With a determined mine, I generated enough energy to deal with cold exposures. Eventually, I was able to build up my stamina by training in snow, ice, ice water, and cold winds. These breathing techniques helped me do that.

Phase three is different from the previous two phases. It is still in cold water, but the experience is much different. Your mindset is crucial to develop absolute control over the body.

The ice-water immersions take determination and visualization. Controlled breaths are essential. When you first slide into ice water, take controlled, conscious breaths. Do not gasp. Try to relax and let the body adapt naturally. Usually, this takes about thirty seconds before the body begins to feel at ease. Once you have relaxed, the mind will do its part and keep the body warm.

Concentrate and visualize heat in your lower stomach. Breathe in and make the heat spread from your lower stomach to the outer parts of your body. When you breathe out, get rid of the cold. When you breathe in, use that breath to generate heat.

Believe in yourself and trust whatever your body tells you. The experience is real and it has been proven using scientific methods.

With these exercises, we can fight disease and begin to live a healthy life. Just go within yourself and tap into your inner nature."

Soon after giving the lecture you have just read, I was asked to give another lecture in front of the doctors of Albert Schweitzer Hospital in Rotterdam. It was my next *big* challenge.

Manely, the man who's doing a documentary on my life, came along as well. Together, we went with Onno, his cameraman. We drove in two cars to Rotterdam. It took us a long time because of the congested traffic, which is a very typical occurrence in the Netherlands considering that every day, there is construction on at least one road.

After a few hours in the car, we had finally arrived at the location, the SS Rotterdam. It's a huge cruise ship in the harbor of Rotterdam.

The ship was very impressive, but I tried to remain focused on what I would say in my lecture.

We grabbed our gear from the cars and went to the reception desk. They sent us to the upper deck where we had a panoramic view over the harbor and the skyline of Rotterdam. Manely and Onno got the cameras ready while I finished preparing the lecture in my head.

The conference room took up the entire backside of the ship. 100 doctors, sitting in comfortable chairs adjacent to little tables, occupied the room. The stage where the lectures were given was nicely done. There was a painted background on the back end that had images of mountains and rocks. Manely and Onno began rolling the cameras and the audience became quiet. An experienced speaker and a cardiologist introduced me.

A microphone and a giant screen were my utensils to speak and visually show what I would normally do in my challenges. We showed three video clips. The first was my barefooted, half marathon ice run in Lapland. The second was my world record attempt, swimming under ice water. The third was the physiological experiment that took place at Radboud University Hospital.

When the video clips ended, I began speaking:

"I have no program, no concrete story in my head that I'm going to tell you, but that is just the way I am. Your energy and attention will help me guide this lecture.

However, I do have a message. I want to show that everybody is capable of influencing the immune system. I don't care about the sequence of my words as long as the message is well understood and can be passed on to you."

The lecture continued that way for a while. Soon, my inhibitions were gone and my words flowed out like a river with a strong current. While I lectured, images and video footage played behind me. Everyone was captivated and listened carefully. The audience remained silent and attentive.

I told them about going deep into myself, about the challenges that present themselves in hard nature, about exerting more effort than we usually can contribute, and about nature as my teacher. I explained that nature is hard, but righteous.

I also told them about how I had learned to breath differently, deeper and more effectively. I explained that my breathing helps me perform better in nature and makes me more capable of taking on "impossible" tasks.

It may sound weird, but going into the extreme cold in nature, especially when you're barely wearing clothes, induces a different state of mind. It's almost intuitive.

I continued:

"Nature rules. Nature learns. Nature lectures.

You have to go deep, deep inside yourself to where the nervous system, immune system, cardiovascular system, heart and mind all work together. When all these systems are working together, it guarantees a tremendous power. I have learned to trust this, whole-heartedly.

The sensation of overcoming the worrisome mind and controlling it is unmistakable. To be able to feel united in body and mind, and not alienated from nature is a powerful thing.

I have no fear of climbing without gear. I have the capability to avoid falling rocks reflexively without consciously seeing them fall. I have the ability to tell a cramp in my leg to go away. I can run a full marathon in shorts, beyond the Polar Circle, without any prior training whatsoever. I have the capability to use *mind* over *matter*.

Deep trust is about knowing that you are fully capable of functioning at your best within your body and mind. The cold teaches you through powerful lessons.

For hundreds of years, we have worn clothes and developed better fabrics to maintain our heat. We have confided in the warmth of our homes and avoided the cold as much as physically possible. We have settled for living comfortably, never testing our boundaries.

To keep our bodies strong, we need to train ourselves in nature. The cold is a powerful voice with a wise lesson. With the right adaptation we can bring back control over the internal workings of our body. It helps us be more alert and reactive to any negative disturbances in our body.

Let us take the cardiovascular system for example. This can be conditioned to function better by doing gradual cold exposures. It is a system that has the ability to become stronger with training. Training the muscular walls of the arteries helps pump blood more efficiently throughout the body. I have found that it lowers 20 to 25 beats off of the resting heart rate! Overall, this aids in making your thoughts more peaceful and coherent.

We are capable of building extraordinary structures, flying into space, and programming computers, yet we continually avoid the opportunity to explore our bodies and push their limits.

Keep this in mind, young doctors, that we are at the forefront of new discoveries within the human mind and body.

My message is that everyone is capable of influencing the immune system and that the cold is a noble, natural force that can help teach us how to regain this ability. Our health is important, why avoid this useful tool any longer?

In medieval times, we thought the earth was flat and we wouldn't dare venture toward the horizon for fear of falling to our deaths. Imagine the fear that thought must have caused -- to be eternally trapped. Yet, we changed our mindsets and discovered new worlds because we were driven to challenge our perceptions. Our perception shapes the way we live. A lot of the time, it can prevent us from reaching our potential.

The cold is a force that must be taken seriously, as we do with the heat. When you're sitting in front of a fireplace, you think it's comfortable and nice. You don't stick your hand into the flames. The same is true for the cold. You don't just dive into ice water, stay there for hours, and expect to live; you must gradually exposure yourself. The best way to start is through cold showers.

You don't need to be a professional football player to enjoy the health benefits of playing football. Just as well, you don't need to expose yourself to the extreme temperatures that I do to reach the immune system. All I am suggesting is that we start fitting in a few cold showers into our weekly schedules."

Feeling that my message was well understood, I thanked the audience for their time. After Manely and Onno packed their cameras, we ate dinner and began our long drive back to Holland.

We had done well. It felt like I had taken a giant step in the right direction.

CHAPTER 39:
THE NEW YEAR

December 2010

After a heavy period of snow here in Holland, daily cold baths and running barefoot through the snow, I had one thing in my mind: Hong Kong. Another opportunity had presented itself where I could travel to Hong Kong to attempt my world record again, encased in ice.

The plane tickets were arranged for me to fly out over Russia, Siberia, China, and then eventually land on an island near a giant status of Buddha. When I arrived, a 54-year-old Japanese man greeted me; his name was Sano.

The temperature was warm compared to Holland. In Hong Kong, the temperature was 19°C (66.2°F) while in Holland it was -10°C (14°F). Despite the warmer weather, a lot of people were heavily clothed. They seemed like they had a natural disposition to "feeling cold" and were in desperate need of staying warm. I was walking around in a t-shirt and felt completely comfortable!

As Sano guided me through the river floating through the city, he pointed out huge buildings with mesmerizing architecture. He escorted me to the giant entrance of a five-star hotel. My room was relatively small, but the view was magnificent. I felt like a king.

I saw many statues of Bruce Lee around the city. There were many photos that showed great respect for him as a martial artist. I feel that he died too young. His statutes gave me inspiration to perform well in the beautiful city full of exotic palm trees and subtropical botany.

Two days after my arrival, the city was blessed with the heat of a warm summer day. It was a heat that could touch the solemnness of the soul. It helped take my mind off the upcoming challenge.

Sano took me all kinds of places. He was a very nice man who was a pleasure to be around. He was also extremely busy because he was helping to organize the events surrounding the countdown to 2011.

Sano arranged a press conference focusing on global warming awareness; I was his protagonist promoting the message. I didn't know anything about global warming, but I tried my best to represent the issue.

There were 15 microphones, 30 journalists, and 10 video cameras while I did a lecture on global warming. Here is what I said:

" I have no knowledge in politics, nor am I someone against the love of the world. I think that children are our future and that the coming generations, who will inhabit this world, need to be raised in a world that is balanced.

We, as humans, can protect ourselves against the changing weather conditions, but animals and plant life cannot!

In the end, we won't be able to turn our back on the world and avoid the consequences of our actions. Exploiting our ecosystem to receive financial gain is not worth it.

I am here to break a world record in the ice and therefore, take the opportunity to raise attention worldwide. I would like to help broaden the vision concerning this delicate matter of global warning. The nature outside of ourselves directly influences the nature within us.

We have become strangers to nature over the years because we are no longer living directly in nature. We are always spending money on clothes and surrounding ourselves with technological luxuries. We have lost our touch with nature.

We have become blind, in a way. Therefore, I am thankful for the opportunity to express my thoughts with you and show you what can be done when you are connected to nature."

Then it was time to immerse myself in a cold ice bath inside of a transparent container.

Click. Click. Click.

A photo shoot was happening outside of the container. My exposed body was being imprinted on the cameras of those around me.

Two days after that, the record attempt was imminent. The plan was for me to begin the full-body ice endurance record at precisely 10:20 PM. When I would get out 1 hour and 50 minutes later, it would be 10 minutes into the New Year, 2011!

A little before the event, I sat down in the audience and tried to relax. The crowd was enthusiastic and many gave me admirable looks.

After some dancers performed on stage, the announcer mentioned that the world record was about to begin. I walked up beside the announcer and he asked a few questions. "How are you feeling?" "Are you confident that you will break the world record?"

My mind was only set on one thing: *Just do it.*

A few of the people lifted the Perspex box and I walked in. They set the box upright and began filling it with ice. It usually takes between 5 to 10 minutes to fill it completely.

The ice poured over my shoulders and I checked how my body was reacting to it. This is what was happening inside of me:

Full of determination, I charged myself up with adrenaline and dopamine. The adrenaline made me feel strong against the cold impact and the dopamine was my pain reliever.

When I was completely covered in ice, the walls of my cardiovascular system contracted and began their search to find a way to work as efficiently as possible, without releasing heat.

The veins around my vital organs contracted and I steered the blood to circulate around them to keep warm. This keeps my core temperature stable.

When all these conditions were met, the time to endure began. The better I was at keeping my core temperature stabilized, the longer I would be able to stay in the ice. Sometimes, I would begin to feel cold in a certain part of my body. By simply concentrating on that spot, I was able transfer heat to that area to warm it back up.

I have two important responsibilities when I am fully immersed in ice. I feel like they are the perfect example of mind over matter. The first is being able to keep the veins and arteries closed, around the core. The second is redirecting heat toward parts of the body when they get cold. Both are done consciously.

This reminds me of a 55-year-old man named Leonard, who had once emailed me. He was interested in some of the articles that he had read about reaching the immune system. Leonard's body was completely paralyzed, save for his head. Despite Leonard's inability to move his body, he still suffered from chronic aches and pains.

I visited Leonard and told him that there is a power in man that can alleviate that pain. Simply direct energy to the aches and imagine them going away. It only took him twenty minutes to figure out how to do it and ever since then, he has been able to relieve his pain using only his mind.

The influence of the mind is powerful. When you are completely fed up with a situation, you are more willing to break through the conditioned mind. Leonard just needed a little push to get him going.

Now, back to the story...

So, there I was, standing on a stage in front of thousands of people, all cheering me on. I was completely in control and winning the fight against the cold!

Groups of performers danced beside me. Sometimes, the steps that they would take on the stage would shift the ice inside of the box, making it harder for me to stay warm.

Every performance in the ice is a different one. I can't ever go in unprepared because if something unexpected happens, there is a huge chance that I will get hypothermia.

I know a perfect example of this. The last time I attempted the record, I was in Tokyo. They had stuck a temperature probe in my mouth to monitor my body heat. It made it extremely difficult for me to breath.

My oxygen saturation fell dangerously low. After an hour of this, I had enough. I made them take the probe out. Immediately, everything felt much better. By the time I had reached the new record time, my oxygen saturation was back to 100%!

I had another problem with this particular ice record when I did it in Austria. The temperature outside was freezing. When I broke the world record and they tried to get me out, they failed. The air had completely frozen all of the ice cubes together. I had become part of an ice sculpture. After they pulled the Perspex box off of me, they needed to chop away at the ice with axes.

So, like those time, I had to deal with something unexpected. I needed to battle against the ice as it massaged my skin. I was determined to break the world record, so I pressed on.

1 hour and 50 minutes after being immersed, I had finally set the new world record! Big cheers from the audience came as I was freed from my icy tomb. It was finally time for my warm bath

I went back to my hotel room, jumped in the hot tub, and fell asleep. Hours must have passed by because when I woke up, everyone who was partying in my hotel room was gone and the wine that was given to me as a gift was empty. In it's place, someone had left a basket of fruit... how kind.

Regardless, I had succeeded once again. The following day, Sano took me to the Chinese Sea. We spent the day walking along the water. When we got back to the city of Hong Kong, there was a surprise waiting for me. There was a Chinese wedding taking place and they wanted me to be the guest of honor! It was a beautiful ceremony.

Sadly, I wasn't able to attend the reception because my plane left at 11:00 PM.

We took the subway back to the airport where we had cheap, but tasty Japanese sushi before we separated. Sano was really nice company and he made the experience feel like a movie. We embraced each other and said our final goodbyes.

CHAPTER 40:
STRENGTH AND HONOR

*M*anely, a talented film director and a good friend of mine, is making a documentary that relates to this book and helps illustrate the point that we can all reach and influence the immune system.

This finding could have huge repercussions on the world and shift the perception of the general population. As I continually show people the health benefits of gradually training in the cold, I hope it leads to a total prevention of diseases.

A few days ago, from the time of writing this chapter, I visited Manely and brought some DVDs of my former documentaries over to him. While he reviewed the DVDs, one particularly clip caught my attention.

"The Superhumans and the Quest of the Fantastic Four," is a series that claims I am a "superhuman." This is the video footage that shows me running a barefooted, half marathon in the snow. Specifically, this is the run that resulted in frostbite.

I can't say that my decision to keep running was only based off of intuition; I had let my emotions get the best of me. I had a situation at home that had left me emotionally distraught. I wasn't thinking properly. Sadly, I let it affect my decision.

I took the challenge offered by the Discovery Channel because it was a quick way to escape from the emotional stress at home. Normally, I don't make rash decisions like that because I know the limits of my body extremely well, but this time I decided to press on despite the imminent damage and signals that my body was sending me.

I was really determined to finish the race, but after pressing on, the medic forced me to stop. She had told me that I was at risk of losing my toes. She also mentioned that it would be foolish if I continued, but it was my decision.

As you know, I ignored her. I desperately wanted to cross that finish line. So I pressed on, regardless of the potential consequences. I know it may sound ridiculous, but I think it was what I was supposed to do. It taught me something about myself that I would have never learned otherwise: *No matter what anyone tells you, you can do anything. Nothing is impossible.*

The doctors told me that I had done "irreversible damage" to my foot and I would never be the same again. Well, they were wrong. I am still doing my challenges, I am still breaking world records, and I am still telling you that because I am capable of anything, so are you. There is nothing "super-human" about me. I am just a man that loves fulfilling human potential.

It can take strength and courage to heal oneself when facing a grim future, but we are all capable of confronting fears and pushing through them. Find that power inside of you and heal your dilemma.

There was a time twenty years ago when I was suffering from a severe case of pneumonia. At the time, I was raising four children on my own and my wife had just passed away. I was extremely emotional and we didn't have much money.

My body could take a lot, but when I became emotionally drained I was susceptible to diseases. Somehow, I had developed pneumonia in the midst of summer. After days of feeling a strange pressure in my chest, I suddenly lost my energy and collapsed against a tree.

At that moment, I decided to go see a doctor. He told me that I was suffering from a severe case of pneumonia and prescribed an antibiotic. He told me that I should be healed in about a month.

I took one capsule and immediately felt better. Once I got that feeling, I wanted to take over the healing process. So that one capsule was the last one I ever took. I grabbed a hold of the wheel and visualized myself getting better. Before I knew it, the pneumonia had left as fast as it had come.

I am not suggesting that you ignore what your doctors or physicians tell you. What I am saying is that we all have an inner doctor that guides us as well.

There's one last story that I would like to share with you about healing. A few years ago, I severely tore my large and small intestines. I could have died from this, but it was not my time. The ambulance transported me to the hospital and cut open my abdomen.

They worked for hours trying to repair the damage. After making a temporary bypass, they patched me up and closed the wound. The doctors told me that my extreme sports career was over and that it would take me at least a year and a half to recover.

That night, they escorted me to my room in the hospital and left me there. When the light was turned off and my door was shut, I began to do a physical examination of my own. I had a gigantic scar on my abdomen where they had made the incision.

I sat there for a while, staring at my wall. Eventually, I made the decision to get out of bed and walk around. It was an enormous task.

My body was in really bad shape but I was extremely determined. Centimeter by centimeter I moved myself from laying down to placing my feet over the side of the hospital bed. It felt like hours!

Finally, the soles of my feet touched that ground. I lifted myself off of the bed and there I was, standing. I was standing!

I checked myself out, observing my condition like a wounded animal. After a bit, I stopped caring about my wound and took interest in my surroundings. I gazed out the window and saw the stars in the night sky.

Even though it had taken all of my effort to move mere centimeters, I was able to achieve my goal. Getting out of bed was my first step in starting up my healing process again. I had won my first battle.

Exhausted, I turned back to the bed and slowly laid myself down. Eventually, I fell into a deep sleep. Every day, from that point on, I continued with the same determination. I couldn't eat for two weeks because my intestines didn't work, but I kept on pushing. Finally, my intestines were able to process food. Another victory!

Three months from the time of my injury, I was performing in the ice again. I was able to perform at ease and my body was in great shape. I didn't have to wait the year and a half that the doctors had suggested. My inner doctor had performed miracles!

Doing something like that takes a lot of courage, strength, and responsibility. You have to trust that there is a lot to gain and that quick healing is possible. It is at that point where the inner doctor will greet you.

Two months after that, I set a new world record for standing in a box where my body was completely immersed in ice. Two months after that, I climbed Kilimanjaro while only wearing shorts.

That's when I returned to the Lapland, the place that had given me "irreparable damage." This time, I ran twice as far and completed a full marathon with no damage to my foot whatsoever!

Despite my injuries and setbacks, I have still managed to press on and take on more challenges. The body adapts if you're willing to test it.

My intestines healed six times faster than the time the doctors told me it would take. It is possible for you to do the same. Trusting that you are capable will make *a lot* of difference. But believing in yourself and knowing that it is possible will make *all* of the difference.

Strength and honor isn't only achieved through sports and challenges. Fighting for life itself makes you a hero. A gladiator doesn't need a sword if his mind is as sharp as a razor blade. Cut through the desperation and dependence and focus on the everlasting possibilities.

CHAPTER 41:
FINLAND

As the temperature dropped and the days grew shorter, I intensified my training. Even though it seemed pointless at the time, with
no hopes of attempting the world record anytime soon, I kept it up.
During the winter months, I added *Cold Runs and *Snow Walks
to my training [*Refer to **Justin's Method** section for more informa-
tion]. I began to see a lot of progress. The amount of time I could
stand and run in the snow was greatly increasing.

As I went on my cold runs, I began hearing my friends call my
name in the streets. A lot of them knew I was training for a world
record. Sometimes, I would still hear profanity yelled at me when I
would run by random strangers, but it didn't get to me anymore. I
just kept imagining what it would be like to finally have the chance
to run my 5 kilometers in the snow.

Finally, my chance arrived. Soon after I had returned from Christmas break, I received an email from Wim, telling me that he would
be willing to pay for me to fly to Finland, if I was willing to attempt
the world records there. I told him that I would have no problem
with going to Finland, as long as there was enough time for me to
inform my professors of my absence.

Exactly three weeks after receiving the invitation, I was standing
in a snowmobile shop in Kittilä, Finland with Enahm and Wim.

"You're finally doing it!" Enahm said to us after handing the clerk
a couple hundred euros. "It's going to happen!"

A year earlier, I never would have dreamed that I would be in
Finland, attempting a world record with the infamous Wim Hof. Yet
there I was, about to rent a snowmobile to transport us to the location. I couldn't believe it.

"Here's your change," the woman said, handing a few coins back
to Enahm. "The man outside will take you to the snow scooters

now."

We walked outside and a man smoking a cigarette called out to us. "Hello, ready?" We jumped into his van and drove to the place where they stored their snowmobiles.

"Here we are," he told us. "The man inside will assist you." I noticed he hadn't shifted his car into "Park." I took that as a sign as he wanted us to leave.

We left the car and entered a small wooden building. There was a man inside as the driver had stated. He fitted the three of us with helmets and gave us the keys. He then directed us outside to a snowmobile with a sled fashioned to its back.

"It's just the three of you, right?" he said.

"Yes," Wim replied.

"All right," the man continued, "Two people sit in the snowmobile, one rides in the sled."

"I'm driving!" Enahm yelled.

"You can ride with Enahm, Justin. I'll ride in the sled." Wim said.

As Wim and I sat in our assigned positions, the man gave Enahm directions to the lake.

"Thanks!" Enahm yelled as he revved the engine. "Hold on guys! "*Yaaaa-hoo*"

The snowmobile screamed, and then lurched forward. I wrapped my arms around Enahm and held on tightly as he increased the snowmobile to 48 kilometers per hour (about 30 miles per hour). We ditched and dodged trees and branches as we flew through the forest. Making our way to the lake, Enahm pushed his new toy to its limits.

A few minutes later, the trees rushing past us began to thin out and open up into a giant, frozen lake. We drove on further, looking for the best place to run. Eventually we came across a ski-trekking course. Luckily, there was a long, straight stretch that had a red pole every 10th of a kilometer, measuring 1 kilometer in length. We decided to use that as a way to measure our running distance. For each record, we would need to run the same kilometer back and forth until we each had reached our record limit -- 10 kilometers for Wim and 5 kilometers for myself.

We stopped the snowmobile and Wim got out to see if the surface was okay to run on. "It's a little rough," he said. "We need to smooth it out."

Wim pulled out a milk carton crate from the inside of the sled and tied it to the back, using a small piece of rope. After fastening the crate to the sled, he sat himself down inside of the crate. "Go!" he yelled to Enahm.

Enahm stepped on the gas and drove around using Wim's invention to smooth out the frozen ice. After making a few laps, I switched places with Wim. "Let's go!" I called to Enahm.

The ride was bumpy. Several times, I found myself being tipped over and dragged by the snowmobile. Luckily, I wasn't hurt. After a few more laps, Enahm stopped the snowmobile and I got out. Wim detached the carton and placed it near one of the poles.

"This will be where we finish," he announced. "Let's get started!"

We all decided that I would be the first one to run. If, for some reason, we were cut short on time, they wanted to make sure that I had the opportunity to break the record.

"I already have enough records. Just in case something goes wrong, I want you to go first," Wim had said.

They drove me back to the starting line and I prepared myself. The temperature was 30°F (-1.1°C) and the air was dry, but I was ready for it. I had spent the last few months training for this moment. I was ready for whatever climate the challenge gave me.

"If I'm going to do this," I said, "I might as well do it... Iceman style." I began taking off my clothes, leaving nothing on but a pair of shorts. As I set my feet down on the chilled, solid ground, I felt the familiar cold tickle my flesh. "Let's do this!"

Wim turned on the camera and prepared the stopwatch. Enahm revved the engine.

"You can do this Justin!" Wim yelled. "Becoming the Iceman! Ready... Set... Go!"

I leaned forward and began pressing my feet against the icy surface. The cool air blew against my exposed chest as I progressed forward. I looked up and saw Wim and Enahm a few feet ahead of me, leading the way on the snowmobile.

Wim smiled while pointing the camera at my face. "Good job, Justin! Keep it up!" Every step of the way, Wim spoke to me. Whether I was looking at him or not, he continued to shout his encouraging words.

As I approached 3 kilometers, I began to feel the roughness of the ice on the bottom of my feet. With each step, the ice tore away at my skin. I had trained for the cold, not for sharp ice, but I pressed on anyway.

"You're over half way, Justin! Keep it up!"

At 4 kilometers the pain grew to excruciating. I would have sworn needles were penetrating the sole of my foot with each step. They seared with pain. I had never run on ice before -- only snow. It was a completely different experience.

"You're going to make it, man! You're almost there!"

With half a kilometer left, my feet turned numb up. I took that as a bad sign, but chose to ignore it. I wanted to reach the end. I was so close. I could see it. Pressing on, I was determined to cross that finish line in under 30 minutes. *Almost... There...*

"Yeahhhhh! You did it!" Wim yelled. "New Record! New World Record!"

I raised my arms in triumph.

"Wim," Enahm said, "the clock?"

"Oh the clock! Here it is, twenty-seven forty six [27 min 46 seconds]" Wim announced.

"Really?" I asked. I couldn't believe that I had actually done it.

Enahm and Wim hugged me out of excitement.

"We are like brothers," Enahm said as he hugged me.

"I'm proud of you man," Wim told me. "I love you. You did it!"

I thanked them for the congratulations and sat down in the sled to examine my wounds. They gathered around to look as well. They were still numb. Both of my feet were severely swollen. Underneath the spot where my callouses had been were large deposits of blood. On my right foot, I had two blood blisters. On my left foot, I had two blood blisters and a large cut beneath my big toe.

"Ahh, nothing to worry about. It is not frostbite," Wim said, trying to reassure me. "Just a few battle wounds. They will heal up in no time."

They looked horrible, but due to my most recent success, I forced myself to believe him.

"All right Wim, your turn," Enahm said, jumping back onto the snowmobile. "We have to finish this before the battery dies on the camera. Let's go!"

We jumped back into the snowmobile and began driving back to the starting position. I readied the camera and positioned my body to get a good angle for when Wim ran behind us.

A few seconds later, Wim was out and ready to run. With the cameras running, I started the countdown. "Ready, set, go!"

I pressed the button on my stopwatch and Enahm revved the engine. While trying to hold the camera steady, we jumped forward once again. As Wim began running forward, I noticed *something* interesting about him. He had a unique look in his eyes. It was as if he *knew* he was going to break the record, even though he had just started running. I could sense his confidence, but not in a boastful way. He just... *knew*.

As Enahm and I led the way, I watched the familiar face I had seen so many times on YouTube and on television, chase after me. Almost a year earlier, Wim had invited me to Poland to train with him. It was a surreal moment to be able to recognize how far things had progressed. He had given me gifts that I would cherish forever. Wim not only taught me how to control my body temperature and survive in the cold, he had also taught me how to live life to the fullest, how to overcome my inhibitions, and how to be patient. These lessons will last me a lifetime and I owe it all to him... My "spiritual brother."

As Wim approached the final stretch with half a kilometer left, I began yelling. "Come on Wim! You can do it! Almost there man! You got this Bro!"

He raised his head, smiled, and gave me a thumbs up. He didn't even look tired!   Just as Wim was about to cross the finish line, he stopped.

"Whoa, whoa, whoa, wait a second," he said. He went to the side of the path and dug his hands into the snow. He picked it up and began rubbing it all over his body.

"I've got to take a bath before finishing, yeah?" He looked at Enahm and I, showing a huge grin. "Okay, that's enough." He crossed the finish line and raised his hands in the air.

"New Record!" Enahm yelled.

"Yeah! You did it!" I added.

"I did it. You did it. We finally did it." Wim hugged me. "I love you man. Becoming the Iceman. We did it!"

IMPORTANT DISCLAIMER: Our world record attempts are currently unconfirmed by Guinness World Records. Therefore, they are NOT official Guinness World Records. If you would like access to the footage of our 5k and 10k runs in Finland, you can contact us at info@innerfire.nl.

CHAPTER 42:
NEW ADVENTURES

After many challenges, I feel like I have finally made it to the level of an extreme sportsman. I provide for my family and myself by living this way. It comes from dedication and conquering the mind. For a while, it seemed like it would never end. Honestly, I don't know if it ever will, but at least things are getting better. I have a peace in my mind that helps me understand life on a deeper level. I would like to pass on to you some lessons that I have learned along the way.

My challenges aren't always amidst freezing temperatures, trying to break a world record. A few of my other challenges are instructing people during my workshops, writing a book, doing my thing while in a scientific setting, and proving that we can do more than we think.

One of my more recent goals has been to teach hundreds of children how to run barefoot over the snow. I would like to instruct them how to bring about the power to resist the cold. Once they see that it is possible, hopefully they will become more prone to embrace the cold and the lessons it can teach.

In a couple of months, I'll be climbing Kilimanjaro again. It will be documented by German television. The amazing thing about doing these challenges is that my way of living, makes me a living. In other words, I get paid to do what I love doing. Their program will be about extraordinary people. I am hoping that this program will help inspire others do confront the cold.

Inspiration is a nice thing to give and I'll do what I can to help others receive that. Despite however many people I try to teach, only those with open ears, heart, and dedication will be able to pursue it.

Another upcoming challenge is my run through the Sahara desert. I plan to go 50 kilometers without drinking any water. I am convinced that it is possible even though all of the doctors tell me otherwise. I worked for eight years in the Spanish Pyrenees during the hot summers. Every day, I carried my rucksack, weighing 20 kilograms (44 pounds), on my back, for the entire day, without drinking any water. I did this because it felt good and my body told me that I was okay.

I believe that at a certain moment when my sweating stops, an auto-circulative fluid system kicks in and begins to regulate my body temperature. At this point, I think my body stops sweating to conserve the fluids and keep the body functioning. When this process would happen to me in the Spanish Pyrenees, I would feel a sort of high, off of natural drugs, comparable to the feeling that one gets when experiencing runner's high. The same happens when I am exposed to the cold.

When Justin and I decided to try breaking two world records together, we had no training. What I mean is, we didn't train specifically for the run. Justin hadn't run much in the snow because there wasn't any snow to run in. Personally, I hadn't done much running either. I had been focused on all of the research and workshops that I couldn't find time to do any endurance workouts.

The thing is, we had faith that it was possible. We knew that we would be prepared when the time came and we were willing to work hard to get there. Justin began using his experiments to simulate running on snow, while I began running slowly. With time, I increased my distance and speed as my body became more accustomed.

For any challenge that comes up, we will find the tools to overcome it. The most challenging thing in life is the mind. Let "opening your mind to new opportunities" be your next goal. When you get there, teach others how to do it. It's a useful technique that all of mankind can benefit from. It's not some spiritual nonsense; it's just a technique to deal with worrisome thoughts.

When you go deep enough, natural drugs, like endorphins and adrenaline, can help your body deal with usually intolerable situations. We can do more than we think and there is still so much terrain to discover.

In many people, the veins and arteries in their bodies are unconditioned. They aren't used to pumping blood efficiently because they're untrained. It causes numerous problems like heart attacks and arthritis. Diseases that deal with blood circulation cause many deaths each year. Millions suffer from bad circulation of the blood. This can all be prevented.

You can easily train your cardiovascular system by taking cold showers. The walls of the vessels transporting blood contract and then dilate because of the cold impact. Start slowly and gradually increase your training as the time it takes for your ability to adapt decreases. It's like any other sort of training that you do for your cardiovascular system: running, swimming, etc.

By training the cardiovascular system, the heart is able to pump blood to the vital parts of your body more efficiently. By taking stress off of your heart, it is quite possible to lower your resting heart rate.

I would like to share with you a short story from my childhood. When I was seven years old I was playing in a pasture near my house, covered from the thick snow of winter. My friends and I built the best igloo a group of seven-year-olds could possibly build. It took us all day to build, but by the end of the day it was majestic.

One by one, my friends went home, to eat, to sleep, or because they were tired. I, however, stayed because I felt attached to the igloo. I felt as if it was my home. My beautiful home. I continued adding snow to it over the next few hours. I molded the walls, built chairs and even a bed!

I then went into the igloo, because it was ready to be lived in. A warm feeling of accomplishment washed over me. I lay myself down on the bed and stretched out. I felt the coolness leak through my layered clothing; it felt nice.

Despite a couple holes in the ceiling, the igloo was perfect. A few rays of sunshine shone through, but it made the experience all the more beautiful. After watching the rays dance off of the walls for a few minutes, I fell asleep.

Hours past before someone shook me. I felt something bringing me back from my slumber. They were tearing at my jacket.

"Wim, wake up! Wim! Wake up!"

The sound felt like it was coming from far away. I couldn't consciously conceive what was going on. Finally, my eyes opened and I became away of my older brother's presence.

"Get up, we have to go home. Mama and Papa are looking everywhere for you," he said.

My feeling was that of a drunken man. Being that I was seven years old, I had no idea what was going on with my body. I had never experienced something like that. I felt very heavy and my movements were slow. I had no control over my limbs. I couldn't even get up! Eventually, I realized that these are the symptoms of hypothermia.

My brother helped me get home by supporting my weight. When I arrived, my parents were relieved of their worries. They escorted me to my bed where I lay shivering and drowsy. Eventually, I fell asleep... cold.

Everyone was worried that day. I had almost slept forever in the cold, thinking it was my warm home. I call it "the white death." It's where people can feel warm and comfortable in the cold, but when they fall asleep they succumb to hypothermia. Eventually, they can slip into a coma and die.

To me, it was a mysterious experience. I look at it as a beautiful, near-death experience. The cold has the power to change the mind. In my case, I was a victim of the cold, yet now I am able to confront it head on. Although to someone unprepared, it is a dangerous force, but simultaneously, it has the power to dig into the deeper levels of the mind.

At the age of 11, I had another dangerous cold encounter. In this encounter, I didn't feel the negative sting of the cold. Instead, it felt like I was going to sleep, nice and warm.

While riding my bike on the way to school one day, that feeling came over me and told me to stop. I stepped off the bike and slept on someone's porch. I was tired and drowsy, but fell asleep cozily. When I awoke, I was being carried into an ambulance. The doctors kept me in the hospital for one week for observation. They couldn't figure out how I had survived.

These mysterious experiences have strengthened my relationship with the cold. I now recognize it as a noble force that teaches me life lessons. Now, I am able to control the impact that the cold has on my body and use it to help keep my body healthy. I have come a long way since I was seven.

CHAPTER 43:
THE FINAL CHAPTER

My mother was a good person, a saint I would say. As a devout catholic, she would consciously, sometimes unconsciously, ask God to tackle any of the Satanic powers related to sickness. During the delivery, while I was still in her womb, she prayed that I would come naturally to the light of God's creation -- the world. Even though I had nearly suffocated, I came into existence. From then on, she promised God that I would become a missionary. I've tried to do my best to fulfill her promise. Thank you God and thank you Mamma. May she rest in peace.

Up until two days before my 52nd birthday, I was unaware of how much this mission controlled my life. It had driven me, sometimes irrationally, through all of my challenges and had brought me near many close encounters with death. Yet somehow, I always found a way to succeed.

I have sacrificed many things in my life. I have had highs and lows, but now I'm finally reaching a peace of mind. There is something within me that is finally settling. I feel that I have finally succeeded in my mission. Knowing that everyone in the world is able to influence his or her immune system makes me believe that I have finally won. It has been a long journey, but I am finally coming home, within myself. The mind can be like an animal at times. Now, I can stand erect like a proud Masai because I have killed the lion inside of me.

From the cold corridor where I was born to this Final Chapter, it has been a great journey. The cold is a warm friend who I hold dear. As it trains the cardiovascular system, it brings about great light, faith, and power.

I am thankful toward God for making the light brighter than the shade. It made my path distinguishable. No longer will my heart be fooled by the tricks of the mind. My heart is full of love and compassion. I choose to serve mankind and to help bring everyone insight through science.

Let us dance on the waves of victory. Let us sing joyously of the blissful presence. Without speculation, the light always wins. The light gives lucidity to the mind, emanates from the heart, and shows true faith.

As I write this, only a week has passed since Justin and I were in Lapland. Together, we ran the 5 and 10-kilometer race against time through the ice and snow. "Becoming the Iceman" is the start of something powerful. I am sure more books will follow. We are on a path to conquer the mind beyond any shred of doubt. We wish to bring the world justice, true knowledge, and the power within.

I apologize if what I'm saying sounds pretentious, but there is no doubt in my mind that it is unjustified to exclaim everything I have just said. It comes from the heart and from my unshakeable faith. This knowledge is not mine to keep. I am merely a messenger that has been given an opportunity. Now, I am giving *you* that opportunity.

Help our method find its way to the world. Bring the knowledge from within and share it. The knowledge is like a safe; only those who know the combination can unlock it. Tell those who are willing to listen and give them the blessing of understanding.

"Just do it!" "Right on!" "Go for it!"

These, among other exclamations, I have shared with most of the people I have encountered. They are simple, like a child, but can bring people out of the world of speculation, the mist of ignorance, disbelief, and helplessness.

Friends, brothers, sisters…. Love will unite us all and overcome our narrowing differences caused by the normal patterns of thought. Let me tell you this… There is nothing more beautiful than the simple peace of mind and conscious sharing of the Good of existence.

CHAPTER 44:
INTRODUCTION TO THE METHODS

As you progress through the stages of the cold exercises, you will begin to understand the body on a deeper level. You will also realize that you can gain better control over your body's physiological response to the cold.

In time, you'll begin to experience something that we, as westerners, thought was impossible, by consciously influencing the autonomic nervous system.

Normally, people view the cold as a negative force, wearing multiple layers to protect their body. Those people that escape the exposure will never recognize the true potential of the cold. We have become alienated from nature, but the cold is capable of bringing us back to what we once had lost. The cold is a marvelous medium, a noble force.

Training and natural adaptation in the cold brings about great changes in the blood circulative processes. The blood circulates around the body to help feed the vital parts that it needs to function.

The cold has the ability to improve the muscular walls of the cardiovascular system. Repeated exposure to the cold causes the walls to flex back and forth, very similar to someone lifting weights in a gym. When the muscular walls in the arteries get stronger, they improve the blood flow throughout the body.

When blood pumps efficiently throughout the body, it helps the immune system stay alert and more able to detect and fight disease. A lot of individuals suffer from the laziness of blood circulation.

By practicing cold exposures, you can learn how to breathe deeper, thus providing more oxygen to the vital parts of your body. This is a crucial understanding of the way cold exposures can help prevent us from disease. We all have the adaptive processes in our body and mind; it just takes a little push to get it going.

Although, it is important to remember that pushing the body too much can put you in extreme danger. So remember that extreme exposures aren't necessary. You can notice big changes in your body by simply implementing cold showers into your life.   Even   as you age, your body can retain the ability to pump blood efficiently. I know people as old as 80 years old who are able to take ice baths because they have performed cold showers daily. It's that easy.

CHAPTER 45:
WIM'S METHOD

*T*hese exercises should be done with heart and conviction to reach the depth of understanding. Only then will you see the effects of the technique.

I have learned to breathe differently in cold-water immersions. It is a natural process; simply because of the impact, you must adapt. You learn to breathe more consciously, deeper and more effectively.

I can stay submerged under ice water for six minuets, without any effort, because of these breathing exercises.

Exercise 1 – Breathing:
*Note: When I put "easy" in parentheses, I am emphasizing that I do not want you to force the explained technique. It is important to stay comfortable and not over exert yourself. Practicing will push you a little more each time. Just try to stay relaxed; don't force it.

Sit comfortably in a peaceful environment (bedroom, living room, back yard, in nature, whatever suits you). Then relax, consciously, and begin to breathe from the abdominal region, not to shallow, not to deep. Think of it like blowing up a balloon.

Do this thirty times. Saturate the muscles and organs with extra oxygen. The goal is to let the oxygen saturate not only the lungs, but also all of the internal organs. It may feel like you are hyperventilating, but just remember that *you have control.*

Whenever you feel saturation throughout your body, exhale completely (easy), then inhale until you can't take in any more air (don't force it), then exhale completely (easy) and hold your breath (easy).

When the feeling telling you to breathe comes, it is because of the depletion of oxygen. At this point, you can inhale fully and hold it for ten seconds with your lungs full of air.

When you complete that, you have completed your first cycle!

Repeat.

By practicing this, over time you will be able to hold each breath longer and get deeper into your system (immune system, nervous system, blood circulation and heart).

After each retention (holding of breath) and inhalation, close your eyes. You may be able to see electrical charges (some categorize these lights as chakras, electric potentials, or even neurons firing). If you go deep inside yourself, you can stimulate this electricity by a pneumatic pressure that goes up the spine toward your forehead. These lights are your aim!

Oxygen aids the metabolism in creating energy for the body to circulate throughout your system. When you empty the lungs of oxygen, hold for retention until you can't anymore, and then inhale. Doing this will give the body new oxygen laced with boosts of energy This provokes the electricity to go up the spine, reaching the nervous system, immune system, blood circulation, and heart. Thus, ending up in the forehead and influencing the brain effectively.

Exercise 2 - Meditation:

Yoga is the silencing of the mind. Only then can we really see the peace inside ourselves. It's no hocus-pocus. The breathing exercise written above will help you get there.

To reach the forehead and see the electrical charges, you must not only be patient and practice, but you must really want it. Controlling the mind is controlling your senses and emotions. When you can do that, anything is possible. By anything, I mean you will be able to still your mind and steer by the intentions to induce the lights.

Once you are able to induce the lights, you will see that the technique is working. Your body will feel lighter and more powerful. This technique can help calm your mind and make it pure.

A pure mind can easily expand and reach its potential. That is when the light will become clear. I could talk about this forever, but what is important is that you truly want to do it. Practice it. That way, you'll come to know and understand the true nature of the spirit.

Abhyasa vairagya bhyah = regular practice and perseverance.

Exercise 3 - Cold Exercises:

It's like I always say, "The Cold is a noble force." If people ask me what that means I tell them, "The cold forces me to generate heat. It makes me feel alive. I see the heat as a warm friend whom I call upon to provide balance." Every Yin has its Yang. The cold is about balance and moderation.

Exercise 3.1 - Adaptation

The first thing you should try doing is taking a cold shower after a hot one. Try to control your breaths as you face the impact of the cold on your lungs. Try to consciously control the lungs to not gasp and breathe at ease. When you are able to do this, you have taken a gigantic step in being able to consciously control the vascular system around your vital organs.

Regularly practicing cold showers can lead to muscle development in your arteries. The entire vascular system altogether will be conditioned as you exercise, but let things adapt and don't force yourself though it. Stay determined, yet patient. Once the adaptation process is complete you can move on to the next phase, which is taking a cold shower without a warm one.

You will need to be determined for this as well.

Before you even begin your cold shower, you may notice a drop in your body temperature. Due to your intentions of taking the cold shower, your body will react psychosomatically. It is all a part of the process.

Once again, when you get in the shower, breathe controlled and let the adaptation happen naturally. You will gain the best results and best control over the body when you are completely relaxed. Eventually you will be able to steer the mind to consciously controlling the autonomic nervous system.

If you try to force it, your body will fight back and try to block you from making any progress. This happens because your body isn't used to taking the impact of the cold.

Once you adapt in this stage, you will feel much stronger. Some have reported an unexpected feeling of happiness. But most of all, your body's cardiovascular system will begin to run much smoother.

Learn to like the cold and you will naturally feel different and eventually have the desire to immerse yourself in cold environments during the wintertime.

Exercise 3.2 – Visualization

In stage one and two we learned to adapt and began controlling the body with the mind. Now, we'll learn how to control the mind and body using the power of visualization. Remember, never force anything; let your intuition guide you. Always listen to what your body is telling you.

The next time you go to perform a cold exercise, like the cold shower, I would like you to visualize heat generating within your body, just before you enter. Hopefully, you will notice that it brings a sensation of warmth and control.

With every breath, intensify this sensation and keep your mind focused on the heat. Don't let it stray away. We can do this with our mind by reconditioning our way of thinking. It's important to focus on this sensation and not dwell on other matters. In time, this focus will come naturally to you.

Once you can feel and control the heat, go into the cold water and control your breathing. Immerse with the power of the mind over the body. When you first get in, you may notice a gasping response. Try to control this, and then peacefully adapt to the water. Continue to keep your mind focused on that heat sensation.

Stay in the cold water for as long as it feels comfortable. As soon as you feel any sort of pain or feel uneasiness, get out.

When you get out of the water, you will probably see steam coming off your body. This is a good thing and a nice result of a focused mind and proper visualization.   Remember, **never force**.

Eventually, when you feel comfortable enough, you can add the breathing exercises, explained in the first section, to your cold-water immersions.

If you want to kick it up a notch, after you saturate with air and are able to hold your breath for a while, place your entire body underwater while holding you breath. I am able to easily do this up to 6.5 minutes everyday without any force whatsoever.

Let your body guide your training and only do what you are comfortable with.

Exercise 3.3 – Sitting Outside

Another cold exercise that you can do is to practice sitting outside in cold temperatures. By using your newly conditioned body that you have developed during the first few stages, you should be able to now visualize a warm sensation coming from the abdominal region. Hopefully, this will allow you to comfortably sit in the snow and control your inner temperature. It is up to you to figure out how long you can sit there. It is extremely important that you **do not force it!**

Now that you have taught yourself how to control the internal temperature of your body, you can attempt to increase your endurance and lengthen the amount of time you can remain exposed to cold temperatures.

Exercise 3.4 – Barefoot Snow Walking/Running
Another cold exercise you can try is walking or running barefoot through the snow. You will find great power when walking and running through the snow without footwear; it is a wonderful sensation.

After you have completed the first few stages of the cold exercises, you will begin to understand the body at a whole new level.

The heat sensation can be powerful. While you control that, you can simultaneously stimulate the autonomic nervous system. It is something that the Western Society once thought was impossible. Usually, people will enter cold environments fully clothed and think that the cold has negative repercussions on the body. Without experience, it is hard for one to understand how the cold can positively affect the physiological processes of our body, including the immune system. The cold has the power to show us true human potential... if we let it.

Training and natural adaptation in the cold brings about great differences in blood circulation. We have to consider this carefully because we now have a way to increase the efficiency of our body's physiological processes.

Everything we consume is processed to stimulate the metabolism to give the body energy. Without an efficient system, the arteries can become clogged and the body can slowly shut down the vital organs.

The cold has a positive effect on all of our bodies; it is our teacher. As you adapt, the muscles in the cardiovascular system are conditioned. The muscles contract and open thus become stronger. When the muscles in the cardiovascular system get stronger, they improve the blood flow throughout the body and press it toward the finest threads of the blood circulative system. This also increases the efficiency of the heart because it doesn't need to pump as hard to force blood throughout the body.

The cold feeds the immune system in the best possible way, keeping it alert and awake. With this newly utilized energy, the immune system can detect disease; specifically the inflammatory marked bodies, and immediately fix the problem. A lot of the western society suffers from a weakened circulation system, therefore causing heart attacks, strokes, arthritis and more.

This method is a way to fix that problem and begin to improve the efficiency of the body. By practicing in the cold, you will learn to breathe deeper. Breathing is also an important factor in influencing the body in order to prevent possible diseases. It can be used to redirect blood flow and maintain warmth. It also helps us focus our attention on what our body is trying to tell us.

Listen to your intuition and never force your practice. It is one of the few ways to bridge the gap between our inner nature and outer nature. At times, we can be overprotective when it comes to deciding what is "bad" for us. Therefore, we miss out on influences, like that cold, that have the potential to help us grow.

It is possible to be one with nature yet maintain a normal lifestyle as you do now. With this method, I hope you can go about your daily lives while using your body's full potential. Just find the time to practice it and your body will live efficiently. We all are capable of using this ability; it is a learning process that we must ease ourselves into. Your body and mind will adapt when you are ready.

I would like to make one final note. You do not have to subject your body to extreme temperatures. You can see big changes in your system by simply implementing cold showers into your daily lives. This is definitely applicable to those that are reaching old age and their cardiovascular system is suffering. These cold showers will help your body remain in great condition.

This training will help keep the heart, body, and mind in shape.

That is the purpose of this technique -- nothing less!

Good luck!
Wim Hof

CHAPTER 46:
THE FOUR STAGES OF THE COLD

*T*he "*Four Stages of the Cold*" is a safety system I have developed from my experiences with the cold. Please note that the stages are only *my* interpretation of how the body adjusts to the cold. Although I have seen most of these patterns in other individuals, I cannot guarantee that you will undergo the same experience. Therefore, I beg you to heed caution when attempting any of the cold exercises. If you are questionable or worried, please contact your family doctor for more advice. Please remember that your safety comes first.

Stage 1 (*The Adaptation Phase*):
Soon after coming in contact with the cold, the exposed part of your body may begin to sting. The pressure could intensify as the seconds pass, making it uncomfortable. Thoughts of aversion, telling you to remove your exposed body part, may flood into your head. These thoughts are natural.

Try to stay calm and relax. If the pressure becomes unbearable, remove your exposed body part. Otherwise, calm your thoughts until the pressure subsides. This will indicate that your exposed body part has adjusted to the cold and is transitioning to *Stage 2*.

It is important to remember that the amount of time it takes for your body to adjust to the cold will decrease with practice, as will the side effects ("*What it may feel like:*").

What it may feel like:
Some have reported feeling intense pressure/pain in joins (i.e. elbows, knees, etc), tightness, dizziness, and an inability to focus on anything else.

Stage 2 *(The Relaxation Phase)*:

This is when the exposed part of the body becomes accustomed to the cold. This can easily be understood as the stage that provides "numbing relief." Sometimes, it's a subtle onset, while other times it can be distinguished as the point in time when you are able to catch your breath.

What is great about this stage is that it reminds you that there is a calm after the storm. Once you reach *Stage 2*, you should be proud of yourself. Most have failed to venture past the uncomfortable part of *Stage 1* and remain exposed long enough to feel *Stage 2*.

Once you feel the calm of *Stage 2*, you should have no problem reaching it in future exercises -- provided that it is the same temperature as your previous attempt.

What it may feel like:
· Absence of pressure/pain
· Dulled pressure/pain compared to that of *Stage 1*

Stage 3:

Stage 3 occurs when you begin to feel tingling in the exposed area. It can start as a warm burn that slowly spreads over the surface of that area. At times, it can feel like your foot is heating up. However, be very careful with this stage. I usually stop a minute or so after reaching this point because I am afraid of doing serious damage. Therefore, **I DO NOT** advise pushing more than a few seconds into *Stage 3*. Once you detect any of the *Stage 3* signs, remove your exposed body part from the cold, immediately.

There have been a few occasions where I tested myself by pushing longer into *Stage 3*, but it took my exposed body part a lot longer to readjust to room temperature and to feel normal again. Once again, I highly advise against doing this.

Your intuition may kick in at this point. If it does, listen to it and pull out immediately. It's better to be safe than sorry.

What it may feel like:
· The feeling that you get when your foot or hand falls asleep (i.e. a tingling sensation)
· Slight burning sensation
· Resurfacing of pressure from *Stage 1*

Stage 4:

This is the stage that you want to avoid at all costs. I have had a few encounters with *Stage 4* and it has always been a terrifying experience. Even though I was only exposed to *Stage 4* for a few minutes each time, it took several days before I had regained all the feeling in my fingers and toes. If, for whatever reason, you are unable to escape from the cold and *Stage 3* has already begun, you are in danger of reaching *Stage 4*. Do everything you can to get out of the cold, *immediately*.

What it may feel like:

After a possible heated sensation takes over, numbness sets in again. It will most likely begin with the toes or fingers, if they are exposed, and slowly spread up the limbs. At this point, it is usually related to a feeling of lifelessness in the exposed body part. Fingers and toes could feel like rocks, as if they are not a part of your body anymore.

Avoid Stage 4 at all costs. Stage 4 has the potential to cause serious damage and irreversible frostbite.

CHAPTER 47:
JUSTIN'S METHOD

Disclaimer:
ATTEMPT AT YOUR OWN RISK. THESE EXERCISES CAN
BE DANGEROUS IF NOT DONE WITH THE PROPER CARE.
LISTEN TO YOU BODY AND NEVER FORCE YOURSELF.
IF YOU DO TRY ANY OF THESE EXERCISES, AS A SAFETY
PRECAUTION, WE ADVISE THAT YOU TRY THIS WITH
SOMEONE ELSE MONITORING YOU — JUST IN CASE
SOMETHING GOES WRONG. ONCE AGAIN, ATTEMPT AT
YOUR OWN RISK. THESE EXERCISES CAN BE DANGEROUS
IF NOT DONE WITH THE PROPER CARE.

Order of Exercises:
  1. *Cold Showers*
  2. *Ice-Water Buckets*
  3. *Ice Buckets*
  4. *Foot Immersions*
  5. *Surface Extremity Exposure*
  6. *Full-Body Immersion*
  7. *Cold/Snow Walks*
  8. *Cold Runs*

Here, I present to you, the fun part of my learning experience --
the training. Developing these exercises and finding the best way
to train gave me great pleasure. I loved having variety and finding
new ways to improve cold endurance.
For each exercise I will provide the following:
A. A quick background
B. How to perform the exercise
C. Comments

Note: It's always important to keep in mind the **Four Stages of the Cold** (refer to previous chapter) when going through any of these exercises. As soon as you feel tingling sensations in any of your fingertips or toes (*Stage 3*), get out immediately.
You never want to reach Stage 4.

1. Cold Showers

A. Background:
This is an exercise that Wim instructed me to try from the beginning. I'll be honest here and say that this was one of the most difficult exercises for me to start, mostly because I took my showers in the morning and I thought that I wouldn't have any time to spare. I thought that it was more important to smell clean than to use the time for cold showers. When I had finally tried it, I realized that it didn't take as long as I had initially thought it would, making me regret not starting sooner.

B. How to:
1. *Take a shower.* Despite my initial delusions, the great thing about this exercise is that it can be scheduled into your daily routine. Wim and I believe that this exercise alone can greatly increase the efficiency of the immune system.
2. *At the end of your shower, gradually turn up the cold water.* After you have completed your normal shower routine, turn up the amount of cold water that flows through your showerhead. When the water changes and begins to chill your skin, focus on staying relaxed and try not to shiver. You may reflexively gasp for air, but try to control it by taking deep breaths through your nostrils. Avoid inhaling water.
3. *Adjust.* Adjust to the water by staying calm and making sure that all of your body gets in contact with the cold water. I suggest slowly spinning in circles. Even though you may not want to, dip your head and face into the water and let it adjust.
4. *Repeat.* Continually drop the temperature and readjust until you feel uncomfortable going any further. With practice, you will progressively be able to do this for longer periods of time. Eventually, the water won't come as quite a shock to you when it first comes in contact with your skin.

C. Comments:
The most important thing you need to know about cold training,

is that each time you do it you will be making progress. It is never as bad as it may seem the first time.

The great thing about the cold is that you will notice results quickly if you stick with it. The problem arises when you don't push past the first few attempts. The key to it all is learning to like the cold. Don't hate it; otherwise you won't want to do it again. Just relax, and try to accept it.

When you can honestly say that you enjoy the cold, you will have broken down one of the most difficult barriers. Only then, will you begin to recognize the potential of the cold.

2. Ice-Water Buckets

A. Background:

When I would walk around from class to class in the middle of winter, I realized that my hands and feet were the first to freeze. When I had asked Wim about this, he suggested that I find a cold surface and condition myself through gradual exposure. He told me that the way he had conditioned his hands was by touching cold rocks while mountain climbing. I didn't have any cold rocks at my disposal, so I tried to come up with another way to train my extremities.

After class one day, when sitting in my bedroom, I noticed a one-gallon garbage can sitting in the corner, so I took out the trash and began my first cold experiment.

B. How to:

1. *Find a container that you can fill with water.* Keep in mind that you will only need enough room to fit one or two of your hands/feet. The less water you use in the container, the easier it will be to chill the water with ice. I recommend only 1 or 2 gallons if you plan on using one hand or one foot, or 3-5 gallons if you plan on using two hands or two feet.

2. *Find a towel and a steady place where you can easily place your extremity into the water comfortably.* If I planned on placing my hands in cold water, I would usually sit on the couch or in a chair, placing the container on top of another chair. If I were going to put my feet into the water, I'd sit on the couch and place the container on the ground with the towel to the side.

3. *Fill the container 3/4 of the way with the coldest water you can find.* I personally use the water from my bathtub faucet. It is the coldest water in my house. The water that comes out of my bathtub is typically 46.8°F (8.2°C) without ice. You could also use the water

from a garden hose, if you'd like.

4. *Pour in a few of handfuls of salt.* In high school, one of my professors taught me that if you put a can of warm soda in a bowl of ice water, add salt, and begin stirring, five minutes later the soda would be chilled. I remember him explaining to the class that salt lowered the freezing point of water, making the temperature much colder. This led me to believe that adding salt to these exercises may aid in dropping the temperature a few degrees.

5. *Throw in some ice cubes.* Don't put in more ice than there is water. You don't want the water to overflow when you put your hands or feet inside. When I do it, I vary between using one or two refillable ice trays. Each tray gives me about 16 ice cubes.

6. *Wait about 5 minutes for the ice to chill the water before doing anything else.* Be consistent if you intend to measure the water with a thermometer before each session. I use a digital cooking thermometer with a metal probe. It's also important to use this time to calm down. If you're anxious or worried, you are going to make the experience 10 times worse. The more panicked you are, the less time you will be able to keep your extremity in the water. Plus, you may imagine more pressure than is actually present. The best way to go into the water is completely relaxed.

7. *Immerse the extremity into the water, take deep breaths, and try to remain calm and relaxed.* When your hand or foot first enters the water, there may be a second or two where you don't feel anything. Assuming the water is cold enough, Stage 1 will kick in rather quickly and the training will begin. Wim told me that during this time, the veins are slamming shut and diverting all of your blood away from the cold area. So at first, you will most likely feel some pressure. It may be uncomfortable, but after a time, the pressure dissipates and your foot/hand readjusts to the water. Now it's important to keep in mind, if it gets to the point where you absolutely can't handle it, take your foot/hand out immediately. **Do not** force your body. Don't feel discouraged if you have to pull out before you get to Stage 2. You can always try it again. Each time you do the exercise, your endurance increases immensely. Gradual exposure is the key to success with the cold. You are conditioning here. You didn't go from learning to walk to running a marathon.

8. *Remain focused on the changes in your body.* You don't want to do any damage, so make sure you're paying attention to every detail. It's important to trust your body and listen to your intuition. The transition from Stage 1 to Stage 2 isn't as important as the transition from Stage 2 to Stage 3. Once you get to Stage 3, you want to get your body out of there immediately. This is where it can get

confusing. If you are unsure of whether or not you feel tingling, or pressure in your fingertips or toes, get out anyway. Like I said earlier, don't force it. Your ability to endure the cold will gradually increase on its own.

9. *Dry off your extremity and warm up after the exposure.* Whether it's simply letting your hands/feet readjust to room temperature, or putting them under a heated blanket, make sure that you're still paying attention to the changes in your body. Whenever I was quantifying how long it took for my hands and feet to return to normal temperature, I would gauge it based on their flexibility. You'll notice that when you pull your hands/feet out of the water, your fingers and toes won't flex as easily as you're used to. Each movement will feel like it's slowed down. I always marked the end of the exercise to be when the lagged feeling dissipated and my flexibility returned.

C. *Comments*:

There is one last thing to note in reference to warming up. I have found that using water that is at room temperature, or even luke-warm, can significantly decrease the amount of time it takes for your body to return to normal. It's very important to remain cautious as to how warm the temperature is. When I first tried using water to warm up my extremities, the water was *too* warm. It felt like needles were penetrating my hands and feet while they were immersed. So if you're going to use warmer water to bring your extremities back to equilibrium, make sure it's not too warm. If it burns, take it out; you don't want to suffer from any nerve damage. Water at room temperature is definitely the best way to go.

3. Ice Buckets

*Note: This exercise should only be performed after you are comfortable with **Foot Immersions** and have tried the **Surface Extremity Exposure**.

A. *Background*:

The **Ice Buckets** experiment was my attempt at making the **Ice-Water Buckets** and **Surface Extremity Exposure** more extreme. I first came up with this exercise when I was training to run the 5 kilometers, barefoot in the snow. The snow in State College wasn't always consistent so I searched for a way to simulate the snow.

B. *How to*:

1. *Find two large containers that can hold both your feet and the*

ice. I'll explain why you need two containers in a later step. I used two large, 5-gallon containers that I had bought from Wal-Mart for $4.00 apiece. They worked extremely well for this exercise.

2. *Make/Purchase enough ice so that it will completely cover your feet inside of the container.* There was a store by my house that sold 10-pound bags of ice for $1.00. Whenever I would walk home from class, knowing that I would do this experiment when I got home, I would buy two 10-pound bags. The two bags were just enough to cover my feet in a 5-gallon bucket. If you're not going to use the bags of ice immediately, make sure they're stored in a place where they won't melt.

3. *Set up the area.* Make sure that you'll be sitting in a comfortable place where your feet can rest comfortably inside the container. Place a towel close to your feet for easy access. I usually sit on my couch and have the buckets sitting side by side on the floor.

4. *Pour half of the ice into each container.* This is why two containers become very important. When I first did this experiment, I used only one of the buckets. After my first few attempts, I found that it was extremely hard to perform the experiment more than once, using the same bags of ice. Once you pull your feet out of the container, the ice collapses into the place where your feet were, making it impossible to get your feet into their original position. You can't slide your feet into the ice as easily as you can into water. Therefore, I came up with the two-container technique.

5. *Place your feet into one of the containers on top of the ice; pour the contents of the other container on top.* Ice is much different than water. When the ice touches your feet, you will notice a slightly stronger feeling of pressure. This is why it's preferable to try the **Surface Extremity Exposure** first. That way, you understand what the ice feels like against your skin, compared to the water. Some people have reported an aching feeling in their knees. This does dissipate.

6. *Try to remain calm. If you see that as impossible, pull out!* Like all of the other experiments, you don't want to do damage to your body. So, it is important to make sure that you don't try to stay in past your pain threshold. If you try this over time, you will be able to gradually stay in longer and longer. Eventually, there is a point where your will feet adjust and the pain goes away for a little while. Meaning, that you will transition from Stage 1 to Stage 2. The onset of Stage 3 comes on much quicker. When you feel any pressure, pain, or tingling in your toes, pull out immediately. As with all of the other exercises, pull out if you sense any sort of trouble. Your body has limits, so listen to them. Once again, **do not force.**

7. *When it becomes too much, or you reach Stage 3, pull out and warm your feet up.* Use the towel to dry off your feet. If you'd like to use a bucket of water to warm up, make sure that the water is no warmer than room temperature. If you would like to repeat the exercise after your feet are warm, as I normally do, you simply have to divide the ice in half between both containers, place your feet in one, and pour the ice back on top.

C. Comments:

This exercise can be overwhelming the first few times you try it. This is mainly because people aren't used to direct contact with the ice. If you want to get better at being in direct contact with the ice, I suggest getting a couple of ice cubes out of the freezer and holding them in your hands until they melt. If you can do that comfortably, then I think you should be able to do this exercise with less difficulty than most people. If it's in the winter, I suggest skipping this exercise and practice walking around barefoot in the snow [*Refer to the **Cold/Snow Walks** section for more information].

4. Foot Immersions

A. Background:

I came up with this idea as an alternative to **Ice-Water Buckets**. This was during the time of my training for the 5-kilometer snow run, barefooted. I realized through **Cold Showers** and the **Full-Body Immersion** that moving water feels much colder than sitting water. Wim explained the reason to me as this:

"When you are sitting in a body of water, a small layer of film develops around you, sort of protecting you from the cold. If you move around, the film is gone! This means you lose heat faster than if you were sitting still."

So, I wanted to use this knowledge and turn it into an exercise. Since my bath water was normally around 46.8°F (8.2°C), I figured the tub was the best place to try it out. My theory was that running cold bathwater over my feet would suck the heat out faster than stagnant water. It worked *magnificently*. I was ecstatic to have found a way to drastically decrease the duration of the experiments, yet still get the full workout.

B. How to:

1. *Check to see how fast your bathtub drains water.* If I turn on the cold water faucet in my bathtub all of the way, the water pours in faster than it can drain. This is ideal for this experiment. If this is

also the case for your bathtub, skip to Step 2.

1.1. *If this is not the case for your bathtub, I suggest plugging up the drain, and filling the tub 3/4 of the way. After it's filled 3/4 of the way, perform Step 2. While performing Step 2, unplug the drain and let the cold water continue to run from the faucet. Repeat this process when the water drops below the top part of your feet.*

2. **Stick your feet in and prepare for Stage 1.** When your feet first enter the water, you'll notice the appearance of Stage 1 rather quickly, much like all of the other exercises. The difference between this exercise and the others is that it will take longer for Stage 1 to end and transition to the relaxed, Stage 2. This is because the water isn't still. The amount of time it takes for Stage 1 to transition to Stage 2 will eventually diminish and adaptation will come much quicker with more training. Remember to stay relaxed. If Stage 1 is unbearable for you, take your feet out and try again later. **Don't force it.**

3. *When you reach Stage 3 and you feel the tingling in your toes, pull them out and dry off.* At this point, your feet will feel extremely cold. Your foot may also feel a little numb; so watch where you are walking to make sure that you don't step on anything sharp.

4. *Walk on your "tippy-toes."* After these exercises, I typically put on a pair of socks, and stand on the fleshy part of my feet right below my toes. Some recall this type of walking from their childhood as "tippy-toes." This helps bring the blood back into your feet and warm them up faster. Like all the other exercises, the amount of time it takes your feet to readjust will decrease with practice.

C. *Comments*:

During the first time I had performed this exercise with my feet, I could only last in the water for 3 minutes before I had to pull them out (Stage 3). After a week of doing this 2 to 3 times a day, my feet were able to withstand 12 minutes of cold, running water before I had reached Stage 3. After a month, my feet could endure 20 minutes of this. I attribute a large amount of my success in the 5k to this exercise.

5. Surface Extremity Exposure

A. *Background*:

The **Surface Extremity Exposure** was the first exercise I came up with to try to imitate walking on snow. When Wim had first suggested that I try walking on snow, it was the beginning of fall. I still had several weeks left before I could try it, so I came up with this technique in an attempt to prepare my feet for walking on snow and ice.

B. *How to:*

1. *Find a rectangular metal container that could store a large amount of water.* I used a lasagna pan that I had found in my kitchen.

2. *Fill the pan with water and store it in your freezer.* Assuming that your freezer is cold enough, let it sit for a day until the water is completely frozen. As long as you put it back in when you finish the exercise, you only have to wait for the water to freeze once.

3. *Set up the area.* Place a towel in the vicinity of where you will be performing the exercise. Grab the ice tray from the freezer and bring it next to you. Figure out whether you'll be training your feet or your hands and place it where it will be most accessible.

4. *When you are ready, apply the palm of your hand, or the sole of your foot to the ice in the tray.* If this is your first time in direct contact with the ice, you'll notice that Stage 1 builds up rather quickly. If the pressure becomes too extreme, take off your hand / foot and try again later. Eventually, you'll get used to it and transition to Stage 2.

5. *Try to relax and take deep breaths.* The **Surface Extremity Exposure**, the **Cold/Snow Walks**, and the **Ice Buckets** are typically the hardest for people to get through. This is mainly because they aren't used to direct contact with freezing temperatures. The rapid onset and the extended duration of Stage 1 can be overwhelming at times. First timers usually recognize pressure in their elbows and wrists when they expose their hands, and pressure in their knees and calves when they expose their feet. The way to get past these side effects is to gradually expose yourself. Don't push past your pain threshold; ease into it.

6. *Know the difference between Stage 2 and Stage 3.* With this experiment, it can be hard to recognize when you are in Stage 2 because the pressure may not completely dissipate. You may question whether or not you ever began Stage 2. For this experiment, Stage 2 is defined as a decreased pressure in the exposed extremity. You may not feel completely relaxed in the first few, so it's important to recognize the little changes. Stage 3 is when the decreased pressure in Stage 2 rises again. Some have reported tingling in the fingertips or toes, but most experience an increase in pressure (Stage 3) after a short period of decreased pressure (Stage 2). *Know the distinction.* If you can't differentiate, take your hand / foot off of the ice and try again later. **Never force.** If you're confused, don't wait and see. If you aren't confident about what is changing in your body, pull away. The goal of these exercises is to understand your body and increase endurance. If you don't understand what your body is doing, repeat the earlier steps until you are confident in the safety of

your body. Your safety comes first.

7. **When you reach Stage 3, pull away and dry off.** Most report an immediate relief of pressure when they pull away from the cold source. Normally the exposed part of your body readjusts rather quickly. When compared to the cold water immersions, the sole of your foot or the palm of your hand can sometimes readjust to room temperature twice as fast as air.

C. *Comments*:

I'd like to reiterate how important it is to never force your body past its pain threshold. If you are unsure of your body's safety, don't proceed. Stop. Forcing can lead to injury; only do what you can handle. In time you will gain experience as well as endurance. With that, you will gain understanding. Once again, if you would like more information, please refer to www.becomingtheiceman.com.

6. Full-Body Immersion

*Only attempt after you have tried **Cold Showers**

A. *Background:*

When Wim first suggested that I find a body of cold water to swim in, I wasn't hopeful. The rivers, lakes, and ponds in the area were either owned by Penn State University or the city. Being that it was the middle of winter, I was afraid that if I tried swimming in any of the waters, I would get charged with trespassing and given a sobriety test.

During one of my dishwashing shifts, I came up with an idea to use one of the inflatable pools that are typically sold in the summer. I called my landlord and described, in detail, the type of research I was performing. I explained my interests and what I had hoped to gain. After a half-hour conversation, I asked if I would be able to place a miniature inflatable pool on my porch to be able to train in cold water during the winter. He told me that it wouldn't be a problem and granted me permission.

Now, at the time, I was extremely low on cash. Instead of returning home to my family for Christmas break, I stayed in State College to work at The Deli, so I could afford my rent. I barely had enough money to feed myself, let alone spend money on an inflatable pool. But I was determined to find a way to perform these exercises to increase my ability to withstand the cold.

Over the following week, I looked around for inflatable pools and came up with nothing. I asked my friends, who had grown up in

State College, if they had an inflatable pool stored at their parents' house. Only one of them had a miniature pool, but it was made of plastic and would be much harder to transport compared to an inflatable pool. After a while with no success, I decided that it was time to move on to something else.

Late one night a few days later, I was texting my friend, Danielle Cardell, about the **Ice-Water Buckets** experiment. That's when the idea finally came to me. The exercise would need to be like the **Ice-Water Buckets**, but on a larger scale. So I ran into my bathroom, examined the tub, and quickly devised a plan to make it work. I asked Danielle if she would like to come over and possibly do the exercise herself; she agreed. About an hour later, I was ready for my first **Full-Body Immersion**.

B. How to:

1. *Check to see if your bathtub is capable.* It's important to note how big your bathtub is and how much water it can hold. Wim says, "Any training is good training." So, as long as your bathtub is capable of retaining water, you should be fine.

2. *Check the temperature of the bathwater.* This will help you decide how much ice you need. My bathtub's water temperature is usually around 46.8°F (8.2°C) without ice. The bathwater at my friends' house varies from as low as 45°F (7.2°C) to 66°F (18.89°C). It's also important to make sure that you are only turning on the cold water. If you are uncomfortable dealing with only cold at first, add a little warm water. Remember, **don't force**.

3. *Make sure help is there if you need it.* Don't try to show how awesome you are by doing this on your own. For at least the first few times, I highly suggest you put on a bathing suit and make sure someone is present. If something goes wrong, he or she could be the difference between life and death. The **Full-Body Immersion** must be in a controlled environment. When I perform the exercise, I still keep a cell phone near me to make sure I can call for help if something goes wrong. Also, make sure there isn't any electrical equipment near the bathtub. This should be obvious, but hopefully this reminder will save someone's life one day. This is training to endure the cold, not to survive an electrical shock. The bathtub is one of the quickest ways to chill your body, so don't take it lightly. Pay attention and if you become afraid or anxious at any point, don't wait and see what happens... Get out!

4. *Block the drain and turn on the cold water; when the water fills up 3/4 of the bathtub, turn it off.* While the water is filling up in the tub, change into your bathing suit, or whatever you're going to

wear in the bathtub. Also, make sure that your towel is next to the place where you will be getting out of the water; think ahead. One of the problems I had when sitting in the bathtub was that my knees would float to the top of the water and stick out. I had found that using a 5-pound weight was enough to hold both of my legs down. Don't use something extremely heavy or something that could get tangled around you; you want to be able to get out of the water at a moment's notice. Please be smart.

5. *Add salt and ice.* Throw in a few handfuls of a salt and whatever ice cubes you have on hand. I vary between putting 1 to 5 ice-cube trays in the water. This also depends on how cold the water is. If you want to gradually adjust, start with fewer trays. Begin by using the tap water provided by the bathtub. If you feel comfortable after doing it this way a few times, add ice and salt to your training regime. The temperature of the water will determine how long you can stay in. With that said...

6. *Never set a timed goal.* If you aren't careful with the cold, it can be dangerous. People die from hypothermia when they are unprepared. This isn't a contest, and you are not trying to break a world record. Your #1 concern should be to monitor what your body is doing at all times. As *soon* as you become afraid, anxious, or feel tingling in your limbs, **get out!** Stay 100% focused the entire time. Never let your guard down.

7. *Take a few deep breaths, relax, and get in.* When I get in the bathtub, I find it's best to submerge my whole body up to my neck. The cold shock is much more when only the hand/foot is submerged in ice-cold water. For some reason, I've found that it takes less time to adjust to the water when the whole body is submerged. Otherwise, if the bottom half of your body is submerged, and your chest/shoulders are exposed, your body will be confused. The top half will try to keep its heat relative to the air temperature, while the bottom half tries to adjust to the freezing water. From my experience -- as well as the people I have taught to do this -- I shiver a lot more when a large part of my body is exposed. So if you can, get in all the way and try your best to relax.

8. *Do your best to relax and breathe normally. Try not to shiver.* After a while, you'll realize that you have the ability to turn off the shivering reflex at will. Not shivering will help you relax, immensely. The shivering is an automatic response that you want to condition yourself away from. It isn't helping when you willingly subject yourself to the cold. My friends and I find it best to focus on our breathing. It helps us relax, as well as control the shivering. Talking can also take away from concentration and bring on the shivering.

If you are unable to stop your shivering after the first 2 or 3 minutes, get out of the water. It's the typical time limit that I give my friends to adjust. If they aren't able to control their shivering by that time, they're in danger of losing a lot of heat. At that point, it's best to get out and try again later.

9. *Pay attention, continuously. When it's time to get out, don't push it; get out!* You'll notice, after the initial shock (Stage 1), that your body will relax and you won't feel as cold anymore. Don't take this to mean that you can stop focusing. You need to be able to understand when your body is ready to get out. If you begin to notice Stage 3, *get out* immediately. If there is any sign of tingling in the toes or fingertips, *get out*. If you are unable to control your shivering, *get out*. If something in your body/mind is telling you to get out, *listen to it*. You can always come back and try it again, but never force it. This can be extremely dangerous if you push beyond what you can handle. So focus on the changes in your body 100% of the time. If you begin to feel lightheaded, or feel any pain other than the initial shock of the cold, get out and contact a physician immediately.

10. *Carefully dry yourself off with a towel and move slowly.* Chances are, your body's coordination is going to be off and your movements will be slower than normal. Your sense of touch also won't be as sensitive as it normally is. Make sure that you don't lean on anything sharp, and watch where you place your foot. When I first did this, I put pressure on my hand, which was leaning against a somewhat sharp shower door. I cut it deep; I didn't notice it until Danielle gasped and told me that she saw blood.

11. *Prepare for the "afterdrop."* Depending on how long you were in the water, you may or may not experience an "afterdrop." It typically appears within 5 minutes after exiting the water. Wim calls the period where your body readjusts to its normal temperature, the *afterdrop*. During this time, you may experience uncontrollable shivering (though you should still try to control it), a cold feeling in the areas where warm clothes are touching your skin, and an overabundance of energy. Wim has suggested taking a bath with water that is slightly warmer than room temperature, afterward, to fix this. I have done it only a few times. Usually, I put on warm clothing and deal with the shivering until I'm back to normal. The afterdrop does shorten in time with repeated exposure. If you notice that you have slurred speech and you cannot think properly, contact someone for help, immediately. You may be suffering from hypothermia. This is why it's important to always pay attention to what your body is telling you.

C. Comments:

During the summer after my first **Full-Body Immersion**, I tried to get my girlfriend, Brooke Robinson, to try it. She has had bad circulation for a while now and constantly feels cold. She's also suffered from sore knees, which Wim said the cold would fix. So after verbally walking her through the steps that I just mentioned, Brooke entered the water. She was extremely nervous and afraid when she first got in. But after a few minutes of exposure, Brooke's body became more relaxed and she stopped shivering.

She was excited, and after just watching me stay in the water for 15 minutes, she believed that she could go longer. So she didn't focus on what her body was doing. Instead, Brooke focused on fighting through whatever happened to try to extend her time. During that time, I constantly asked her to give me updates so I could pull her out when she began to reach Stage 3. After 6 minutes passed, I asked Brooke to tell me what she was feeling. She replied, "I'm fine, it's comfortable."

I waited for a bit, thinking that she'd tell me when something changed. After 8 minutes of being in the water, I noticed that she was shivering again, so I asked her how she felt.

"Fine, I'm warm," she said.

Something seemed off, it appeared as if she wasn't able to control her shivering. So I asked her to get out.

"No, I don't want to get out; it's warm in here."

That's when concern washed over me. Her logic didn't make sense and she wasn't thinking clearly. I kindly asked her to get out so that I could warm her up. She reverted to a childlike state and seemed afraid. She began crying. When she got out of the bathtub, I dried her off with the towel. Her speech was significantly slower than it was a few minutes before and her facial expressions weren't matching up with her sentences. I was filled with fear because I had never seen this before. I was worried and wanted to make her better as fast as possible.

After the cold water drained from the tub, I turned on the faucet to produce a lukewarm temperature. I flipped the shower switch and made her get inside. I know what it's like to get inside a warm shower after you've been exposed to the cold for a long time... it burns. It feels as if you're getting into a hot tub. It can be very uncomfortable. So I put on my bathing suit and got into the shower with her.

She was hysterical, crying, sobbing, and constantly asking, "what is wrong with me?" I tried to be brave and tell that her it was going to be okay, and that she'd be better soon. I began rubbing her back in an attempt to soothe her. I also tested her memory by asking her questions about her childhood. Her answers were slow, but correct. I then proceeded to give her multiplication problems to test her ability to solve problems. She was slow to give the answers and appeared to need to think really hard, but she answered correctly. Sadly, she was still shivering.

A few minutes later, she told me that she was starting to feel lightheaded. So I turned off the warm water, dried her off, and then had her get dressed while I went into my bedroom. Her speech was still slow, but progressively improving.

I put her in my bed and covered her up with three blankets. I began rubbing her back, trying to make her feel more comfortable. Finally, 90 minutes after her exposure to the cold, she returned to normal. Her speech was coming back and the tears had stopped. The shivering faded and her facial expressions matched the emotions that she was trying to convey.

It was the scariest moment of both of our lives. I never want anyone to experience what she did. So I implore you to heed caution when attempting any of these exercises, especially with the **Full-Body Immersions**. Take heed and always keep safety as your main priority.

7. Cold/Snow Walks

A. Background:
One of Wim's first suggestions to me was to try walking around barefoot in the snow. He told me the following:

"When I am teaching people how to walk around in the snow, barefoot, I tell them to just do it. After a couple minutes of walking in the snow, they feel pain. So I tell them to go inside and warm their feet. After they're better, they come back into the snow again and can walk for as long as they want."

Now, this was during the time when the only training I had done was the Tummo experience in California. Besides that, I hadn't done anything beyond walking home from class without a jacket. So when the first snowfall of the season came, I was excited to try walking through it barefooted. From Wim's story, it seemed easy and I was eager to try.

An hour later, I was sitting on a bench, in the middle of a secluded park, a mile away from my house with my feet on the brink of frostbite. I had no experience with the cold, no knowledge of what was going on inside my body, and I was convinced that I was going to lose my feet. Luckily, I was able to get home in time to warm up my feet in the bathtub. I didn't suffer from any permanent damage, but my spirit was broken.

I remembered Wim's advice to "learn to like the cold." That night, I hated it. I was ready to leave all hopes of becoming The Iceman behind me. After the pain subsided, I realized my ignorance and laughed at it. I decided to give it one last try. I knew nothing about the cold, but I wanted to learn. Wim claimed that it was an ability anyone could be trained to do. It *seemed* possible, and that was enough for me to try.

This experience led me to start making controlled experiments to find exercises where I could increase my endurance. Making it controlled provided me with a way to get out of a bad situation quickly, if I needed to. If it was going to be something that people could be trained to do, I wanted to make sure I devised exercises that could be replicated easily.

So, here is my safer method of conditioning yourself to walk through the snow. Or, if there isn't any snow, you could do cold walks.

B. How to:

1.a. *Snow - Find a flat surface covered in fresh, powdered snow.* The ideal spot should be your backyard or your driveway. You want to be in a place that's close enough to your house so that it would take you about 30 seconds from the time you decide to get out to return to the confines of your home.

1.b. *Cold Surface - Find a flat surface outside that is cold to the touch.* The concrete or cement in your driveway, or a sidewalk, will do. Personally, I used the ceramic tiles that make up my front porch.

2. *Clear the area.* You want to make sure that the path you will be walking/standing on does not have any sharp objects. Clean up any broken glass, sticks, mulch, and anything that may be able to somehow penetrate your skin. When your feet are that cold, the first thing you want to do is step on a warm surface; the last thing you want to see is a trail of blood following in your footsteps.

3. *Just do it.* When you're ready, just go out and stand in the snow or on a cold surface. There's no meditative state you have to be in before doing it. Just do it.

4.a. *Standing - If you're just starting out, practice standing in one spot.* This will help you get used to the cold feeling, and warm up the spot below your feet. You'll still go through the same stages (1-3), but it'll take longer for you to progress through the stages than it would when walking around. Try to remain focused, take careful breaths, and stay relaxed. Standing in the snow, or on a cold surface, is the first step to take when beginning this exercise. If you feel like you aren't getting any colder after standing there for a while, take a step anywhere else and the process will restart. When you reach Stage 3, don't restart the process anymore; go inside. When you feel the tingling or aching in your feet, go directly inside your home.

4.b. *Walking* - Walking around through the snow, or on a cold surface, is like pushing the reset button. With each step, you restart the Stage 1 process. It will progressively feel as if each step is getting colder. Try to remain focused, take careful breaths, and stay relaxed. Eventually, as you continue to walk through the snow, the feeling will dissipate and you'll enter Stage 2. A slight, numbing feeling will help you recognize Stage 2. When Stage 3 presents itself as an ache in the foot, tingling in the toes, or simply as intuition, get out immediately and walk into the warmth of your home.

5. *Warm up.* Whenever I finish these exercises, I walk around on my "tippy-toes." It feels like it's warming up faster than if I was walking around flat-footed. I believe that the amount of pressure I'm putting on the forefront of my foot helps the blood recirculate to that area. Jogging in place has also worked well for me. This is also a time where you should watch where you are walking and avoid sharp objects. If the inside of your house isn't warm, put on socks. Otherwise, your feet will readjust to room temperature over the next hour. Some may experience aching in their feet while they readjust to room temperature. This will dissipate with time. If you stayed out too long and the pain does not dissipate within an hour's time, seek medical help.

C. Comments:

I used to do this exercise several times a day. It rarely snowed, but when it did, I took advantage of it. Sometimes, I would go out as often as ten times a day. I would like to mention that the **Foot Immersions** exercise greatly aided in my ability to walk in the snow and stand on cold surfaces. I performed the cold surface exercises a few times, but not as much as the snow walks.

If you get to the point where you are comfortable walking around in the snow, try jogging. Just be careful to watch your feet and make sure you don't step on anything sharp.

8. Cold Runs

A. Background:

Running in the cold was a learning experience. I made a lot of mistakes when I first began, but I eventually grew to understand them. Since I had started running in the cold before I trained with Wim, I had to develop my own technique to keep warm; it still works perfectly to this day. Now, I can run comfortably in 32°F (0°C) weather for over an hour, wearing only shorts and sandals. Out of all my training, the **Cold Runs** are my favorite. I love the **Cold Runs** because it is the workout that quickly proved to me that the adaptation to the cold was easily attainable. The ease of running in the lower temperatures continually inspired me to press on with the cold research.

B. How to:

1. *Plan a jogging route.* If it's your first time running, keep the distance and time that you'll travel short. You can gradually increase the time you're exposed outside as you become more comfortable. It's also better to plan a route that doesn't take you too far away from your house. If you're far away from your house when you reach Stage 3, you could be in danger. Learn to understand your body and don't push your limits. Start out with one lap around the block. As you feel more comfortable, you can increase the distance. Always have a plan for what you'll do if something goes wrong; don't run unprepared. Also, make sure that you'll be running on dry, solid surfaces. Running through snow or water will chill your feet extremely fast. Last winter, I ran around downtown because the city kept their sidewalks clean. It made for a great running course.

2. *Check the weather conditions.* There are a lot of variables you need to take into account before you run.

2.a. *Temperature.* The temperature will determine how long you'll be outside. You will last much longer in temperatures that are over 60°F (15.5°C) compared to temperatures below 32°F (0°C).

2.b. *Wind speed.* The wind can greatly decrease the amount of time you spend outside, especially in colder temperatures. It's preferable to run outside if the wind speed is below 5 mph (8.04 kilometers per hour). Any wind speed higher than that may cause problems if you run for longer periods of time.

2.c. *Precipitation.* Honestly, I love doing **Cold Runs** while it's snowing, but the choice is up to you. I highly suggest not running while it's raining. I enjoy the snow because it's much more entertaining. I usually last longer if running in a dry environment, but the snow makes the run interesting. If you choose to run while it's snowing, be careful. The last thing you want to do is slip, fall down, and lose focus. Watch your steps if you decide to go running in the snow. If it's raining outside, being wet will make you lose heat faster.

3. *Pick a time of day to run.* If your jogging route consists of running in the middle of the road, don't run at night. You want to be visible at all times so a car doesn't hit you. If you're worried about people making fun of you while you run around wearing less clothing than they are, either use a secluded route to run during the day, or run in a safe area during the night. For a while, I only ran downtown at night. People thought I was a drunkard who had lost a bet, but it didn't turn me away from my training. After a while, once I began to feel more confident, I would run in the afternoon after my classes. I received a lot of crazy looks and many people beeped their horns, but I wanted to get to the point where I was comfortable being myself around other people. I had hoped that if they ever saw The Iceman on television, or eventually found this book, they would understand.

4. *Carefully select your clothing.* If it is your first time running in the cold, start with what's comfortable for you. As you grow more accustomed to it, you can reduce the amount of clothing you wear to something that you would wear in the summertime.

4.a. *Headgear.* If you want to wear a hat or something like that, I'm not against it. It's your call. I never ran with a hat, nor ever regretted it. If you're a woman with long hair, make sure to keep it out of your face. When running in the cold, you want your focus to only be on your running and your breathing.

4.b. *Shirts/Sweatshirts.* If you're just starting out, try going outside and running in a t-shirt. If you're too cold, try it with a long-sleeve shirt. If you're comfortable, try wearing a tank top. Personally, if I'm running in the cold, I don't like any article of clothing to be touching my chest. I feel like I adjust faster when my chest and arms are completely exposed. Men, this is the point that you want to get to. Women, if you can get down to your sports bra, or even a tank top, that's perfect. Only do what you are comfortable trying.

4.c. *Shorts.* If you can, always go in shorts. Your legs will be moving and generating more than enough heat to keep them warm. If you're self-conscious about your legs or have a condition where you need to wear pants, then by all means, wear pants. Otherwise, wear shorts that are comfortable to run in.

4.d. *Shoes.* Find running sandals. I found a pair of $100 running sandals online two years ago that I still wear today; they're perfect. You can wear them year-round and they can greatly increase the foot's ability to endure the cold. However, if it's snowing or raining, wear athletic running shoes. They'll give you traction you need on a slippery surface. If you are uncomfortable running in sandals, you can still do the running in tennis shoes and get a great workout.

As much as I'd like to encourage barefoot running, I must advise against it. There could be broken glass or gravel that could easily cut into your skin. If you'd like to simulate running barefooted, I strongly suggest the Vibram FiveFingers, specifically, their KSO design. I like them because they let the cold come in and chill my feet, while still protecting my sole from any sharp objects. They were my greatest investment.

4.e. *Gloves.* I never wore them and I suggest you don't either. One of the most important indicators that let you know when you should get out of the cold are your hands. When your hands tingle or hurt, get out of the cold inside immediately. During my cold runs, my hands were the things I paid attention to the most. As soon as I had felt discomfort, I changed my course immediately and headed for home. In the next section, I'll describe the method I developed to regulate heat in the hands to make them last longer.

5. *Warm your hands.* My fingers have had their share of close encounters with frostbite. After much trial and error, I developed a technique that will not only regulate heat in your hands, but also allow you to last longer in the cold. Here's the method:

5.a. *Thumbs.* Place your thumb in the palm of your hand. Bend it so that the knuckle is directly between your pointer finger and your middle finger. The tip of your thumb should be directly below the ring finger.

5.b. *Fingers.* Close your fingers around your thumbs. Each fingertip should comfortably rest around your thumbs, touching the palm of your hand. Your pointer fingers may not be able to reach the palm of your hand, but as long as they're not exposed, they should be fine. It may be uncomfortable for you to run like that in the beginning, but you'll get used to it, especially because it warms up your hands and reduces the chance of getting frostbite on your fingertips. *Remember*: This does not make your hands invincible to the cold. As you're running, the wind is pushing against the rest of your exposed hand. After a long period of running like this, you can still get frostbite. This is why I mentioned earlier that it's important to check out the wind speed. If the wind speed is high, it will increase the amount of cold air brushing against your hands, and you'll have to return home sooner because Stage 3 will come on much faster.

6. *Continuously breathe through your nose.* When you run, you want to run at a comfortable pace where you aren't overexerting yourself. Breathing only through your nose helps you do just that. It's a technique that I learned on my own and has helped me immensely during all my cold training. During the first few attempts, it may be difficult to do a cold run while only breathing through

your nose, but keep at it. At first, your nose will probably run, but still keep a steady breath. You can sniff occasionally to keep the fluid from escaping your nose, but really focus on having a steady rhythm to your breathing. Practice breathing during your other physical activities as well. Really try to focus on not breathing through your mouth for any reason. Eventually, when it becomes a habit, it will help you relax in the cold, keep you warm, give you better control over your air supply, and prevent you from overexerting yourself.

7. *Get out there and run.* In the beginning, before each run I would stand at the door and think about what was going to happen. I don't mean I was planning out what I was going to do. No, I was trying to rationalize the fear that was building within me. The anxiety never completely left me until I sucked it up, went outside, and started running. It's like getting a shot from the doctor when you were a child. The anticipation building up to the shot is much worse than the shot itself. The cold is the same way. The only difference between the shot and the cold is that with the shot, you can't decide when it's coming; it's happening on the doctor's time schedule, but with the cold, you are the one in control. You are in charge and it is a powerful feeling. Know that it will be okay and that Stage 1 will go by much quicker than you think.

8. *Adapt and pay attention.* When you first step outside, your body needs to readjust. The time it takes to readjust to the temperature is, typically, a lot quicker than any other exercise. When I first started running, it was in temperatures between 28°F (-2.2°C) and 32°F (0°C). When I did my first cold run, it only took my body about 15 seconds to adapt. Though it's important to note that as soon as I left my house, I was jogging. If I wasn't moving faster than a walking pace, my body would adjust very slowly. So, remember to keep moving.

9. *Know that it's possible.* If you perform your first run safely, chances are you really enjoyed it. If you ran into some difficulties, just remember it is possible. The side effects that come with running in the cold like, runny nose, sore throat, or even a burning sensation in your chest, all dissipate with practice. I've taught people how to run comfortably in the cold before, and they've all adjusted perfectly. After the first few times, they lose all signs of discomfort. Surviving in the cold is about conditioning and adaptation. If you aren't willing to accept the change, your body will fight you every step of the way. Keep an open mind and just try it.

10. *When you enter Stage 3, if your hands burn, you begin to feel anxious, or you begin shivering after a period of being comfortable, return home.* Don't push your luck by seeing if you can go a little

farther. Return home so that you can try it again later with no fear of frostbite.

11. *Get warm.* When you get home, you can either warm up naturally or take a lukewarm shower or bath. Before you get in, test the water with your hand to see if it burns. If it burns, you need to turn down the heat. You may experience shivers as you adjust to the water, similar to the afterdrop experience you get when doing the **Full-Body Immersion**. Continue to take normal, steady breaths, and you'll be back to your regular temperature in no time.

C. *Comments*:

For my birthday this year, I asked my father to do a **Cold Run** with me. The temperature was 8°F (-13.3°C) outside and it was one of the coldest days of the winter. I told him that it would only be a quick 10-minute jog around the block. At first, he told me that it was impossible and that someone of his age and shape couldn't do it without some sort of training first.

"It's too cold; are you kidding me?" he would repeatedly state.

"This *is* the training," I would reply.

After reassuring him that we'd take him to the hospital if something went wrong, he accepted the challenge and said he was only doing it because it was my birthday. In case something did go wrong, my father hugged and kissed each member of my family and told them that he loved them.

Several minutes later, we were shirtless and standing in shorts by the front door. Before we left, I reminded my father of the technique to use when outside. I warned him of the changes that would happen to his body in the next few minutes and told him to let me know if he began having trouble.

With that, we ran out the front door and into the street. Breathing solely through the nose was something that was new to my father, so we ran at a slow pace. Several times I asked questions to check on him; he seemed to be all right. After 2 minutes of being exposed, he told me, "It's not that bad, I feel warm!"

When we got back to the house, I kept close tabs on my father. Ever since Brooke's episode when she almost became a victim of hypothermia, I have been very cautious with the people I train. My father wasn't any different. He kept professing to my family how awesome the experience was.

"It didn't feel that cold!"

"I was warm the whole time!"

"I could have gone longer!"

The only parts of his body that he said were cold were his hands

-- and that was only at the end of the run! He didn't even experience any shivering. Within 15 minutes, my father was back to his normal state, warm and energetic. It meant a lot to me that he had trusted me as much as he did. It gave me confidence in my ability to teach others and to help them understand the cold's potential.

ABOUT THE AUTHORS

For more information on
Wim and Justin, please visit:
www.becomingtheiceman.com

For Wim's official website, please visit:
www.innerfire.nl